DISCIPLING

———◆———

*God's Plan
to Train and Transform
His People*

GORDON FERGUSON

DISCIPLING

*God's Plan
to Train and Transform
His People*

One Merrill Street
Woburn, MA, 01801
1-888-DPI-BOOK Fax (617) 937-3889
www.dpibooks.com

Discipling
©1997 by Discipleship Publications International
One Merrill Street, Woburn, MA 01801

Printed in the United States of America

Cover design: Chris Costello
Interior design: Chris Costello and Laura Root
Cover photo: ©W. Morgan, Westlight

ISBN 1-57782-031-2

To the newest members of our family: our son, Jeff, and our daughter, Joy. Because we are disciples in the kingdom together, you are not "in-laws" but a true son and a true daughter. Theresa and I prayed for you decades before we met you and now are most delighted with the way you have completed our first son and first daughter as their mates for life.

A SPECIAL INTRODUCTORY NOTE

Some of you reading this book are veterans of discipling relationships. Others are new Christians in churches practicing discipling. However, some will be spiritually minded people for whom this whole concept will be quite new. It is to those of you in this last group that this note is addressed.

I want you to understand that what you will find described here is not theory. It is something I have seen in practice for the last fifteen years of my life. I have personal knowledge of more than 250 churches in more than 120 nations that are wholeheartedly practicing what I am describing in this book. Lives from Moscow to Manila, from Paris to Perth are being radically changed by a return to this biblical practice. Churches emphasizing these principles are growing incredibly and are currently the largest churches in many nations worldwide. The fastest growing church in the United States for the past two years is a church totally committed to the kind of relationships you will read about here.

You are likely in much the same place that I was a number of years ago. My prayer for you is that you would step out on faith and discover the same blessings that have flooded my life. If I can be of any help to you, you can reach me through the publisher of this book.

Gordon Ferguson
Boston, Massachusetts

CONTENTS

Part 1

BIBLICAL FOUNDATIONS

Part 2

BEING A DISCIPLE OF JESUS

Part 3

BEING A DISCIPLER FOR JESUS

Part 4

ISSUES, CHALLENGES AND OPPORTUNITIES

FOREWORD

Few topics in Christianity evoke such a wide range of emotional responses as does that of discipleship. Comfortable pew-warmers, safe in their protective cocoons of mediocrity, are sure that Satan himself is corrupting the church with religious fanaticism. Disciples who are eager to have the daily encouragement and challenge to become more like Jesus Christ, however, cannot sing the praises of discipleship loudly enough.

Gordon Ferguson has written a book that has something for everyone who claims to be a Christian. For the skeptic who suspects that discipling is nothing more than manipulation and the invasion of personal space, Gordon shows that Jesus was the Master Discipler and expects us to imitate his example. For the novice who wants to grow as a Christian and help others to grow, he shows both the theory and the "how to's." And the mature disciples are not left out; plenty of pointers are included to help them to keep on growing. All of the basic facets of discipling are covered: one-on-one discipling, group discipling and family discipling. Also, Gordon does not sidestep any of the issues commonly raised, such as authority and confidentiality.

Much of the power of the book is its realness. Gordon has been a close friend for ten years. He is an outstanding Christian man, husband, father, church leader and teacher. His openness and vulnerability have been a constant upward call for me. He is writing from the strength of having experienced the frustration of trying to follow God while caught in a maze of conventional mainline Christianity, with no discipling available. He knows first-hand the freedom and power that comes from eagerly inviting devoted disciples into his life to help him become what God wants him to be.

I wholeheartedly recommend this book to you. The principles presented here will change you, your friends and the world. Discipling works!

Al Baird
Los Angeles, California

ACKNOWLEDGMENTS

To write an acknowledgment page is a daunting task, for so many have contributed to my becoming a disciple, a discipler and a leader in the kingdom of God. I mention in the introduction a friend from long ago, whose name is Richard Hostetler. Another early mentor was J.T. Bristow, who influenced my preaching passion and evangelistic zeal in a significant way.

My connection to the discipling movement traces back most directly to a special brother named Tom Brown. He reached out to me and first invited me to speak at an evangelism seminar in which the entire audience was committed to the principles described in this book. Thankfully, I never recovered from that first dose of discipling! Once I tasted it, I could not be satisfied without it.

Joe Woods was a fellow student in graduate school who became involved in discipling before me, and then loved me, served me and patiently answered an abundance of early questions.

My first foray into a discipling church came after a call from George Havins, who was then an elder in the San Diego church. George, his fellow elder, Ron Brumley, and their wives Cleo and Linda, as leaders loved us in a way simply incomparable to anything I had ever experienced in my former denomination. Gregg and Cathy Marutzky completed our leadership team in that church and will always be as my own children.

Kip McKean, who appointed me an evangelist and elder, gave me the respect and concern I needed but did not deserve, and it changed my heart and the direction of the rest of my life. His elders in the Boston church at the time, Al Baird and Bob Gempel, with their wives Gloria and Pat, contributed much to my training as a leader and an elder in the kingdom of God.

Wyndham Shaw, my first discipler in Boston, is now a fellow elder and a friend *par excellence*. He endured the worst of me and helped to bring out the best of me.

Randy McKean has contributed more to my role of teaching and writing than any other man—by far. He appointed me as a teacher, has used his abundant gifts to help shape me, and continues to call me much higher by his own spiritual growth.

Tom Jones has been my disciple and editor, and consequently, one of my best disciplers in life and in writing. Of all the men in Boston, he and I are the most alike in background and interests, making him a refreshing friend indeed.

Finally, my most influential discipler, other than God himself, has been my wife, Theresa. Without her, quite simply, I would not be me. Only heaven will be able to reveal the power of her influence in my life for time and eternity.

Scores more are left off this list, but not out of my heart. You know who you are and what you have done. Like the ones mentioned by name, you have been tools of God to help me live for and write about him. May he bless all of you for your grace to me.

INTRODUCTION

THE MISSING INGREDIENT

It was a brisk and clear afternoon in February 1967. I was pushing my boat away from the shore of my favorite lake for a fishing trip designed to last all night and most of the next day. Ordinarily I would have been filled with joyful anticipation, but on this particular day, I was filled with apprehension. You see, the man who had invited himself along on this trip was a minister, and the thought of being his one-man audience for a day and a half was more than a little terrifying!

At that time I was just beginning to attend church regularly as an adult. (As a kid, I attended regularly but not of my own free will—Mom had the only free will in that decision.) And although I was going to church just about every Sunday, it was much more to placate my wife than to please the Lord. Much of the world was still in my heart and in my life. Without question, I found being stuck in my boat with this preacher guy to be a scary proposition.

However, my discomfort began to fade rather quickly. For one thing, the fish starting biting immediately upon arriving, and we began filling up the ice chest with dinner. A fighting fish on the end of the line had a way of dissipating anxieties, even the anxiety of having to act much more like a spiritual person than I was.

For another thing, this preacher guy began evidencing some very intriguing and winsome qualities. He loved to fish and shouted and laughed with glee every time one of us caught a fish (and we caught many). Beyond that, he didn't preach at me, even though he seemed to be aware that my life-style included drinking, smoking, foul language and assorted other pagan practices. However, he did talk about a wide variety of subjects with perfect ease and naturalness. Clearly he was cut from a different cloth than any other minister that I had ever been around.

My impression at that time was that preacher types had dropped in on our planet from another galaxy. Their "stained glass" clergy tones and seemingly sinless lives did not strike me as real. But my *buddy* (we got close quickly, didn't we?) at the other end of the boat was not like that at all. He talked very candidly about his own life with its struggles, sins and victories. He talked about God and the Bible as if they were among his closest and most exciting friends. By the time we fried our fish over that old camping stove and settled back in our lawn chairs with steaming mugs of coffee, my heart had started feeling some new things which were unsettling and thrilling at the same time.

However, it was a mere beginning of a spiritual awakening, made clear when he suddenly looked up at the starlit skies and remarked about how wonderful it would be if the heavens were to split open and reveal a returning Jesus! I was shocked into absolute silence outwardly while my heart was crying out, "No, God! Not that! Don't listen to this fella! I'm not nearly ready to meet you yet!" Other than that little glitch, though, the entire trip was to be etched into my memory as one of the highlights of my life. Unexpectedly, as I write these very words, I find my eyes filling with tears as poignant memories and tremendous appreciation flood my soul.

What was that trip all about? And the scores of other times spent with that man—fishing, eating fish, praying, studying the Bible together and with others, laughing, and most of all, just talking about everything in our hearts and lives? Those marvelous times were all about what we are calling in this book "being discipled": two men sharing just about every aspect of their lives in a manner that blended the so-called sacred and secular sides of life into a spiritual learning situation. I was changed forever.

This unusual man became my mentor, my friend, my advisor, my teacher, my role model. In spite of his human imperfections, he was the flesh and blood demonstration of Christ to me. He was being used as God's tool to help lift me up from a spiritually aimless life. He was helping me get to a vantage point from which I could finally see enough of God to make me want him—and want him badly. It was discipleship as the Master practiced it himself. It was the God-designed way of molding lives and training men for the task of changing the world. It was the missing ingredient from my life in all the years before, and the missing ingredient from all of the religion I had ever seen or experienced. One of the key reasons I am a disciple of Jesus today (as the Bible describes it) traces back to those early experiences with my friend. He planted seeds in me that never died through the years, seeds that kept me looking for a church that practiced discipleship as the Bible depicts it and as I had known it with him.

The word "disciple" is very important biblically. Although the term "Christian" is most often used in our current age to describe one who professes allegiance to Christ, it is used only three times in the Bible and is never even defined within it. In fact, every occurrence is a reference to what those *outside the church* called those who follow Jesus. On the other hand, "disciple" is used nearly 300 times. As the term of choice of Jesus and those who were committed to him, it is quite well defined, as we will soon see.

Jesus said to go into all nations and make disciples (Matthew 28:19-20). A useful and descriptive term for the process of making and maturing disciples into Jesus' image is "discipling." The Greek text in Matthew 28:19 literally says, "going, therefore, disciple [a verb] all the nations." The rest of the verse makes it clear that "teaching them to obey everything I have commanded you" is a part of the discipling process. Thus, a "discipling" relationship is one in which a disciple helps another person to become more obedient to Jesus in attitude, life-style and mission. A main tenet of this book is that discipling is the forgotten art, the missing ingredient, in so many efforts to build churches and practice what is commonly known as Christianity.

Perhaps, as you read these words, a red flag is going up. Perhaps you have heard religious and irreligious people express specific misgivings about these kinds of relationships. Admittedly, such an emphasis on developing intimate spiritual relationships between disciples, designed to help them become more and more like Christ, falls on ears and hearts often unprepared by experience and training for the concepts. Two thoughts may be helpful here at the outset.

First, we are beginning the book with a study of what the Bible says about the subject. Rest assured that if the Bible doesn't teach what I am going to write about discipleship generally, or discipling relationships specifically, you are free to discard it. On the other hand, if the Bible does teach these principles, then you cannot ignore them and be pleasing to the God who inspired them. The real concern can never be what people (even religious ones) have said about a subject; the only ultimate concern is what God has said about it in Scripture.

Second, real problems have occurred in connection with the practice of discipling relationships, and potential challenges are always inherent in such relationships. But what of it? The same is true of all relationships, isn't it? It is especially true of the closer ones, and relationships in the kingdom of God are to be close. After thirty-two years of marriage, I can tell you that my wife and I have some relational challenges periodically. We misunderstand one another and even hurt each other. But we both treasure the relationship and would die before we would give it up. The issue is not "Could I be hurt?" in a discipling relationship. Growth in character will never be painless, and truthfully, it seldom occurs in quantity without someone else lovingly administering challenges (that feel painful). Did not the writer of Proverbs state: "Better is open rebuke than hidden love. Wounds from a friend can be trusted, but an enemy multiplies kisses"? (Proverbs 27:5-6). Looking back, the teachers I had in school whom I most appreciate now were the hard ones, the ones who challenged me to be my best. Relationships which don't help us to "take it higher" end up as the ones least appreciated (if we have much in the way of goals or ambition to better ourselves).

Nor is the issue "Will someone make mistakes in our relationship?" Of course they will! Have you been free of mistakes in all of your relationships? Have you never given bad advice or hurt someone, even with the best of intentions? Sure you have, if you have real relationships.

Relationships will always have challenges and problems because they involve humans. But a life without deep relationships is empty, and a life without deep spiritual relationships will be stagnant at best. With the kinds of relationships described in Scripture, life is more joyful than most can imagine, and the resultant growth keeps us "on the edge" as disciples whose commitment and zeal are not dimmed by the passing of the years. And that phenomenon, you will have to admit, is a rarity in a religious world most often characterized by lukewarmness and downright indifference.

The kinds of relationships we will discuss in this book are humbling, challenging and risky, but if they are what Jesus had in mind when he sent out the disciples, we will be blessed if we embrace them; we will miss his plan altogether if we do not.

I will always be grateful for those early days of adventure and exhilaration as I walked with another man who both taught me and showed me the way. I am grateful for the learner's spirit instilled in me which kept me searching for the exact path followed by the Master, that I might follow him ever more closely. Today, at age fifty-four, I have come to understand some key principles of discipleship, which I am anxious to share with you, the reader. But my understanding of the principles makes me acutely aware of how much more I need to grow in their appreciation and practice. And that understanding helps me to see how urgent you and I must be in pursuit of the Principle Maker's heart and mission. In the humility of a learner, whose life is *at best* a work in progress, I would echo these words of Paul, the consummate disciple:

> Not that I have already obtained all this, or have already been made perfect, but I press on to take hold of that for which Christ Jesus took hold of me. Brothers, I do not consider myself yet to have taken hold of it. But one thing I do: Forgetting what is behind and straining toward what is ahead, I press on toward the goal to win the prize for which God has called me heavenward in Christ Jesus (Philippians 3:12-14).

Part 1

BIBLICAL FOUNDATIONS

Discipling relationships work because they are thoroughly grounded in biblical principles. They are not contrived by human wisdom to meet psychological needs; they are part of God's plan to meet our spiritual needs. This section of the book will establish the scriptural and theological basis for such relationships, and will help us to see that they are absolutely essential for all who would obey Jesus' teachings and imitate his example.

1

JESUS
THE MASTER DISCIPLER

✠

If you have the world's most important message and you want to get it to the most people, how do you do it? Jesus had that conviction, and he had that concern. However, most Bible readers make some very erroneous assumptions about the ministry methods of Jesus. For years I was one of those people. I was very impressed with the times the Master Teacher worked with large crowds. I thought about how great it was for him to have exercised such magnetism that he was able to attract thousands at one time.

As a minister, I yearned to have such opportunities to influence the masses. I knew that the big campaigns by well-known speakers had short-lived results, but I thought it was due to the failure of their message, not their method. I found myself getting much more excited about speaking to hundreds than to tens, and the prospect of being before smaller groups left me wallowing in disappointment. My enthusiasm level rose and fell in direct proportion to the size of the group I was to address. *How unlike Jesus I was!*

You see, Jesus spoke to the crowds more as a means of his training of the apostles and other future evangelists (such as the seventy-two) than to "convert" the crowds. Of course, he was vitally interested in sharing God with those multitudes, but he wasn't naïve enough to suppose that teaching in those large groups was going to really do the job of changing their lives. He realized that a more individualized approach was going to be necessary, and he was preparing some very special men to provide just that approach.

Do those statements shock you? Just stop and think about how ineffective the crowd appeal actually was in the long term. The multitudes met him with joyful acclamation at the triumphal entry and a few days later were yelling "Crucify him!" Their real understanding of him and his mission was almost nil. It was going to take a more personalized approach if they were to understand the real Jesus. After his ascension back to heaven, he left only 120 in Jerusalem and about 500 in Galilee who were still faithful followers. Does that not strike you as incredible? The masses simply were not "converted" by the greatest Preacher in the world—at least not through his preaching to them *as* multitudes! He had a better way, which was, in fact, the *only* way.

How We Learn Spiritual Truths

At this juncture, let's stop and examine the way that we learn the spiritual principles which change lives at the deepest level. (This point is *immensely* important, and we must grasp it well. Keep your thinking cap on, and stay focused.) How do men learn to know God, to really know him? A related question would be to ask how well those who lived during the OT period understood God. With some notable exceptions, not many understood him very well at all. The way we humans learn is at issue here. We are not good at learning abstract truths in the absence of a physical demonstration, which explains just how essential the coming of Jesus was in helping men to understand God.

Most of what we learn in life is learned by OJT (on-the-job training). We watch big brother tie his shoes, and then we imitate him. We watch Dad change the tire on the car, and we quickly know far more than if we had spent a couple of hours reading the manual. Becoming a carpenter is a process: A journeyman repeatedly shows an apprentice how to do carpentry. Just about everything we learn in the early years of our lives is learned in this manner, as is most of what we learn in the later years. It is the fastest and easiest way, and in many cases the only way, to learn.

I'm reminded of the story I heard about a Harvard professor of home economics trying to teach some basics of cooking to women living in the backwoods of the Arkansas Ozark mountains. Nearly all of the women were raising families already and had cooked for years. But the professor was showing them how to separate the yolk of the egg from the white without breaking the shell. Her instructions went something like this: "First, we perforate the basil end of the egg, and then we repeat the procedure at the apex. Place the mouth on the aperture, compress the air and cause the crystal liquid to exude." One of the women looked at another and exclaimed: "Well, whatta you know! All these years I just knocked a hole in both ends and blowed!" Now how did those Arkansas women learn how to do that? By watching their moms, of course, just like we learn nearly everything else in life: from example. Nowhere is this principle more important than in learning spiritual truths.

The Gospel of John rather systematically develops the grand theme of "God with us." We read in John 1:18, "No one has ever seen God, but God the One and Only, who is at the Father's side, has made him known." The New American Standard Version (NASV) translates the last phrase as "has explained *Him*" (emphasis added), thus describing Jesus as the explanation or demonstration of God. As stated in John 1:1-3, Jesus as the eternal Word (*Logos* in Greek) was with the Father and is himself Deity. He became flesh and lived among men in order to reveal God to us (John 1:14). He told Philip clearly that "anyone who has seen me has seen the Father" (John 14:9). Until men could see God in flesh and blood, they could never really understand him. Colossians 2:9 informs us that the fullness of God dwelt in Jesus, meaning that the complete picture of God could be seen in him, and without that flesh and blood demonstration, men could not see the whole picture.

Remarkably, the church is described as the fullness of Christ (Ephesians 1:22-23), the natural implication being that men cannot get the complete picture of Christ without seeing him dwell in flesh and blood in every generation. So this is the role of the church! To make the point perfectly clear, the Israelites in the Old Testament could not gain a complete understanding of God simply from reading the Law—they needed to see a flesh and blood God (in the form of Jesus). People today cannot gain a complete understanding of Christ simply from reading the New Testament; we now have to see a flesh and blood Jesus in the form of his body, the church of his disciples. No wonder Paul said he was in birth pangs until Christ was formed in the Galatia Christians (Galatians 4:19)! Unless we are that demonstration, the world will never really see Jesus. *Amazing!*

We can see from all the biblical evidence above that there can be no "loner" Christians. We play an absolutely essential role in each other's lives. The gospel cannot be spread effectively without the human demonstration at the heart of it, nor can those who accept it be brought to maturity without those relationships (Matthew 28:19-20). Regarding the initial conversion process, just stop and think about how God chose to communicate the gospel to man. He didn't choose to drop leather-bound, gold-edged Bibles from heaven. He knew that the gospel had to be communicated by humans, because those receiving the message had to see it in writing *and* in lives: Enter King Jesus! And enter true disciples of Jesus.

The Book alone is sufficient to reveal the content of the truth to man, but to grasp its power, we must read it both in black and white (pages) *and* in black, white, brown, red, and yellow (people). The Bible has been the best-selling book in America for decades, but who is naïve enough to think that all those who own a copy will read it, let alone put it into practice? Most sinners will never read it until they see it lived out in a person. And they will never really see it in a person until that person is getting discipled according to the directions in the Book of books. Can you see the point here? Discipleship has not been tried and found wanting; it has simply been found difficult and not often tried. However, when it is put into practice, lives change radically, and others are drawn to that magnet of visible change. Discipling works! And it is all that works! It was and is, without question, the plan of Jesus Christ for the salvation of the world.

The Plan of the Master

Years ago, when I was first learning about discipling, I read a very helpful little book entitled *The Master Plan of Evangelism*.[1] Looking back over it recently, it seems quite basic, but when I first read it, I was affected significantly. (If you have not read it, I highly recommend it.) Coleman shows quite conclusively that the Master's method was men, plainly and simply. He poured his life into men, especially the Twelve, and when he returned to heaven, he left them to evangelize the world. They very effectively carried out his mission because they followed the same plan of pouring their lives into the lives of others, who repeated the same process over and over and over.

Christ's purpose was never to personally convert the masses, for in a physical body he was limited to one place at one time. However, through his spiritual body, the church, he could be everywhere at once. The masses are converted one by one. As I shared my faith yesterday with a young couple in a restaurant, disciples all over the world were doing the same. And as I slept last night, members of Jesus' body were carrying out his mission all over the world. Yes, the plan of Jesus was certainly the *master* plan!

The basics of his plan were as follows. First, he called men to follow him (Mark 1:14-18). They understood the commitment well enough to leave their personal priorities behind them and to accept his priorities. Following him was (and is) a lifetime commitment with no limitations set by man on the nature of the relationship; for to be his *follower* is to be his *slave.* Responding to his call is neither for the fainthearted nor for those with shallow commitment. It was, and will forever be, a complete surrendering of our lives to him.

In the second element of his plan, he kept men with him in order to train them and later send them out to share his message (Mark 3:14). He demonstrated all aspects of the spiritual life, from prayer to preaching. His training program was no seminary of academic intellectualism; it was a following in his steps as he loved, served and taught men. He knew that the communication of abstract principles was not the need, for the Jews had been exposed to quite enough of that.

His disciples had to see love with skin on it, compassion enough to break down walls of personal interests, personal problems, personal prejudices and all other self-focused pursuits. Self-denial is the fundamental prerequisite of following Jesus, but it is a radical quality that goes against the grain of our human nature and can only be learned by seeing another person practice it.

Jesus spent huge quantities of time with those early disciples in order for them to observe his total self-denial day after day. Then and only then would they be able to imitate it and pass it on to others. Transfer of knowledge was not his focus; transfer of heart was his task.

Third, the training process included practical assignments, for we truly learn and retain only that which we practice. Thus we read about Jesus sending out the Twelve to drive out demons and preach (Luke 9:1-6), and later the seventy-two were dispatched to do the same (Luke 10:1-16). Jesus had demonstrated how to do those things, and now he provided them the opportunity to imitate his example. Being the master Teacher, he spelled out very specifically exactly what they were to do and how they were to do it. After completing their assignments, they reported to Jesus how everything had gone with them, and he helped them gain the right spiritual perspective about their accomplishments (Luke 9:10, 10:18-24).

With Jesus, the classroom was life, and classes were always in session. His joy over the success of those returning disciples fairly *jumps* from the page when we read it. Doing great things for God is highly fulfilling, but training others to do the same yields the greatest reward possible. Jesus systematically taught his disciples by example, gave them assignments, complete with careful instructions, and then held them accountable for following through. He taught, demonstrated what he taught, observed them putting it into practice, and evaluated what they had done—over and over and over.

Finally, Jesus gave his life for what he had taught. Until we have something worth dying for, we have nothing worth living for. Unless others see an unlimited commitment in our lives, they will not commit their lives. Just as Jesus' bearing of his cross drew all men to himself (John 12:32), the bearing of our crosses will continue to draw those of our day to him. Paul understood this ultimate drawing power of suffering quite clearly, as may be seen in these statements: "We always carry around in our body the death of Jesus, so that the life of Jesus may also be revealed in our body" (2 Corinthians 4:10); and "Now I rejoice in what was suffered for you, and I fill up in my flesh what is still lacking in regard to Christ's afflictions, for the sake of his body, which is the church" (Colossians 1:24). Nothing in Christ's afflictions was lacking in paying the price of our sins, but again, until people see his qualities in the church, his spiritual body, they are not going to get the point. And the ultimate point is that we are willing to bear our crosses as we follow him. Only that level of dedication and determination in our lives will provide the supreme drawing power. Human beings must attract other human beings to Christ.

After Jesus had been resurrected from the grave, he spent forty days preparing his trained men for the coming of the kingdom and the task of spreading it all over the world. He then ascended back to heaven, leaving these few ordinary men with the extraordinary task of *being* (not just preaching) Jesus to the world. As Paul put it in 2 Corinthians 5:20, "We are therefore Christ's ambassadors, as though God were making his appeal through us." Jesus' method was to pour his life into men, and once they were fully trained, they would be like him (Luke 6:40). Having been thus discipled, they were able to "go and make disciples of all nations, teaching them to obey everything I have commanded you" (Matthew 28:19-20). It was a simple plan with a high price tag (a tremendous personal investment in training individuals), but it worked. It remains the same simple plan, and the price tag is just as high. No other plan has ever worked, can ever work, will ever work. We either do it his way, or we fail miserably.

Levels of Relationships

Jesus was the master relationship builder, and he built relationships at a number of different levels.[2] He had many interactions with the crowds, at the largest level. He had groups of disciples of various sizes: the most numerous mentioned was more than 500 (1 Corinthians 15:6); next in size were the seventy-two sent out on the limited commission (Luke 10:1); then the twelve apostles; and finally, the three in the inner circle (Peter, James and John). At the most intimate level would perhaps be his relationship with John. Regarding the last two levels, the three were with Jesus in a number of settings without the rest of the apostles, and John mentions himself several times as "the disciple whom Jesus loved." Certainly Jesus loved all of the apostles more than any of them could possibly grasp, but John seemed able to accept greater amounts of his love than could the others. He felt comfortable enough with Jesus, the God-man, to lean on his breast at the Last Supper (John 13:23).

These different levels of relationships were developed according to a plan. Jesus did nothing accidentally. He took only three years to ready his followers for his death, resurrection and return to heaven. They were left behind to carry on his mission of world conquest—to preach the gospel to the entire world and make disciples of all nations. Suffice it to say at this point that he left nothing to chance, especially his discipling of men to prepare them for their future monumental task.

In the simplest of terms, if we imitate Jesus, we will have relationships on the same levels that he had them. And each level will have a valid purpose, just as it did with him. What are the levels for us? Starting with the largest size, we rub shoulders with our multitudes in the world daily and must figure out ways to influence as many as possible in order to get them into a relationship with God. We attend church, which would approximate the 500 in Jesus' life. We have our smaller groups within that group, perhaps a group placed together for geographic or other reasons (age, interests, etc.), which would correspond to the seventy-two. Then comes the dozen level: the Bible-study group or discipleship group. The level of three (or something very close to it) might be the men or the women of the Bible study group spending time together. Finally, at the most personal level comes what we are calling "the discipling partner"—a person of the same sex with whom you have a special relationship for the purpose of growing and maturing in Christ. This would constitute one of the most intimate of our spiritual relationships.

Jesus' Discipling Imitated

Jesus called men to be with him, and then to be sent out to preach (Mark 3:14). The apostles predictably followed the same pattern. After Philip had been with them, he was sent out to preach in Samaria, with great results (Acts 8). After Barnabas had been with them, he was sent to Antioch (Acts 11:22). He, in turn, went to find Saul (later known as Paul), a man of great potential, and discipled him in practical ministry. Jointly, they discipled many other leaders there in Antioch and, through the missionary journeys, made disciples and raised up leaders all over the world.

One of Paul's most influential disciples was Timothy. Their discipling relationship began when Timothy was a young disciple living in Lystra (Acts 16:1). Paul took him with him and Silas on the remainder of the second missionary tour for training and later sent him to lead the very influential church in Ephesus. While there, Timothy received this very special charge about discipling from Paul: "And the things you have heard me say in the presence of many witnesses entrust to reliable men who will also be qualified to teach others" (2 Timothy 2:2). In Chapter Three we will examine this passage in more detail. Suffice it to say for now that establishing a *chain of discipling* is the intent of God in carrying out his mission on earth.

Paul had discipled Timothy, and Timothy was to disciple other reliable men, who would be able to teach others. Converting someone is never the ultimate goal of a disciple. The goal is to convert and train them to convert and train others, so that the chain will continue. In the case of Timothy, we have four spiritual generations implied in the above passage: Paul, Timothy, reliable men and others. When discipling is passed down through several generations, we can be assured that the discipleship concept is understood and will continue in the pattern Jesus envisioned.

Notice the same multiplication principle in the church at Thessalonica. Paul, Silas and Timothy had established the church there, as recorded in Acts 17:1-4. Later Paul wrote two letters to guide the young congregation in his absence. In 1 Thessalonians 1:6-8, Paul recounts how their discipleship had indeed spread rapidly to other places. It began with them imitating their original leaders, and then passing on what they had become to Macedonia and Achaia and ultimately to those "everywhere." Several spiritual generations were encompassed here, as discipleship followed its intended course. We see something similar in Acts 19:9-10 as Paul taught disciples daily in the lecture hall of Tyrannus over a two-year period, with the result being that "all the Jews and Greeks who lived in the province of Asia heard the word of the Lord." (Although Paul used a setting here which may remind us of a more formal type of ministry training, his training program included all of the practical ministry activities Jesus used. See my comments on Acts 20:17-38 in Chapter Three.)

When he was writing to encourage the young evangelist Timothy, Paul made it abundantly clear that his discipling was not simply academic, but quite practical.

> You, however, know all about my teaching, my way of life, my purpose, faith, patience, love, endurance, persecutions, sufferings—what kinds of things happened to me in Antioch, Iconium and Lystra, the persecutions I endured (2 Timothy 3:10-11).

Through his efforts at Ephesus, men were trained and sent out to lead churches all over Asia Minor. The multiplying ministry multiplied until Asia, and indeed the whole world, heard the message (Colossians 1:6).

Unity Produced by Discipling

The training of leaders as Jesus had done it not only set the stage for multiplication of disciples, it also set the stage for brotherhood unity like nothing else could have. An absolutely essential ingredient to the success of his mission was total unity among his followers (John 13:34-35; 17:20-23). When men have their hearts and entire lives discipled to become like Jesus in life and mission, the pride that normally divides men is dealt with decisively. The importance of this leadership training cannot be overestimated! It produced a brotherhood unity which in turn produced an evangelized world. Each member of the church saw himself as a part of one body on a brotherhood basis. They worked together with an amazing lack of sinful competitiveness. They cooperated in the prime mission God had given the church, and as a result, the entire world heard the message of Christ in about thirty years.

The church in the first century considered leaders to be "brotherhood leaders," rather than simply "congregational leaders." A careful study of Acts will demonstrate that key leaders had a striking non-attachment to any one congregation. They went where they were most needed at any one time. They were sent to the places where they could best serve. They were *world Christians,* not simply Philippian Christians or Ephesian Christians! And they instilled these concepts into all disciples, whether they were church ministry staff or not. A notable example of such world Christians is seen in Aquila and Priscilla, to whom we are first introduced when they are in Corinth. They are later sent to Ephesus, then to Rome, and then back to Ephesus (Acts 18:2, 18-19; Romans 16:3; 2 Timothy 4:19). Disciples of Jesus are those in any age who will go anywhere, do anything and give up everything for the advancement of the only Cause that really matters!

Blessed Are My Eyes

God has allowed me to live to see these principles reinstated in a marvelous way. I am often reminded of these words of Jesus:

> "But blessed are your eyes because they see, and your ears because they hear. For I tell you the truth, many prophets and righteous men longed to see what you see but did not see it, and to hear what you hear but did not hear it" (Matthew 13:16-17).

After many years in the ministry, I had all but lost my dream of an evangelized world. I had nearly given up on finding a church in which total commitment was a standard rather than a mere ideal. Unfortunately, the constant disappointment and disillusionment of my years as a preacher had taken their toll on me spiritually, and my eyes were not blessed nearly as soon as they might have been.

I needed to understand the distinction between a discipling model of evangelism and a preacher-centered one. For purposes of illustration, suppose that a highly effective preacher were to convert one person every day of the year. At the end of one year, he would have a church of 365 members. (And he would likely be acclaimed as one of the more successful preachers alive!) At the end of year two, his church would have 730 members and so on. Impressive performance, wouldn't you say? The discipling model, on the other hand, would not begin nearly so impressively. Suppose the discipler would make and train only one disciple the first year. The second year he and that newer disciple would each make and train one other. After one year, their "church" would number only two; after year two, only four; and after year three, just eight. But geometric progression begins to make its mark, and at year thirteen, the discipler model would have produced nearly twice the number of the preacher model (8,191 vs. 4,745). In thirty-two years, the preacher model results in 11,680 and the discipler model in over five billion! Sure, the illustration isn't perfect. In a real world there will be some attrition, not just additions, and not every disciple will reproduce himself. But, there can be no doubt that the discipling model produces amazing growth that cannot be matched by other methods. It is the plan of God for the salvation of the world.

By God's marvelous grace, I now hear stories of modern-day miracles practically daily, as lives are changed through the discipleship practiced all over the world just as Jesus and the early church practiced it. Examples of multiplying disciplers in the Bible are wonderful to read about and learn from, but seeing present-day examples seems more wonderful. Jesus is once again present in the flesh and blood examples of disciples making disciples who make disciples, in churches that multiply and send out, multiply and send out, as the world hears about our King Jesus the Christ! His simple, yet highly effective, plan for conquering the world spiritually cannot be improved upon, and it is time that all who would follow him really start to follow his approach to discipleship! Praise God that we are out of the realms of theory and into the concrete examples of those who are doing it!

2

DISCIPLING AND ONE-ANOTHER RELATIONSHIPS

✠

"A new command I give you: Love one another. As I have loved you, so you must love one another. By this all men will know that you are my disciples, if you love one another."

John 13:34-35

We have already seen that Jesus' plan to reach the world involved working through relationships. Now in this statement we see that in unique relationships, Jesus' disciples would show the world the uniqueness of his work. When the prophet Isaiah, six hundred years before Jesus, had looked forward to the coming Messianic kingdom, he had envisioned just such unusual relationships:

> See, a king will reign in righteousness
> and rulers will rule with justice.
> Each man will be like a shelter from the wind
> and a refuge from the storm,
> like streams of water in the desert
> and the shadow of a great rock in a thirsty land
> (Isaiah 32:1-2).

Everything Jesus taught was designed to create a church in which people would be this faithful and this helpful to one another in real life, as Isaiah describes poetically. The remainder of the New Testament shows that the apostles and others who penned the authoritative documents did not miss or misunderstand Jesus' message.

As you can see from the passages listed at the end of this chapter, the New Testament has a long list of directives about how those in the church are to relate to each other. All in all there are fifty-six verses with either "each other" or "one another" in them, and five of these verses have two such mentions, bringing the total to sixty-one. The number in itself is quite impressive and certainly makes the point that life in the family of God is all about relationships—close, caring, responsive relationships. Some in the list tell us what we should be doing, and some tell us what to avoid. It is important to note that there are scores of other verses concerning relationships besides those which use this specific phraseology. However, these provide a fairly comprehensive description of godly relationships.

The focus of this book is on discipling relationships. In one sense, *all* relationships in the body of Christ are to be "discipling" relationships. That is, in all our relationships, we are to be concerned with helping our brothers and sisters be faithful disciples of Jesus. However, we are talking here about a more specific relationship in which, for some period of time, one disciple makes a special commitment to the growth and encouragement of another disciple. As we look at these one-another commands, we would never argue that one-on-one discipling relationships are the only way to observe these instructions. Certainly, "body life" in general must be based on them. None of these can be ignored in any spiritual relationship, but some of them are most readily put into practice in one-on-one discipling relationships. Discipling has been rediscovered and reinstituted in modern times by those who have a passion to restore the relational nature of biblical Christianity. They see how imperative it is that every church be a demonstration of these passages. They are right when they recognize that some one-another commands are easily omitted from our lives in the absence of best-friend discipling relationships.

For example, just think about how few church-goers confess their specific sins to another person (James 5:16). Think of those who never spiritually instruct other people (Romans 15:14), or admonish them (Colossians 3:16), or encourage them on a daily basis for the specific purpose of keeping their hearts soft and resistant to the hardening effects of sin (Hebrews 3:13). Oddly, many religious people have less than positive feelings about the discipleship-partner arrangement, yet their own lives are devoid of obeying many of these one-another commands. Whatever religious activities they may be involved in, they are not involved in the practice of these passages just mentioned. Such a lack of conviction and subsequent neglect surely must be seen by God as willful disobedience. Why would we find fault with anything that helps us more fully love, help, encourage and train one another?

Discipling and One-Another Passages

In the rest of this chapter we want to take just a few of these important one-another passages and look at how a special discipling relationship gives us a unique, but much needed, opportunity to put into practice the biblical commands in a very consistent and life-changing fashion.

John 13:34-35—Love One Another

> A new command I give you: Love *one another*. As I have loved you, so you must love *one another*. By this all men will know that you are my disciples, if you love *one another* (John 13:34-35, emphasis added).

As we mentioned earlier, the love demonstrated between disciples is to have a profound effect on the world who sees us together. Most often we think of assemblies of the body of Christ as the most appropriate way of making this demonstration. But this is not necessarily accurate. For example, in the Boston church of which I am a part, our assemblies make a powerful statement about race relationships. We have members who represent just about every race and combination of races possible. When nonmembers attend and see the hugs and warm greetings between races, it makes quite a powerful impression. Boston is characterized by its share of racial tensions, especially between blacks and whites, but the church strives mightily to be color blind. Therefore, attendance at our assemblies will allow visitors to experience the effects Jesus had in mind in John 13:34-35.

However, more impact is possible in smaller settings. For a number of years, I discipled Hardy Tillman, a noted professional counselor, who happens to be black. (I'm white.) We are best friends, our families are best friends and we have been for many years. The Tillmans are a part of our family, spending most major holidays and many other occasions with us. We don't *look* like family, but we *are* family and we *act* like family! We are expressive and demonstrative in our love for one another. Now don't you imagine that the impact of our relationship is more striking to onlookers than it would be when simply seeing us attend the same church? I think so. Some of my best spiritual friends are of different races than I, which makes some very strong statements to my neighbors, their neighbors and to all who see us together. While John 13:34-35 is fulfilled in many ways, to see best-friend discipleship partners loving as Jesus loved probably makes the point in the most dramatic fashion.

Hebrews 3:13—Encourage One Another Daily

> But encourage *one another* daily, as long as it is called Today, so that none of you may be hardened by sin's deceitfulness (Hebrews 3:13, emphasis added).

Sin is deceitful. Our own sin deceives us into thinking we are doing better than we are, and we then proceed to deceive others around us into thinking we are doing better than we are. We are pretty clueless about the lives of the people we see only in larger church settings. We have to know people well to know how they are doing spiritually and to be able to tell when they are becoming blind to their spiritual condition.

Certain people cannot be fooled. Children are not often fooled about how their parents are really doing. They read them like a book. Wives are not oblivious to their husbands' spirituality level. After thirty-two years of marriage, I sometimes think that Theresa knows me better than I know myself, and quite often she does. I desperately need her input, because she loves me most and knows me best. My sin seldom deceives her. And she seldom fails to tell me what she sees! (Praise God!)

Discipleship partners develop the same types of insight into our spiritual lives because they are around us a lot and know us. Our relationship is to be based on honesty and vulnerability. We all need people in our lives who know us and love us enough to help us when we are veering off the narrow path. Even when we are mostly deceived by and about our sins, we sense that something is unsettled in our souls. Then when our discipleship partner says, "How are you doing?" we might answer quickly "Fine," but if he (or she, if you are a woman) knows us well, he won't leave the issue too quickly. The next question is often, "How are you *really* doing?" At that point I start getting in touch and being real. If I truly don't know what is wrong with me, talking with him usually drives it to the surface, and I am on my way back to an even keel.

Of course, then, in Hebrews 3:13, we have to deal with the "daily" encouragement issue. With whom do you have a *daily* relationship? If you can't answer that question, then you are probably right now making excuses and trying to find ways to explain away what the verse plainly says. Maybe you are thinking about cultures with poor transportation and few telephones. So now you feel better, because you have found an exception! (Please spare me.)

I'm not trying to be legalistic about the matter, but neither am I willing to discount the passage. I have daily contact with my discipler and/or disciples virtually every day of the year, and I try to share exactly what is going on in my life (as much as I am aware of it). I have seen many Christians lose their first love, become lukewarm and ultimately leave God. I have seen many leaders follow exactly the same path. Satan knows much more about your spiritual condition and the exact ways in which you are vulnerable to temptations than you do. I don't intend to be one of those who becomes hardened by sin and then loses his faith. I need people in my life at close range—I *want* people in my life at close range. I need all the help I can get, and I need it daily! And so do you!

Hebrews 10:24—Spur One Another On

> And let us consider how we may spur *one another* on toward love and good deeds (Hebrews 10:24, emphasis added).

Now this is an intriguing passage. The original Greek word translated "spur on" *(paroxysmos)* has an interesting history. It has a very definite connection with anger. At best, the word carries the idea of being very passionate about something to the point that becoming heated about it would be a natural response. It was not a word used for conflict avoiders and people pleasers. We find it twice in the New Testament: once in this passage and once in Acts 15:39. In the latter it is translated "sharp disagreement," as it describes an encounter between Paul and Barnabas when they were discussing the role of John Mark in their mission efforts. The disagreement was so sharp that these two great missionaries parted company!

Hebrews 10:24 is saying that another's spiritual life is worth fighting for, if need be. Surely this is the language of relationships, close relationships. Barnabas discipled Paul in the early stages of their relationship, and Paul loved and respected Barnabas immensely. They were secure enough in their love to lay all of their cards on the table. All indications are that they kept the highest regard for one another, even after their disagreement. Interestingly, near the end of his life Paul requested Mark's help in his ministry (2 Timothy 4:11). With whom do you have this kind of relationship? The person you only greet in the foyer before or after a church service? No, we must have close relationships for these kinds of potentially heated interchanges, and no relationship lends itself to it more than a discipling relationship.

James 5:16—Confess to One Another

> Therefore confess your sins to *each other* and pray for *each other* so that you may be healed. The prayer of a righteous man is powerful and effective (James 5:16, emphasis added).

Confession of sins is vital if we are to overcome Satan's power in our lives. He is a creature of darkness, and thrives well only in his native environment. If we get ourselves out into the light, he runs. James promised in James 4:7 that if we resist Satan, he will flee from us. But how do we resist him? With light. The more light, the more he is rendered powerless. The Bible is light, and studying it definitely limits Satan. Spiritual activities and spiritual relationships limit him. The closer we are to God, the less the devil can do to hurt us. The more we surround ourselves with spiritual things, the less he can get a foothold in our hearts.

What is hidden inside us remains in the darkness. Only by getting it out and exposing it to other people do we ourselves see it clearly. When sins are confessed, the light destroys sin's grip. The world has this concept exactly backwards, which is not surprising. Confessing one's sins is considered lunacy by most. So they keep sin hidden in darkness, and its effects multiply mightily. Read John 3:19-21 in this vein, and ask yourself whether you love coming out into the light or staying hidden in darkness.

But now, what about the confession of sins in James 5:16? In context, a sick person is told to send for the elders of the church, who can anoint him with oil and pray over him. If he has sinned, it says, he will be forgiven. When we are seriously ill, we are very conscious of our spiritual condition. Asking elders to pray about our spiritual condition at the same time they are praying about our physical condition is quite natural. But verse 16 adds several very important insights.

One, confession and prayer brings healing. It may well improve physical health, for our spiritual condition definitely affects our bodies. A number of statements in Psalms, such as 32:3-4, demonstrate that point decidedly. But confession and prayer brings healing to our souls like nothing else does. We don't confess to another person for forgiveness (unless we have sinned against them); we pray to God for that. But healing of the soul comes from this whole process of confessing and praying with other people.

Two, the grammatical construction of the Greek in James 5:16 shows the need for a habitual, continual confessing of sins. "Be in the habit of confessing" is the idea—don't wait until an illness and the presence of church leaders motivates you. Be in the habit of doing it, for surely confession is good for the soul. With whom do you consistently confess your sins?

Three, we are to confess specific sins, not just that we have sinned. The more specific, the more light and the more victory over them. Years ago when the magnitude of this principle dawned on me, I came up with a plan to defeat the sins in my life. First, I would confess very specifically and graphically to God, to the point of embarrassment. That in itself introduces copious amounts of light onto the situation. Then I would confess to a brother. If no victory came at that point, then I made my confession to a *group* of men. I determined to confess to larger and larger groups until the light blinded Satan and ran him off (at least on that point). The first time I tried it in those years before I was a part of a discipling ministry, I ended up going all the way to the whole congregation with the confession. As my face blushed with embarrassment, Satan cowered with light overdose and left me alone! The practice works if we have the conviction to work it.

But one more word on confessing specifically. While preaching, I often use stories from my own life, as you would suspect after reading this far. I want to model openness for others, and I want the benefit of throwing the light in Satan's eyes. Mentioning in a general way that I struggle with lust is not out of place in a congregational setting. But mentioning the specifics of it would be. Yet, if I am to have a victory, I need to confess the specifics. To whom should I confess? To Theresa? Probably not. My own opinion on this sensitive area is that wives don't quite understand men's struggles in this regard, because for women lust typically involves more of an emotional attraction. Therefore, they may assume that we are emotionally attracted to someone when we are not, and that assumption can affect them detrimentally.

The discipleship partner is the ideal one with whom to share my inmost struggles. If you are a man, he is a man and understands what you are going through and can help you. In this illustration, the wife would be protected and the man helped by specific confession. The only exception I normally make in this approach is to recommend a brother confessing to his wife if other measures don't produce repentance. For example, I have known of men who needed to confess to their wives repeated late-night channel surfing on TV and using the computer to view pornography on the Internet. Confession to the wife would certainly increase the wattage of the light exposure! (And it normally works wonders in inducing repentance!) We need to have a natural avenue of confessing all temptations and sins. The sensitivity of the area mentioned above shows the need and the wisdom of having these close one-on-one relationships with what we call discipleship partners.

Ephesians 5:21—Submit to One Another

> Submit to *one another* out of reverence for Christ (Ephesians 5:21, emphasis added).

Mutual submission is part of the foundation of spiritual relationships between all brothers and sisters in Christ. Nevertheless, Paul reiterates this command for mutual submission before addressing the husband/wife relationship. He may have done so to tie this passage in with the earlier part of the chapter; indeed, the command fits all relationships in some way. In the marriage relationship, wives are to submit to the *leadership* of their husbands, and husbands are to submit to the *needs* of their wives by loving them as Christ loves the church. (Modern society may take offense at God's teaching, but God takes offense at their teaching and the divorce rate it produces!)

Submission comes in many forms, as leadership and followership is a part of all of our lives. In some areas I lead, and I expect others involved in those areas to submit to my leadership. In other areas I am led, and I willingly submit to those leading me in those areas. For example, Randy McKean is my lead evangelist, and I submit to him in that role. I am his teacher, and he submits to me in that role (and does quite well on ministry training exams, I might add!). Submission is a part of orderly life, and the less of it any society, group or family has, the more chaos will reign.

But what does all of this have to do with discipling? Let's appeal to the same logic we used with the commands we have already discussed. Submission to one another is quite vaguely expressed in a large-group setting, except for the role of the leaders and those under them. It comes into play between "one another" at the more intimate levels of relationship. Certainly the discipleship-partner relationships require this kind of submissive heart. We cannot be discipled without a willingness to be discipled, and that certainly involves some type of submission. (We will clarify

some related issues later in the book regarding differences in spiritual maturity, age or experience that exist between discipleship
partners. Until then, don't start jumping to convulsions!)

I was discipled for a couple of years by Jimmy Rogers, who
is nearly fifteen years younger than I. Once in a sermon, he
mentioned that discipling me was a major two-lane road. In
other words, the discipling went both ways. Actually, it should
always go both ways to some extent (unless, of course, one of
the dp's is Jesus!). Jimmy and I are both in the leadership group
of the Boston church, and we both wear many "hats" of leadership. But back then I still strove to have a submissive spirit
toward Jimmy and looked at him as a tool of God in helping me
grow.

Authority and submission are most often viewed negatively.
However, we must learn to see them biblically as very positive.
I deeply appreciate those in the kingdom of God who will accept leadership roles because I know that Jesus demands that
his leaders be servants—submissive to the needs of those they
lead. I am grateful to submit to godly leadership. I am grateful
for those "willing volunteers" (Judges 5:9) who submit to my
leadership. Our submission in discipling relationships is not
really submission to the authority of the discipler; it is submission to the authority of God, who has chosen to work in our
lives through human tools. (There are roles with authority at
some leadership levels in the church, which we will clarify in
Section Four of the book. On the discipling level, think friendship, not authority—but also think submission and humility,
and enjoy the blessings!)

Romans 15:14—Instruct One Another

> I myself am convinced, my brothers, that you yourselves
> are full of goodness, complete in knowledge and compe-
> tent to instruct *one another* (Romans 15:14, emphasis
> added).

Competency to instruct one another, according to this passage, is based on two things: being filled with goodness and being
complete in knowledge. Just what does being "complete in knowl-

edge" entail? Certainly it would include a knowledge of the word of God. We cannot instruct, counsel or advise without a basic understanding of the biblical issues involved in helping one another spiritually. But this knowledge would necessarily include our familiarity with the person we are trying to help. *Those who know me best are able to help me most.*

Recently in a men's discipleship group of eight leaders, we spent some time talking about our personal spiritual lives. This was followed by a brief evaluation of each person by others in the group who noted one strength and one area most needing improvement. (We will examine group discipling in Chapter Fifteen.) Randy McKean, who was leading the group, asked us to share only about the person sitting to our right. Although that method of selection was purely arbitrary, I was glad that I was sitting to the right of Randy, since he disciples me at this point in my life and knows me better than some others in the group know me. He picked the weak point I most needed to hear at that time (although others could have been selected!).

Later that night, as Theresa and I were driving home from our discipleship groups, I shared with her the gist of Randy's comments. She became quiet, and after about a minute I looked over at her and noticed that she was crying. My first thought (obviously an *unspiritual* one!) was that she felt defensive for me! That was hardly the case. Upon hearing about Randy's critique, she started getting in touch with some emotions that totally validated the critique. In a word, the sinful tendency which had been pointed out in me (essentially, impatience and irritability) was the very sin that had hurt her. Because of the demanding schedule I had been under for several months, she had "stuffed" her feelings, not wanting to add more pressure on me, but now she was beginning to get in touch with the pain. We spent several hours talking that night and on the following day. She was able to have her heart healed and her husband repentant. The level of conviction produced in me has enabled me to make some great strides, thank God, but the beginning point was that d-group. More than that, it was a defining moment brought about by the loving critique of a brother who was "complete in knowledge" about the man he discipled.

Ephesians 4:32—Forgive One Another

> Be kind and compassionate to *one another*, forgiving *each other*, just as in Christ God forgave you (Ephesians 4:32, emphasis added).

Forgiveness is a wonderful, godly quality, but its presence is needed only when ungodly qualities have entered the scene! Sin must occur before forgiveness is needed. Now, against whom do you most sin—those you are around most or least? Those who see me only in a larger church setting often seem to think I am *Mr. Wonderful* and *Mr. Perfect.* Why is that? I often mention in lessons that I am far from perfect, and share instances in my life (like the one above) to demonstrate it. But most of them are not in my life at the more intimate levels, and we don't have many opportunities to sin against each other. Those who are in my life at the closer levels see and are hurt by my sins more readily, and since they have more expectations in our relationship, are more prone to be disappointed by me.

Therefore, although forgiveness is vital in all relationships when sin occurs, the fact remains that relationship sins occur most in the closest relationships. I'm reminded of an old song with this phrase in it: "You always hurt the one you love." (No surprises there—they are about the only ones who will put up with you long enough to get hurt by you!) And the more love there is, the deeper the hurt can be. You could never wound a casual friend as deeply as you can an intimate friend. I am persuaded that Ephesians 4:32 is needed and exercised most in the relationships which are the closest to us. And of all of our spiritual relationships in the church, those with a discipleship partner will be among the closest. I remind you that I am not saying that any of these one-another passages *only* applies to discipleship-partner, "d-p," relationships. I'm simply saying that some of the passages have their greatest application in the closer settings.

Philippians 4:2—Agree with One Another

> I plead with Euodia and I plead with Syntyche to agree with *each other* in the Lord (Philippians 4:2, emphasis added).

Agreement with each other, in the case of Euodia and Syntyche, was needed due to some disagreement between them which had affected the church. We have to assume that these women were key leaders, or else Paul would not have mentioned their names publicly. They, in fact, had been co-workers with him when he had been in Philippi, according to Philippians 4:3. Such disagreements could only occur between those with a close relationship. Whether they were what we are terming "discipleship partners" or not, they must have been functioning in a similar manner. We generally do not have disagreements like this one without first having a close working relationship.

Just last evening I was speaking with a brother about a disagreement he had experienced in the past. He felt badly about the disagreement (which, in this case, involved some incorrect assumptions), but I was not alarmed by it, especially since he and the brother had worked it out. My comment to him was that disagreements, when resolved correctly, bind us closer together. My closest relationships are those in which some rather heated disagreements have occurred and been resolved.

When we first moved to Boston and Wyndham Shaw was discipling me, I was unsatisfied with only one thing in our otherwise good relationship. I was quite open with him about my life (including my sins), but he didn't reciprocate. Once I asked if we could take a long walk together around a lake, and during the walk I expressed my disagreement with his approach on this one point. My ultimate issue was that no relationship can ever be really close without both people being vulnerable. He began the conversation disagreeing with me, saying that he was open with his discipler, just as I was with him, and that was sufficient. He said that what we really needed to get closer was to get more time playing sports together! Our disagreement continued for most of our walk around the lake. After some fairly intense exchanges, he changed his mind. He then changed his practice immediately, and by example, called me higher in that very area! We were more bonded that day through our frank disagreement and resolution than we would have been after ten days on the basketball court!

While discipleship-partner relationships are not the only way to put into practice these vital one-another passages, they are often the best. And without such relationships, my experience is that some of the passages will be seldom practiced, if ever. We all need each other in the church, every member, for we are a family. But as in a physical family, we need that special one with whom we can pour out our hearts freely in a confidential setting, who will be able to handle our heart and its problems because of the closeness of the relationship. I thank God for discipling relationships!

New Testament One-Another Passages

1. Mark 9:50 – Salt is good, but if it loses its saltiness, how can you make it salty again? Have salt in yourselves, and be at peace with *each other*.
2. John 13:34 – A new command I give you: Love *one another*. As I have loved you, so you must love *one another*.
3. John 13:35 – By this all men will know that you are my disciples, if you love *one another*.
4. John 15:12 – My command is this: Love *each other* as I have loved you.
5. John 15:17 – This is my command: Love *each other*.
6. Romans 12:10 – Be devoted to *one another* in brotherly love. Honor *one another* above yourselves.
7. Romans 12:16 – Live in harmony with *one another*. Do not be proud, but be willing to associate with people of low position. Do not be conceited.
8. Romans 13:8 – Let no debt remain outstanding, except the continuing debt to love *one another*, for he who loves his fellowman has fulfilled the law.
9. Romans 14:13 – Therefore let us stop passing judgment on *one another*. Instead, make up your mind not to put any stumbling block or obstacle in your brother's way.
10. Romans 15:7 – Accept *one another*, then, just as Christ accepted you, in order to bring praise to God.
11. Romans 15:14 – I myself am convinced, my brothers, that you yourselves are full of goodness, complete in knowledge and competent to instruct *one another*.

12. Romans 16:16 – Greet *one another* with a holy kiss. All the churches of Christ send greetings.
13. 1 Corinthians 1:10 – I appeal to you, brothers, in the name of our Lord Jesus Christ, that all of you agree with *one another* so that there may be no divisions among you and that you may be perfectly united in mind and thought.
14. 1 Corinthians 7:5 – Do not deprive *each other* except by mutual consent and for a time, so that you may devote yourselves to prayer. Then come together again so that Satan will not tempt you because of your lack of self-control.
15. 1 Corinthians 11:33 – So then, my brothers, when you come together to eat, wait for *each other*.
16. 1 Corinthians 12:25 – so that there should be no division in the body, but that its parts should have equal concern for *each other*.
17. 1 Corinthians 16:20 – All the brothers here send you greetings. Greet *one another* with a holy kiss.
18. 2 Corinthians 13:12 – Greet one another with a holy kiss.
19. Galatians 5:13 – You, my brothers, were called to be free. But do not use your freedom to indulge the sinful nature; rather, serve *one another* in love.
20. Galatians 5:15 – If you keep on biting and devouring *each other*, watch out or you will be destroyed by *each other*.
21. Galatians 5:26 – Let us not become conceited, provoking and envying *each other*.
22. Ephesians 4:2 – Be completely humble and gentle; be patient, bearing with *one another* in love.
23. Ephesians 4:32 – Be kind and compassionate to *one another*, forgiving *each other*, just as in Christ God forgave you.
24. Ephesians 5:19 – Speak to *one another* with psalms, hymns and spiritual songs. Sing and make music in your heart to the Lord,
25. Ephesians 5:21 – Submit to *one another* out of reverence for Christ.
26. Philippians 4:2 – I plead with Euodia and I plead with Syntyche to agree with *each other* in the Lord.
27. Colossians 3:9 – Do not lie to *each other*, since you have taken off your old self with its practices

28. Colossians 3:13 – Bear with *each other* and forgive whatever grievances you may have against *one another*. Forgive as the Lord forgave you.
29. Colossians 3:16 – Let the word of Christ dwell in you richly as you teach and admonish *one another* with all wisdom, and as you sing psalms, hymns and spiritual songs with gratitude in your hearts to God.
30. 1 Thessalonians 3:12 – May the Lord make your love increase and overflow for *each other* and for everyone else, just as ours does for you.
31. 1 Thessalonians 4:9 – Now about brotherly love we do not need to write to you, for you yourselves have been taught by God to love *each other*.
32. 1 Thessalonians 4:18 – Therefore encourage *each other* with these words.
33. 1 Thessalonians 5:11 – Therefore encourage *one another* and build *each other* up, just as in fact you are doing.
34. 1 Thessalonians 5:13 – Hold them in the highest regard in love because of their work. Live in peace with *each other*.
35. 1 Thessalonians 5:15 – Make sure that nobody pays back wrong for wrong, but always try to be kind to *each other* and to everyone else.
36. 2 Thessalonians 1:3 – We ought always to thank God for you, brothers, and rightly so, because your faith is growing more and more, and the love every one of you has for *each other* is increasing.
37. Hebrews 3:13 – But encourage *one another* daily, as long as it is called Today, so that none of you may be hardened by sin's deceitfulness.
38. Hebrews 10:24 – And let us consider how we may spur *one another* on toward love and good deeds.
39. Hebrews 10:25 – Let us not give up meeting together, as some are in the habit of doing, but let us encourage *one another*— and all the more as you see the Day approaching.
40. Hebrews 13:1 – Keep on loving *each other* as brothers.
41. James 4:11 – Brothers, do not slander *one another*. Anyone who speaks against his brother or judges him speaks against the law and judges it. When you judge the law, you are not keeping it, but sitting in judgment on it.

42. James 5:9 – Don't grumble against *each other*, brothers, or you will be judged. The Judge is standing at the door!

43. James 5:16 – Therefore confess your sins to *each other* and pray for *each other* so that you may be healed. The prayer of a righteous man is powerful and effective.

44. 1 Peter 1:22 – Now that you have purified yourselves by obeying the truth so that you have sincere love for your brothers, love *one another* deeply, from the heart.

45. 1 Peter 3:8 – Finally, all of you, live in harmony with *one another*; be sympathetic, love as brothers, be compassionate and humble.

46. 1 Peter 4:8 – Above all, love *each other* deeply, because love covers over a multitude of sins.

47. 1 Peter 4:9 – Offer hospitality to *one another* without grumbling.

48. 1 Peter 5:5 – Young men, in the same way be submissive to those who are older. All of you, clothe yourselves with humility toward *one another*, because, "God opposes the proud but gives grace to the humble."

49. 1 Peter 5:14 – Greet *one another* with a kiss of love. Peace to all of you who are in Christ.

50. 1 John 1:7 – But if we walk in the light, as he is in the light, we have fellowship with *one another*, and the blood of Jesus, his Son, purifies us from all sin.

51. 1 John 3:11 – This is the message you heard from the beginning: We should love *one another*.

52. 1 John 3:23 – And this is his command: to believe in the name of his Son, Jesus Christ, and to love *one another* as he commanded us.

53. 1 John 4:7 – Dear friends, let us love *one another*, for love comes from God. Everyone who loves has been born of God and knows God.

54. 1 John 4:11 – Dear friends, since God so loved us, we also ought to love *one another*.

55. 1 John 4:12 – No one has ever seen God; but if we love *one another*, God lives in us and his love is made complete in us.

56. 2 John 1:5 – And now, dear lady, I am not writing you a new command but one we have had from the beginning. I ask that we love *one another*.

3

BIBLICAL PRINCIPLES
OF DISCIPLING

✠

Biblical discipling is a good idea, but it is more than that. I believe we will see in this chapter that discipling is a matter of absolute necessity for anyone who would take seriously the teaching of the New Testament. We will examine biblical passages which show the basis of having such relationships and provide the directions for gaining the most benefit from them.

The first murder in the world was committed because of the breakdown of brotherly relationships. When God asked Cain about his brother Abel, Cain replied "Am I my brother's keeper?" (Genesis 4:9). The remainder of the Bible shouts "Yes!" Of the thousands of truths taught in the Bible, none is clearer than the fact that we emphatically are to be our brother's keeper. The greatest command in all of Scripture is to love God with our entire being and to love our neighbors as ourselves (Matthew 22:36-40). Must we love our spiritual brothers? Absolutely! But how does that love show itself? In myriad ways, but one of the most important is to love enough to help each other grow and change to be more like Christ. Jesus said, "Those whom I love I rebuke and discipline" (Revelation 3:19). How much do you love—enough to lovingly confront sin in the life of your brother? Enough to "spur one another on toward love and good deeds"? (Hebrews 10:24).

Discipleship demands that we put our laziness behind us and serve another for his highest good. It demands that we put off our pride and humbly submit to the leadership of others and to the needs of others. It demands that we put aside our people-pleasing, conflict-avoiding natures and reach out to those who need our direction and correction. It demands that we follow the One who set the pattern for it and died for it and spelled it out in his Word for us. Are we willing? Since "faith comes from hearing the message, and the message is heard through the word of Christ" (Romans 10:17), let's go to that message and deepen our convictions about the subject of discipling relationships.

Old Testament Principles

Many passages show the value of close relationships which challenge us to be our best for God. At a later time, we will mention a number of Scriptures, particularly in Proverbs, that talk about seeking advice and responding wisely to correction. Characteristic of such verses are these: "Whoever loves discipline loves knowledge, but he who hates correction is stupid" (Proverbs 12:1) and "Listen to advice and accept instruction, and in the end you will be wise" (Proverbs 19:20). These are general discipleship verses, for they show the importance of having others in our lives to advise, instruct and correct us.

The most classic passages in Proverbs on the subject are in chapter 27:

> Better is open rebuke
>   than hidden love.
> Wounds from a friend can be trusted,
>   but an enemy multiplies kisses (Proverbs 27:5-6).
>
> As iron sharpens iron,
>   so one man sharpens another (Proverbs 27:17).

Such verses presuppose really close relationships that call out the best in each other. I don't particularly *enjoy* open rebuke, but I have grown to *appreciate* it. Some of the most valuable lessons in my life have come from the mouth of someone willing to lay out the truth to me. I neither enjoy nor appreciate hidden love, or hidden displeasure, or any other hidden agenda. Bottom line, I appreciate honesty. Whatever you are really thinking about me, just come out with it! Real relationships are just that—real (open and honest).

I remember a time when my daughter, Renee, was a teen and we were having difficulties in our relationship and we needed help. Randy McKean suggested that he come over so he could disciple us both together. I asked Renee how she felt about going this route, and she said "Fine, because I know you will get yours too!" Randy was evenhanded, and sure enough, we both got ours. Afterwards, Randy asked if he had been too hard on me (not wanting to show disrespect to me as an older man). I told him that he had been very honest and straightforward, but impartial, in his correction. I expected nothing less and would not have been satisfied with anything less.

Both Bryan, our son, and Renee are happily married to disciples and doing great. My relationship with them and their spouses is superb, thanks to several friends "wounding" us with the truth through the years. Probably the most helpful aspect of the times when I asked others to disciple us together was in the kids seeing my heart and knowing that I was more interested in being *right with God* than being *right* about the issue at hand. No one will ever love correction without first having an overriding desire to please God and to be his best for him. If becoming more and more like Jesus is our greatest aim in life, then even corrective discipling will be a joy to us.

But be prepared: When iron sharpens iron, some sparks are going to fly. I have forgotten thousands of pleasant conversations through the years, but I have some heated conversations firmly etched in my memory. They may have seemed tough at the moment, but the closest relationships have been forged at the anvil of tension and resolution. Do you find yourself recoiling at words like these? What would you have done had you been in Peter's shoes and been called "Satan" by God in the flesh? Some of us have been hurt by worldly rebukes which were given to damage and destroy. But now, if we are in the kingdom, we are going to have to develop new attitudes about relationships and the confrontational nature that all spiritual relationships are going to have on occasion. Let's develop the heart of the psalmist when he wrote:

> Let a righteous man strike me—it is a kindness;
> let him rebuke me—it is oil on my head.
> My head will not refuse it (Psalm 141:5).

A passage seldom used in this context, but one which is none-theless full of discipling principles is Ecclesiastes 4:8-12.

> There was a man all alone;
>> he had neither son nor brother.
> There was no end to his toil,
>> yet his eyes were not content with his wealth.
> "For whom am I toiling," he asked,
>> "and why am I depriving myself of enjoyment?"
> This too is meaningless—
>> a miserable business!
>
> Two are better than one,
>> because they have a good return for their work:
> If one falls down,
>> his friend can help him up.
> But pity the man who falls
>> and has no one to help him up!
> Also, if two lie down together, they will keep warm.
>> But how can one keep warm alone?
> Though one may be overpowered,
>> two can defend themselves.
> A cord of three strands is not quickly broken.

This passage is often applied to marriage and is thus used as a part of wedding ceremonies. We can certainly make such an application, but in context, it is simply describing the need we all have for close relationships. Take a closer look at the wording of the passage. A man alone, without family or close friend will never be satisfied with a career and wealth (verse 8). Life is about relationships, not possessions or accomplishments. We need a buddy to help us work and to help us up when we fall. Teamwork not only increases accomplishment, it makes work much more enjoyable. Who helps the average person get up when he falls?

Years ago, I remember facing some personal struggles of a fairly ordinary nature. I had no one with whom I talked about such things, but I dared venture out to talk with a good fishing buddy. After pouring out my pain, he just looked at me and said "Oh." No more, no less—just "Oh." You can bet that I didn't try that openness stuff again for a long time! Certainly not until I found the kind of friend described in the above passage—namely a spiritual friend. In verse 12, "the cord of three strands" may simply refer to three close friends, teaching that if a relationship of two is helpful, then three together is even better. Peter, James and John would agree with that one! A deeper meaning may be that two spiritual friends bound to God are unstoppable. I like that idea better, though I am not sure that the writer had it in mind.

While the Old Testament taught in principle the need for close relationships designed to call each other higher, the New Testament teaches this much more directly. Let's take a look at some of the key passages in it.

Key New Testament Passages

The Commission

Although I believe many, many passages show the need for discipling relationships, Matthew 28:19-20 is, in some ways, the clearest.

> Therefore go and make disciples of all nations, baptizing them in the name of the Father and of the Son and of the Holy Spirit, and teaching them to obey everything I have commanded you. And surely I am with you always, to the very end of the age.

Several foundational lessons are contained in this passage. First, we are to make disciples—not simply church members, religious people or nicer humans. This means that before any person is a biblical candidate for baptism, he must have made the *decision* to be a disciple (and he must have learned enough of what this means to make an educated decision). This decision is called "repentance" in Acts 2:38. But what is repentance?

To properly understand repentance, we first have to properly understand sin. Sin, from the Greek *hamartia*, is derived from an archery term, meaning "to miss the mark." Since our mark is being like Jesus (1 John 2:6), it should be obvious that the mark can be missed by doing things that he would not do, or by *not* doing

things that he would do. Either way, we miss the mark! Therefore, repentance is making the firm decision to stop doing wrong
things and to start doing right things. Most religious people focus only on the first part of repentance and not the last part. They
make a commitment to stop sins of *commission* but not to stop
sins of omission. So their repentance, being only partial, is not
true biblical repentance.

At one point in my life, after learning about discipleship, I
preached and taught much to the traditional church for which I
was serving as a minister about our responsibilities as disciples.
For a long time, the reluctance of the members to put into practice the things I was teaching was a mystery to me. Finally, it
dawned on me that they had originally been baptized for different reasons than to be disciples! They had missed the teaching of
Matthew 28 by a long shot and had not signed up for a commitment which was that serious! The only conclusion that I could
reach regarding them was that they had not biblically repented
and therefore were not really disciples. A hard teaching? You bet
it is, but it is also biblical. No one who draws lines in his life and
says "This much and no more" is a disciple of Jesus Christ. He
may be a church member, or a religious person or a nice guy—
but he's not a Christian!

Second, Matthew 28 teaches that we are to baptize them.
This would have to be with the one baptism of Ephesians 4:5.
This baptism in *form* is a burial in water (Acts 8:34-39; Romans
6:3-4). It, in *intent,* is a decision to be a disciple in all of the ways
described in the New Testament. It should be rather obvious that
no one can be biblically baptized until they are old enough to
make such a decision and then follow through with it. Choosing
to be a disciple is just that: a choice.

Third, the passage shows that we are to teach them (the baptized ones) to obey everything that Jesus commanded the apostles.
Just like every child born into a family has to be trained, every
child in God's family must be trained. We are not simply to *teach*
everything Jesus commanded, but to teach to *obey.* Consider this
difference in the rearing of children. It is a very large difference!
For example, Eli, the OT priest, taught his sons, even to the point
of rebuking them, but he did not train (restrain) them (1 Samuel
2:25, 3:13).

I remember my experience of planning the curriculum for the traditional churches of which I was a part. We had our five-year plans for teaching through the Bible, but I assure you that we never had any intentions of teaching the members to *obey!* They had not made a disciple's commitment, and they were not about to have anyone disturb their complacency. Had anyone come close to *insisting* on obedience to everything Christ taught, we would have lost members quickly!

But we need to examine this passage more closely, especially verse 20 and its directive to teach disciples to obey everything Jesus taught. What is the most effective way to teach a person initially to come to Christ—in a group or as an individual? Obviously, the smaller the setting, the more personalized the teaching. Agreed?

After baptism, what is the most effective way to train them to obey everything—in an assembly of hundreds, or in an individual manner? Isn't the answer obvious? Why would anyone think that the conversion and training in Matthew 28 would be done in two different ways? Making disciples initially and training them as disciples gives us two sides of the same coin. In both phases, the goal is forming Christ in them. I realize that I'm belaboring the point a bit here, but some religious people have argued at length that discipling relationships are actually unbiblical. Is that not absolutely incredible, in light of Jesus' example and his commission here? Would not those disciples who heard these words have remembered just how Jesus had worked with them? Would they not have employed the same methods that he employed?

I'm reminded of the person who heard about discipling relationships and commented thus: "Well, that may sound good to some, but how do you square it with the biblical teaching about personal privacy?" When my children were young and didn't want their parents in their lives training them, they would have liked that personal-privacy doctrine! However, it was not a part of my parental doctrine, because I was intent on training my children to be responsible, righteous adults. Nor is it a part of God's doctrine, for he is intent on all disciples being trained, and therefore all who are a part of his family are responsible for each other's spiritual well-being and growth. The isolation and independence of church members from one another in traditional religion is just about the most unbiblical practice one can imagine. Those biblical passages on personal privacy are not easy to find!

I have yet to see how Jesus' commands in Matthew 28 can be carried out except when someone is directly responsible for the training in every disciple's life. Just attending church could not possibly accomplish what is being commanded, for it takes a specific person to train another specific person in the specific commands of Jesus.

Another vital point in this text concerns the *standards* of being a disciple. Our standard is Jesus himself (1 John 2:6), and this standard is the same for every disciple. No person in the church is to have more commitment to Jesus and his cause than any other person. We are all to obey *everything!* And the discipling-partner arrangement is the most effective way to obey these injunctions and is the natural outgrowth of evangelism. When each of us initially studies with a person to help them reach the point of baptism, it will seem obvious that the same training relationship should continue as we strive to help them mature in Christ. In the event a new disciple is passed off to another discipler for a valid reason (and there are valid reasons), the best practice is for that person to be in on the studies prior to baptism in order to build the needed relationship.

The Leadership Provision

Leadership has been planned and provided by God to ensure that his mission for the church is accomplished.

> It was he who gave some to be apostles, some to be prophets, some to be evangelists, and some to be pastors and teachers, to prepare God's people for works of service, so that the body of Christ may be built up until we all reach unity in the faith and in the knowledge of the Son of God and become mature, attaining to the whole measure of the fullness of Christ.
>
> Then we will no longer be infants, tossed back and forth by the waves, and blown here and there by every wind of teaching and by the cunning and craftiness of men in their deceitful scheming. Instead, speaking the truth in love, we will in all things grow up into him who is the

> Head, that is, Christ. From him the whole body, joined and
> held together by every supporting ligament, grows and
> builds itself up in love, as each part does its work (Ephesians
> 4:11-16).

These few verses encapsulate most of what has already been said
about discipleship and the role it must play in God's kingdom.
Leaders are to prepare God's people for works of service ("works
of ministry," Revised Standard Version—RSV), not do the work
for them! The goal of this training is for the church to be built up
in unity and knowledge, becoming like Christ. When the church
is matured into the fullness of Christ, the on-looking world can
be attracted through us to him. We must note the emphasis on
every disciple being trained. Such maturity comes only when all
disciples are fully trained to obey all that Jesus commanded, just
as he taught in Matthew 28. The unity necessary for effective
evangelism (John 13 and 17) comes when leaders train disciples
as Jesus did. Then the church grows because every part does its
work, with Jesus himself being the standard for every person's
spiritual life—nothing less will do.

Contrast this discipleship passage with what is seen most often in the organized religion of modern Christendom. A small
minority in churches do a large majority of whatever work gets
accomplished. Leaders are actually hired to do the work, not to
train others to do it. The serious pursuit of biblical knowledge is
reserved for the clergy (if, in fact, they seek it), and they spend
little time figuring out how to pass it on to their group. The idea
of leaders raising up a united body of believers, mature in love
and knowledge, spreading the gospel through teaching and living
the gospel is thought to be impossible. And it *is* impossible without discipling, God's process of training and maturing disciples.
However, when leaders are personally involved in training others
to personally train others, amazing things happen. The next passage shows how this works.

The Discipling Chain

Paul gave very specific and practical advice to his own young
disciple in 2 Timothy 2:1-7:

> You then, my son, be strong in the grace that is in Christ Jesus. And the things you have heard me say in the presence of many witnesses entrust to reliable men who will also be qualified to teach others. Endure hardship with us like a good soldier of Christ Jesus. No one serving as a soldier gets involved in civilian affairs—he wants to please his commanding officer. Similarly, if anyone competes as an athlete, he does not receive the victor's crown unless he competes according to the rules. The hardworking farmer should be the first to receive a share of the crops. Reflect on what I am saying, for the Lord will give you insight into all this.

This text not only outlines the process of establishing a chain of discipling relationships, but it also describes the qualities demanded of both the discipler and the disciple in order to make the chain function effectively. (We will reserve comment on most of these qualities until later chapters, since these considerations fit more naturally into those discussions.) Paul does provide some great insights into the discipling process, although he informs us that we will have to open our hearts to it by doing some reflection on it (verse 7).

Paul had committed everything he knew about the heart and soul of ministry to Timothy, and now he asks Timothy to pass these things on to reliable men. "Reliable" men (or "faithful"—KJV) were to be Timothy's focus. Paul and Timothy were following Jesus' example of focusing his efforts on fully training a few in order to not dilute his long-term impact. No one—not even Jesus—can fully equip the multitudes, and thus choices must be made. Leaders today need to ask themselves, *Who can I best train to affect the most other people for Christ in the most dramatic fashion?* Timothy undoubtedly had to determine how *many* men he could effectively disciple, and then *which* were the most reliable (or *faithful:* "full of faith").

Several lessons may be gleaned from this need to be selective. First, although we love everyone in the church and would enjoy deepening our relationship with each of them, we who lead cannot afford to spread ourselves too thin, nor can we allow other disciples to be overloaded. Jethro's admonition to

Moses in Exodus 18 will help clarify that issue. A leader must wisely choose those whom he will disciple in order to multiply his influence most effectively.

Second, everyone must be discipled, but not everyone can be discipled by leaders (at least not when we first become Christians). Paul chose Timothy as one with great leadership potential, and then told Timothy to make similar choices. Those who were chosen by Timothy in turn had to make choices about who they would pour their lives into. It's an issue of maturity: Ideally, everyone should be discipled by someone more spiritually mature than they are. As someone ahead of us in maturity helps to lift us up, we reach down and help someone who is behind us in maturity (just like siblings in a family). The ideal may not always work out precisely at all levels due to the composition of a ministry group, but it will in most cases. (We will discuss some of the possible exceptions in a later chapter.)

Third, in both phases of making disciples (bringing them to Christ and training them in Christ), all leaders should be reaching out to those with leadership potential. Every disciple has comfort zones in his evangelism, meaning that he finds it easier to share Christ with some types of people more than with others. But we all need to reproduce ourselves by converting others *like ourselves*. Particularly, leaders should make sure that they are studying with and discipling those who have leadership potential. If they don't, everyone ultimately will suffer, for not enough leaders will be available to train the church.

Fourth, by adopting the selection process we are not encouraging cliquish relationships in the church. We are merely focused on the ultimate mission of the church—to win as many as possible (1 Corinthians 9:19). It is not a question of loving some more than others, but rather an issue of trying to see the body of Christ matured in the fastest and most effective way possible. In Timothy's case, he was to pass on what he had directly observed from Paul's life. A good commentary on this process is found in 1 Corinthians 4:16-17, as Paul writes:

> Therefore I urge you to imitate me. For this reason I
> am sending to you Timothy, my son whom I love, who is

> faithful in the Lord. He will remind you of my way of life in
> Christ Jesus, which agrees with what I teach everywhere in
> every church.

The things Timothy had heard from Paul were not abstract theological precepts; they were issues involving the life-style of disciples who were imitating Jesus.

When Timothy received his letters of instruction, he was leading the church in Ephesus. Since Paul had established the church, Timothy was well aware of how the church had been led by Paul, and he was intent on imitating his leadership. In Acts 20:17-38, Paul recounted his days in Ephesus. They were characterized by him teaching publicly and from house to house (large settings and small). As he lived among them, he warned them and pleaded with them to live the life of disciples. He worked hard, pouring out his life for them and into them. And he put his whole heart into it, which was shown by his mention twice of serving them "with tears." Discipling other people is no easy matter! It isn't possible unless we make a disciple's commitment to Jesus, for the sacrifice is great. But the cause is the most important on planet Earth, and it cannot be successful without the entrusting of our hearts and lives to others.

The Commitment to Perfection

Our final passage to examine in this chapter is Colossians 1:27-29:

> To them God has chosen to make known among the
> Gentiles the glorious riches of this mystery, which is Christ
> in you, the hope of glory.
> We proclaim him, admonishing and teaching everyone
> with all wisdom, so that we may present everyone perfect
> in Christ. To this end I labor, struggling with all his energy,
> which so powerfully works in me.

These verses reiterate the extent of dedication needed to disciple others to maturity in Christ. Paul said that he taught, proclaimed and admonished everyone with his God-given wisdom.

His goal was to present every disciple perfect ("mature" in the RSV) in Christ. Only when this maturity is our goal can the fullness of Jesus be seen in us (Colossians 1:27); only when this fullness is seen will the world be attracted to him; and this fullness is only possible with the kind of focused discipling mentioned in this passage. Regardless of which passage about discipleship we read, the same points are made, emphasized and implied.

What kind of discipling is taught by Paul here? It is a purposeful kind: "to this end," meaning the maturity in Christ we are to attain, making "Christ in us" a reality. It is a sacrificial kind, requiring "labor" (literally "toil which exhausts"), "struggling," and "energy" which only God can supply. Paul further describes this strenuous type of discipling in this way:

> I want you to know how much I am struggling for you and for those at Laodicea, and for all who have not met me personally. My purpose is that they may be encouraged in heart and united in love, so that they may have the full riches of complete understanding, in order that they may know the mystery of God, namely, Christ (Colossians 2:1-2).

Why did he want them to know how great a struggle it was discipling others to Christ? Because they all were to imitate it (see 1 Corinthians 4:16, 11:1).

Paul does not mention the discipling-chain process here, but it was definitely involved. Neither he nor any other person, including Jesus, could present the masses perfect in Christ. He could work closely with kingdom leaders like Timothy and Titus and pour his heart into them. They in turn could pour their lives into others under their leadership, who could do the same with yet others, and on and on until every person could be matured in Christ. When a discipling passage does not specifically mention this chain process, we must conclude that it is presupposed because it was evident in the lives of Jesus and the apostles and common sense tells us no other method would have worked. The world cannot be reached unless the church is matured enough to demonstrate Jesus' fullness to them, thus attracting them to him.

And the church cannot be matured without following Jesus' example of maturing disciples.

After looking at the biblical examples of discipling, examining the specific discipling passages, and logically connecting the premises, do you have any doubt that what we have termed "discipling relationships" are absolutely needed in order to fulfill Scripture and to bring about the evangelization of the world? It didn't take nearly this much evidence to convince me fifteen years ago, even though I knew the implications of accepting discipleship. I was compelled by Scripture and logic to embark on a journey that took me far, far away from familiar surroundings and lifetime comfort zones. The price I paid seemed high at the time, but the rewards have been beyond description, and even comprehension. The Scriptures are quite clear to all who would read them with a heart to obey.

Ultimately, we are discipled by God. Passages like Romans 8:28-29 and Hebrews 12:5-11 make it clear that God works through every aspect of our lives to help us become more like his Son. However, the discipling of one person by another is an integral part of God's plan for our lives and a key to fulfilling the mission of God on earth. I am my brother's keeper, and I am to let someone be my keeper. This has been God's will from the beginning. Let's pull out all the stops and dedicate ourselves to it as fully as did Jesus, Paul, Timothy and all others who have been determined to change their world. Lost souls are waiting for us to do it.

4

A THEOLOGICAL BASIS FOR DISCIPLING RELATIONSHIPS

✠

Special Note: The material in this chapter is in some ways "deeper" than that in the preceding chapters, being more theological in nature. Newer disciples may find it more difficult to understand and may want to skip it now and come back to it later. I think that more mature disciples will find it highly stimulating and challenging.

God is a God of order and harmony. The various aspects of his revelation to us fit together like the pieces of a puzzle. He does not arbitrarily tell us that something is good for us or that he wants a kind of behavior from us when it does not, in fact, fit beautifully with other realities. What is good for us always grows out of who God is, who we are and what it takes to live together in love and harmony. So it is with discipling.

Close relationships in general, and discipling relationships in particular, fit perfectly with what we know about God and about man. These relationships first find their basis in the nature of God himself. The vital need for these relationships is further seen by looking at the nature of man. Then finally we can look at the nature of the church that God dreamed to establish, and we can see how essential these relationships are to that church. If we properly understand God, man and the church, there is nothing surprising about our need for the kind of relationships we are describing in this book.

The Nature of God

What do we know about God that would lead us to anticipate that discipling relationships would be a part of his plan for us? Several of these "theological" foundations come to mind.

First, God himself is all about relationships. Even though we intellectually limited creatures cannot really comprehend the Person of God, we do know that he has revealed himself as a Father, Son and Spirit. This one God is thus wholly relational *by definition*. Of course, the concept of the trinity is beyond our understanding, but this insight from Lanier will perhaps help to clarify.

> We do not affirm that one God is three Gods; we affirm that there is but one infinite Spirit Being, but within that one Spirit essence there are three personal distinctions, each of which may be, and is, called God; each capable of loving and being loved by the others; each having a distinct, but not separate, part to play in the creation of the universe, and in the creation and salvation of man.[1]

Since God is somehow "Three within One," then our capacity for relationships grows out of the very essence of his nature. This fact provides the ground-zero basis of theology behind all spiritual relationships. The biblical definition of Deity is the very foundation of relationships. And if our relationships are to be patterned after who he *is*, do we need comment about the required closeness of spiritual relationships? Yet, where are the relationships within mainline religious groups that can be accurately described as "deep" and "close"—patterned after the nature of God? It would certainly be challenging to find such relationships in the average church that meets on Main Street, USA!

I don't doubt that exceptions to this sad rule exist, but when they do, it will be in spite of the nature of the church group involved, not because of it (if my experiences in those churches is any indication). Deep, close relationships cannot be developed in large-group settings, on which most churches totally rely. The more intimate the setting (the fewer people), the more intimate the relationship can become but only if the parties involved are committed to such development. Otherwise, our closest friendships will be no closer than a good "golfing buddy" relationship.

Second, God in his very nature has a heart that moves toward relationships. John simply wrote, "God is love" (1 John 4:8). The Old Testament abounds with passages that show that the heart of God is full of love. Psalm 32:10 is typical: "Many are the woes of the wicked, but the LORD'S unfailing love surrounds the man who trusts in him." His love is variously described as faithful, unshakable, unfailing and steadfast. God's heart is full of divine *agape*, "unconditional love," and love always has to do with relationships. What is found in God clearly shows us what needs to be found in us.

I may have thought I "fell" in love with my wife Theresa, but I can assure you that we did not build our relationship on some euphoric feelings which caused our hearts to soar and even skip a few beats when we were at close quarters! It took time together, sharing our hearts, doing things as a team and working through all kinds of differences to establish a true *agape* relationship. *Agape* is the Greek word used most often for "love" in the New Testament, which means "a commitment to another person at all costs for their good, not our own." My relationship with Theresa has not come out of simply doing "what comes naturally." Who could claim that the qualities described in 1 Corinthians 13:4-8 are "natural" or accidental? "Falling in love" can only refer to the *eros* type of love, which has to do with physical attraction or perhaps the *phileo* type, the warm affection of a friendship. In a marriage, developing an *agape* relationship takes intent, planning, self-denial, sacrifice, time and just plain old hard work.

Did it not take all of those things for God to build that kind of relationship with us? Now he wants us to have this kind of relationship with each other. But what settings most naturally "grow" such closeness? While you will find it difficult to build such close relationships with hundreds, you can do it with smaller numbers. You cannot learn to love everyone without first learning to love someone. As we are helped to learn how to build one such relationship, we will be able to duplicate it with others as time goes by (just like a baby begins with the parents and branches out to others in the family). With whom in the church do you share this type of relationship? Without the plan and intent, it will not happen, which is the logical reason that discipling relationships are so vital. The more we learn to love, the more we will become like God; and the more we are like him, the more people we can love more deeply.

Third, God's nature of rewarding certain qualities logically makes discipling relationships the object of his graciousness. Two of the qualities he rewards most are faith and humility. He is less patient with pride and unbelief than with many other sins, and conversely, he takes special delight in those of his creatures who possess humility and faith. But what does this have to do with discipling relationships? A great deal, to be sure.

Allowing someone to disciple you requires faith. Our prideful and independent natures say, like some two-year-olds, "I can do it all by myself." We have confidence that we know best and that we do not need input or guidance. We naturally distrust others who would get too involved in our lives. We fear that if we are not independent and self-preserving, our lives will not end up in a good place. But God says something different. He says we will be much better off getting counsel, advice, guidance and even rebukes from others. To let that happen, you must show more faith in God's plan than in your own knowledge and intuition.

Do you remember the admonition given to Christian wives in 1 Peter 3:1-6? They were to trust God to work through even their *non-Christian* husbands to lead them. And the model for their submission was given in the previous chapter where Jesus trusted God to work even through the *Herods* and *Pilates* of the world (1 Peter 2:21-23). The idea that God cannot work through a well-intentioned brother or sister who disciples us is a faithless idea indeed. And without faith, we can neither please God (Hebrews 11:6) nor be blessed by him (James 1:6-8).

What about the quality of humility as it relates to discipleship? To place ourselves in the hands of an older brother or sister in the family requires a great deal of humility. And the nearer we are to that older sibling in age and maturity level, the greater the challenge. Think of the situations in physical families where the older kids baby-sit the younger. The less the age difference, the greater the challenge. How humble are you in the family of God?

When we first moved to Boston in January of 1988, Theresa and I were asked to disciple Tom and Sheila Jones (current editors of Discipleship Publications International). After several months, Tom expressed appreciation for the discipling relationship and made some nice comments about how much I had helped him. His humility humbled me, for we are near the same age (I know I'm a few years older, Tom, but not very many!) with much the same experience in ministry. In fact, he had been more in touch for a much longer time with many of the principles of discipleship than I had. Yet, in humility he was happy to be discipled by me. A truth dawned on me that day. I expressed it to him in terms similar to this: "Tom, I think I understand why discipleship works so well. It is not because all of the advice and direction given is the very best available; it is because to be discipled by another demands humility, and God blesses humility. It wouldn't matter in our case whether I discipled you or you discipled me—what really matters is the level of humility, which determines how much God is able to bless."

In March of that year, after many talks and prayers, I advised Tom to step out of the ministry position he was in because of the physical and emotional effects of having multiple sclerosis. I wasn't sure what he would be able to do, but I had become convinced of what he could not do any longer. His immediate response was one of humility. He started working in the church office, and after several years, God raised him up to be the editor of a fast-growing and widely influential publishing company. His influence far exceeds what it did in earlier years, and only eternity itself will reveal the extent of that influence. How did all of that happen? Great discipling? I would like to say yes, since I was the discipler then and am once again, but we now know better, don't we? It was Tom's humility that caused God to abundantly bless him.

You see, the material in this book is not some dry, dusty theory written by a theologian wearing a clerical collar. It is written by a disciple who disciples others, who is himself discipled by others, and who has discovered that the answers in the Bible do work in the laboratory of life. Because God is God, discipleship works, and because his Word is irrevocable, we cannot receive the quantities of the blessings which he longs to shower on us until and unless we practice what he has preached!

The Nature of Man

What about man's nature makes discipling relationships essential? Of course, the Bible teaches that we are to have them, which makes them essential. But God, as our Designer and Creator, prescribed in his Word everything which exactly corresponds to our nature. Why then, did he prescribe discipleship?

Two Potentials to Develop

First, since he is made in God's image, man has tremendous potential for relationships. Just as Deity is three in one and one in three (in some totally inexplicable way!), man is designed to be bound to others like himself with the closest of bonds. Our nature will always be crying out for incredibly deep relationships with other humans, whether or not we are aware of it. And usually we are not aware of it, are we? At the earliest stages of life, these inherent longings are stifled and redirected (or worse), with the result being that most adults are not *remotely* aware of their relationship needs or potentials.

Why is it that we feel and say things at times of tragedy (the death of a loved one, for example) that we aren't normally aware of and certainly don't express? Where do those amazingly deep feelings come from—sentimentality gone awry? Absolutely not. The emotions and expressions at such times are quite genuine, but until something breaks through our shells, we just don't let them out. In fact, we most likely don't even know they are there. This is especially true of *unreal* men (real men are that very small minority who are *real*—vulnerable and honest about who they are!).

As a young man, I knew I needed a wife, but I didn't have much of a clue about how much I needed *real* relationships with other guys. Honestly, I am not often in touch emotionally with those needs even now, except when something pierces the protective coating (of fear and selfishness, I think) around my heart. However, intellectually I know what I really need, and I am trying to become more like God in developing deeper relationships. You male readers are going to have to think about this one for a while to really get it, but keep trying—your wife or girlfriend or coleader or sister friends will be grateful to you if you do get it, to say nothing of how God will feel when you start functioning more like he designed you to function! Without question, discipling relationships with brothers have helped me far more than any other type of relationship to grow in being a deeper, more loving man.

Second, another potential we have as those made in God's image is our creative ability. We have the capacity and the inner drive to create. We may exercise this drive in careers, hobbies or other avenues, but our inner prompting toward creativity is actually aimed at reproducing ourselves in the lives of other people. Why is it that even in our self-focused society the large majority of us want to have children? Simply because they are so cute and cuddly when they are little? Hardly. The most naïve person has figured out that babies eventually become teenagers. And the thought of raising teens in our dangerous world scares responsible parents and potential parents enough to make them soberly count the cost before embarking on the trail of family development. Why then do we still have such a deep-seated desire to reproduce? Because we have an inborn drive to create something that will outlast us!

Discipling fulfills this need more than anything else, with the exception of parenting. Did not Jesus say to go "make disciples" and then train them to become like him (Matthew 28:19-20)? To pour our lives into others is to expend our creative "juices" in the most rewarding way possible, reproducing our lives in the lives of those who will make a real difference in time and in eternity. What kind of legacy will you leave behind when you die? Most people will leave very little that really matters, and the most successful in the eyes of the world will leave some business with their name on it! What a horrible waste of creativity. Just imagine someone who knows you describing you a week after you die. "Well, he made lots of money, lived in this fine house, drove this expensive car, and founded a multimillion dollar business." *SO WHAT? WHO CARES?* What a hollow reason for existing on this planet! Never give up your life for anything that death can take away!

On the other hand, what if you were a disciple making disciples: How would you then be described? "He loved God with all his heart, and he taught his family, friends and scores of others to do the same. On the Day of Judgment, only God will be able to show all the influence exerted on many lives by this dear brother." You would have understood the basic spiritual value system, but unlike many religious people, you also would have understood the true purpose of discipleship—reproducing Christ-like qualities and values in others.

What does Scripture have to say about such desire to create or reproduce? Paul wrote: "My dear children, for whom I am again in the pains of childbirth until Christ is formed in you..." (Galatians 4:19). "Even though you have ten thousand guardians in Christ, you do not have many fathers, for in Christ Jesus I became your father through the gospel" (1 Corinthians 4:15). Many similar passages could be noted, but these are sufficient to make the point. By sharing Christ and by pouring his life into new disciples, Paul was bearing spiritual children. God has stamped on our hearts the need to create—the need to make a difference and leave a legacy. Discipling fits our need: It allows us to live a life in a way that our influence will outlive us in the most significant way. Without it, our potential for creativity will be squandered on something transitory and valueless.

Two Weaknesses to Offset

Our potential makes discipling vital, but so do our human weaknesses. For one thing, we tend toward blindness about ourselves. Without looking in a mirror or appealing to another person's view, we can't tell if we have egg on our face or not. This is true both physically and spiritually. God's word is one type of mirror (James 1:22-25), and close, spiritual friends are yet another, functioning as our "eyes" to help us see ourselves as we actually appear. At the risk of sounding a bit blasphemous, the Word alone will not provide us with the complete picture of ourselves. There is nothing wrong with Scripture, mind you. It is just that we read it sometimes through our distorted lenses. We need help seeing ourselves—honestly.

When I moved to Boston just over nine years ago, my view of myself was distorted. But thankfully, for the very first time I was being discipled by other men. I will never forget a leaders' discipleship group of men at the home of one of my disciplers,

Wyndham Shaw. (I needed two strong disciplers in those days!)
In that group I was given input regarding my critical edge. Of
course I knew that I was very outspoken and direct, but I thought
that only demonstrated my amazing honesty and ability to see
people clearly! I actually told them something like that, but they
didn't buy it. When asked for the evidence behind their evaluation, they had only to repeat some of the statements I had made
that night in the group. Those same statements coming out of
their mouths sounded sharp, abrasive and unloving. Their loving
input cut to the innermost part of my being and hurt terribly. But
the pain was like that inflicted by surgeons performing a life-sav-
ing operation, whose scalpel was the sharp sword of the Spirit
(Hebrews 4:12).

My picture of myself wasn't yet quite clear. I had lived with
my sinful nature for a long time, and my image of myself was still
out of focus. Shortly after the discipleship group described above,
I had a discipling time with my other discipler, Kip McKean. Kip
and I were walking in his neighborhood talking about the ministry and related items. Somewhere in the course of the conversation, he said something that reminded me of my recent spiritual
critique. His statement was little more than a passing comment,
but now my antennas were up. I was becoming more aware of my
weaknesses, so I asked what he meant by the brief comment. He
was quite willing to elaborate! A few minutes prior, he had asked
me about an evangelism seminar I had just attended, and I tried
to give him a full description of both its strong and weak points.
He explained that he had just received a similar evaluation from
another brother who had attended, and although both of us mentioned both the positives and the negatives, he was left with two
different impressions of the overall quality of the seminar. From
the other brother's description, Kip thought that it must have
been great, but from mine, that it had been pretty mediocre.

Wow! The scalpel was out again and my self-image was bleed-
ing again. By that night I thought I was about to have a heart
attack—weak, dizzy, chest pains. This physical distress gave way
to spending three days in bed with the flu. Was I really sick? Well,
yes, with the flu, but thankfully not with a heart problem (physically). Why was I hit with the psychosomatic heart problem and

the actual illness of influenza? Because of the major emotional hit of seeing myself more clearly than I had ever seen myself. How did I feel at that time? Devastated. How do I feel about it now? Unbelievably grateful for disciples who were willing to be honest with me!

Most people in the world never experience being discipled, and they simply do not change once their adult character is developed. When I visit old friends who are not involved in discipleship (though they may be religious), I know exactly what to expect of them. They remain the same year after year, with the same character sins and personality quirks. On the other hand, I have changed remarkably because of discipling. My blindness has given way to sight, and with the help of others, the man God designed me to be has emerged more and more (and the work on me continues).

After the discipling described above, I came to the rather obvious conclusion that I did not see myself as I really was, and I decided to take the challenging and narrow road of humility. I asked those brothers who had given me the godly critiques (along with many others in my life) to point out quickly and clearly all such ungodly qualities as they saw them appear. They did (and do), gently and lovingly, and my life has soared with eagles as a result. We need to be discipled—badly.

A second weakness of our nature with which we need help is our strong tendency to turn away from the spiritual to the worldly. Something much like the second law of thermodynamics is evident in our personal lives: Order gives way to disorder; spiritual strength to weakness; resolve to doubt; conviction to sentimentality; righteousness to sin. Surely we don't need much proof of this one, do we? We can look at David, Solomon, Moses, Peter, or just at ourselves in the mirror. The Hebrew writer quoted these words from Psalm 95: "Their hearts are always going astray" (Hebrews 3:10). In the original context, the psalmist was describing the faithlessness of those who wandered in the wilderness for forty years. However, note how the writer applies it to Christians:

> See to it, brothers, that none of you has a sinful, unbelieving heart that turns away from the living God. But

> encourage one another daily, as long as it is called Today,
> so that none of you may be hardened by sin's deceitful-
> ness (Hebrews 3:12-13).

What is the antidote for this strong tendency toward going astray? Discipleship of the daily variety. Now who in the church is going to encourage you daily, if not someone specifically responsible for doing so? We will have more to say about the whole process of discipling relationships, but I have personally never seen this one passage obeyed by a majority in any church I have ever been a part of before coming to a discipling ministry.

The Bible frequently describes human beings as sheep—usually sheep who have gone astray. There's a good reason for that comparison: Sheep are notoriously dumb. They wander off and do stupid things which endanger their lives. So do we, and therefore we need all the help we can get! We simply cannot afford to look at commands such as Hebrews 3:12-13 as optional. Discipleship, as described quite plainly in this passage, cannot be ignored if God is to be pleased and our spiritual lives protected!

The Nature of the Church

If you were to describe the nature of the church, what would you say? How do you think most religious people would describe it? Picture a woman going to the most popular type of church in her area. (I chose to describe a woman for two reasons. One, women seem to be more naturally attuned to the spiritual side of life; and two, most traditional types of churches have far more women members than men.) Our average church attendee arrives only a few minutes before the service is scheduled to begin. As she comes into the sanctuary foyer, she might or might not greet other worshipers. She thinks that it's nice to be friendly, and should she meet anyone she knows, she will exchange pleasantries for a minute or two.

But now she must hurry into the sanctuary and find her pew. As she awaits the clergymen's entry, she meditates quietly yet intently. You can almost picture a vertical shaft of light connecting her to heaven. After the fairly brief service, she quietly leaves the sanctuary, goes to her car and drives home. Perhaps she exchanged a greeting or two leaving the building, but she has done what she came to do—spend time focused on God in the midst of her busy life. Therefore, she leaves feeling much better for having come. She has been raised to view church attendance as a spiritual duty, a moral responsibility, and having fulfilled this spiritual obligation, she returns to her mostly "secular" world. But she feels spiritually cleansed, for she has done what she believes to be right before God.

Now, I'm not trying to be critical here; I'm just trying to describe the religious reality of most of our modern society. Several observations from the illustration are in order. First, religion is seen as a very important part of life, but really only a small part. It is a slim slice of the pie, in terms of time spent, while the other "slices" (job, family, entertainment) may be much larger. Spirituality is a segment of life, but it is an isolated segment. Second, religion is mainly vertical in nature, an experience with the Divine, and other people are an incidental part of it. Many faithful churchgoers have virtually no relationships in their congregations, and they certainly have no relationships which remotely resemble those we are calling discipling relationships. Third, the atmosphere of a religious assembly is very quiet and "reverent." I have attended funerals at some of these kinds of churches, and occasionally arrived early enough to stand in the back of the building to observe the last part of the regular church service. I honestly could tell little difference in the atmosphere of the regular service and the funeral service.

Is that what the Bible teaches about the nature of the church? Folks, we are talking different planets or galaxies here. The church described in the New Testament does not remotely resemble what has become the norm for churches in our day. Let's just consider the three observations mentioned above in light of the Bible's description of church. First, religion is not simply a part of life— it is life. It is not a slice of one's weekly pie—it's the whole pie. Consider just this one passage:

> Therefore, I urge you, brothers, in view of God's mercy, to offer your bodies as living sacrifices, holy and pleasing to God—this is your spiritual act of worship (Romans 12:1).

Our lives are everyday sacrifices to God, and that living sacrifice is described as "spiritual worship." The purpose of attending a church service is not simply a coming together "to worship"; we come to worship *together*. In other words, we don't worship only at a church service; we worship every day, for our whole lives are worship, biblically understood. And one key reason our lives can continue to be worship is because of the spiritual relationships we must develop and maintain every day with people in and out of the church.

Second, religion was never intended to be vertical only, or even mostly vertical (man and God). It is quite horizontal at the same time, uniting us with others in the church. Even a casual reading of the account of the beginning of the church will provide proof positive that the church was a *family* (Acts 2:36-47). If I am a son of God, then other sons and daughters of God are by definition my brothers and sisters. A one-sentence greeting in a church foyer doesn't quite equate with family relationships! Because we are a part of the body of Christ, "each member belongs to all the others" (Romans 12:5) and "its parts should have equal concern for each other" (1 Corinthians 12:25). The New Testament is replete with "one another" and "each other" responsibilities (which was looked at more in detail in Chapter Two). If we are family, we must function as family. In a church setting, where members may be quite scattered geographically, there must be some kind of plan for the organization and function of the group and because of the preeminence of love in Christ's group (John 13:34-35), the organization and function reflect a focus on relationships as described in the Bible. The family nature of the church demands discipleship as an integral part of its life.

Third, the atmosphere in the church should be like that found in a family. Acts 4:32 gives us an intimate glimpse of the early church: "All the believers were one in heart and mind. No one claimed that any of his possessions was his own, but they shared everything they had." Certainly this sounds like family, and family metaphors used in connection with the church abound in the New Testament. No less than five NT letters talk about disciples greeting each other with a holy kiss or a kiss of love. Church assemblies should be much more like family reunions than funeral services.

Discipling relationships fit with the biblical church like a hand in a glove. Everything about the relationships we are describing in this book enrich the church and help her to be all God planned her to be.[2]

———◆◆———

Discipling relationships are not contrived by man, nor are they optional. Just as biblical morality finds its basis in the nature of God and the needs of man, so the close spiritual relationships found in discipleship grow out of God's triune nature and man's need. Without discipleship, church members become lukewarm, churches stagnate and entire societies die. In America, we are in that downward spiral and picking up speed. The only thing that can turn the tide is a return to biblical discipleship, which alone can produce disciples radical enough to be the leaven, light and salt of God—and to once again be used by him to turn the world *upside down*—in a good sense! (Acts 17:6, King James Version).

Part 2

Being a
Disciple of Jesus

Christianity is a taught religion. No one can become a disciple of Jesus without first being taught. No one can mature as a disciple without continuing to be taught. But the method of this teaching is of paramount importance. How can we become more and more like Jesus for the rest of our lives? It requires other people in our lives committed to teaching us to obey all things that Jesus originally trained the apostles to obey (Matthew 28:19-20). It requires discipling relationships as defined by the Bible, which are only made effective by our desire and determination to take full advantage of them. This section of the book will provide the needed direction to obtain the most growth possible as we seek continual maturation into his image.

5

BEING DISCIPLED
JESUS
IS THE FOCUS

Being discipled is a "Jesus thing," in that we are doing what he modeled and commanded for the purpose of becoming more like him and helping others to do the same. He is our example to imitate and the constant focus of all discipling efforts. Without this focus discipling will become no more than a tradition at best and a burden at worst. In this chapter we will focus on Jesus and pose the question: "What does it mean to be a disciple?" His answer: to follow a leader, to follow on his terms and to follow for training. As the voice from heaven in essence told other would-be disciples, "This is God's Son, listen to him."

To Follow a Leader

During the centuries leading up to Christ, the idea of following a leader for the purpose of becoming like him was quite in vogue. Aristotle had his disciples, and Plato had his. Their disciples committed themselves to following these famous leaders, intent on learning everything about them, imitating their behavior and espousing their philosophies. We independent Westerners have a difficult time with the concept. We pride ourselves on not becoming very much like those from whom we learn. We want to be our own man, to make our own unique mark in the world. At the very least, we are eclectic in our learning approach, taking a few ideas from one person and a few from the next.

The Jews in Jesus' day employed much the same method of training as did the famous philosophers. Leading rabbis had their little groups who followed them through the daily tasks, straining to pick up every tidbit of wisdom that might drop from their lips. Paul had been tutored in this fashion at the feet of probably the most famous rabbi of his time in Jerusalem. He spoke of this training in Acts 22:3:

> "I am a Jew, born in Tarsus of Cilicia, but brought up in this city. Under Gamaliel I was thoroughly trained in the law of our fathers and was just as zealous for God as any of you are today."

John the Baptist had a definite group of disciples who followed him and learned from him. In Mark 2:18 it was mentioned that John's disciples fasted; in Luke 11:1 that they were taught to pray by John; in John 3:25 that they argued with a certain Jew over the issue of ceremonial washing; in Matthew 11:2 that they were nearby while John was in prison; and in Mark 6:29 that they buried John's body. Therefore, when Jesus came on the scene in his public ministry, it was not unusual that he would have had his own entourage of disciples following him to learn from him as their Master.

Certainly he came forward like a rabbi, calling men to follow him. Unlike his Jewish counterparts, he broke through racial, ethical and national barriers in gaining adherents. To follow him meant facing the same dangers he faced because you would be identified as his disciple and thus treated exactly as he was treated. Thomas understood this principle, once remarking to the other apostles "Let us also go, that we may die with him" (John 11:16). Similarly, Peter and the other apostles understood the implication of being his disciples, as seen in Matthew 26:35: "But Peter declared, 'Even if I have to die with you, I will never disown you.' And all the other disciples said the same."

The key concept to learn from these examples is that following someone as his disciple did not simply mean that you followed only to acquire some good philosophy. You were committing your life to being very closely identified with him to the point that whatever victories and defeats he had, you shared. In a real sense you gave up your identity and became an extension of him.

In the Jewish system, given time and growth, you could advance to your master's status, but in Christ's system, you would always be his disciple.

With this background in mind, certain passages become crystal clear:

> I have been crucified with Christ and I no longer live, but Christ lives in me (Galatians 2:20a).

> "A student is not above his teacher, but everyone who is fully trained will be like his teacher" (Luke 6:40).

> "Remember the words I spoke to you: 'No servant is greater than his master.' If they persecuted me, they will persecute you also. If they obeyed my teaching, they will obey yours also" (John 15:20).

And the beauty of following *this* Rabbi is that we end up not only becoming like him in this life, but being with him in the next:

> "Whoever serves me must follow me; and where I am, my servant also will be. My Father will honor the one who serves me" (John 12:26).

> "And if I go and prepare a place for you, I will come back and take you to be with me that you also may be where I am" (John 14:3).

Men discipling other men has only one aim: to help disciples of Jesus become more like him. He is the ultimate leader that we are to follow and emulate. Today, in one sense we have disciples, but they are only ours to train for him. He is the focus and not we ourselves. Paul was a father (with a small *f*) to those whom he converted, and a teacher (with a small *t*) to the Gentiles, but he knew that there was only one Father and one Teacher (Matthew 23:9-10). We must keep in mind that although we are disciplers, there is only one Discipler, and all of our efforts must be to exalt him by discipling those in our care into his image.

To Follow on His Terms

Defining Relationships

Since Jesus is also the one Rabbi (meaning "master") of Matthew 23:8, we must follow him on *his* terms. In this vein we must understand his terms by both definition and commitment. John's gospel provides us with three specific definitions of what it means to follow Jesus. All three passages in which the definitions are found have to do with relationships (not a surprise!).

Relationship with Christ

The first has to do with our relationship with Christ:

> To the Jews who had believed him, Jesus said, "If you hold to my teaching, you are really my disciples. Then you will know the truth, and the truth will set you free" (John 8:31-32).

Jesus makes it clear that our relationship with him is dependent on our following his teachings. None can claim to be disciples who are not studying and obeying his Word. In Luke 6:46, he stated "Why do you call me, 'Lord, Lord,' and do not do what I say?"

It is only when we are obedient to his teaching that the truth can be known. Contrary to the approach of Jewish rabbis, his approach was never intellectual but always experiential. The truth of Jesus is pragmatic—it works. Since the basic definition of the word "disciple" is "one who follows in order to learn," we cannot really learn the deeper spiritual truths without first obeying as a *means* to learning. Do not expect everything taught by Jesus to make sense unless you are willing to obey it. He has orchestrated discipleship to demand that we must go beyond logic before his truths become apparent. Once we make the necessary "leap of faith," we are blessed with both understanding and the freedom which it brings. Therefore, let's make sure we comprehend the sequence of being a true disciple of Jesus: (1) initial belief in him, (2) holding to his teaching (studying and obeying it), (3) understanding it at the deeper spiritual level through experiencing it, and then (4) being freed from the bondage to sin that ignorance produces.

Relationship with Other Disciples

According to Jesus, a second aspect of discipleship has to do with our relationship with our brothers and sisters in the church:

> "A new command I give you: Love one another. As I have loved you, so you must love one another. By this all men will know that you are my disciples, if you love one another" (John 13:34-35).

The injunction to love was not new, in that the whole Old Testament was based on it (Matthew 22:36-40), but the type of love taught by Jesus was new. It was a love between brothers patterned after the depth of love he had demonstrated to them. Such love went far beyond anything the apostles had ever imagined. Once when Jesus had shown them the extent of forgiveness inherent in such love, they could only reply "Increase our faith!" (Luke 17:1-5).

Further, this "new" love was a love designed to convince others that followers of Jesus were really his disciples. In order for this to happen, the love between believers has to be radically different than the love experienced in the world, even in the closest of families. How can it be this radically different? In a passage that is clearly Messianic, Isaiah prophesied about these kinds of relationships:

> The wolf will live with the lamb,
>   the leopard will lie down with the goat,
> the calf and the lion and the yearling together;
>   and a little child will lead them.
> The cow will feed with the bear,
>   their young will lie down together,
>   and the lion will eat straw like the ox.
> The infant will play near the hole of the cobra,
>   and the young child put his hand into the viper's nest.
> They will neither harm nor destroy
>   on all my holy mountain;
> for the earth will be full of the knowledge of the LORD
>   as the waters cover the sea (Isaiah 11:6-9).

Isaiah 2:1-4 (when compared to Acts 1 and 2) helps us see that the "holy mountain" in Isaiah's vision is God's kingdom established by Jesus. As we see in the powerful metaphors of Isaiah 11, the relationships in this kingdom were going to be strikingly unique. In it would be found all kinds of people relating as brothers and sisters who could never have been united in the world.

The apostles were a great demonstration of the principle. There was Simon the Zealot, who hated everything about the Roman empire, and Matthew, who worked for the Romans exacting taxes from his own people. In the world, these two would have been the worst of enemies, but in the church, they united for a greater cause. Within the group were two sets of brothers, who in the world would likely have been consumed with jealousy and envy, but who in the kingdom were brothers twice born, laboring side by side.

About a year ago, I listened as a brother named Curt shared at a church service about growing up as a black child in the South. As he described examples from his life about the racially prejudiced treatment he had received even as a boy, I was shocked and saddened. He talked about how he had grown to hate whites, a hate which continued until he was middle-aged. Finally he was invited to visit a meeting of the body of Christ by a friend. While there, he saw a very racially mixed crowd, but he wasn't favorably impressed—he just wanted to leave and never come back. But some time after he had visited that Sunday, his wife Carol had a baby, and some people from the church (blacks and whites) kept bringing food to them and serving in other ways. Finally, the walls of hatred began to fall, and Curt's heart began to soften. He started attending church regularly and began studying the Bible. After a while both he and Carol were baptized into Christ as disciples.

I didn't know Curt well, but after he had finished sharing, I felt compelled to talk to him. I found him in the foyer and started trying to talk with him, but my emotions were welling up in me so strongly that all I could do for awhile was hug him and cry. My feelings were mixed, but very strong. I felt something of the hurt he must have felt to have been treated terribly simply because of his skin color. I felt grateful to my parents, who did not burden me with racial prejudice, although we were Southerners. Mostly, I felt wonderfully thankful to be in the kingdom of God, experiencing the love of disciples, who are determined to reject all of the world's prejudices by loving like Jesus commanded. Since that time, Curt and I have become very good friends and have shared some great times together.

As I think about the make-up of the church of which I am a part, I marvel at the depth of the relationships, which transcend the barriers of race, age, education, nationality and economic status. I've never before experienced relationships like these, nor have I seen them. Politics has not produced them; education has not; sports has not; and the arts have not. Divisions in our society are as dramatic as ever. Only Jesus in the heart of disciples, who share his love for God and for the lost, can *cultivate* such love for one another. And it must be cultivated. Simply being religious and a part of a church will not produce this crop. Only the commitment of discipleship, to follow the heart and mission of Jesus at all costs, combined with the practice of discipling one another, can ever make Isaiah's prophecy come true. But for those of us who have returned to the Master's pattern for discipleship, we are seeing daily the love between the wolves and the lambs; the leopards and the goats; the calves and the lions; the cows and the bears; and the children and the cobras. This Jesus-love is a reality, not a theory, and may God be praised for it!

Relationship to the World

The third aspect of discipleship that we find in John's Gospel concerns our relationship to the world whom we are trying to reach for Christ.

> "This is to my Father's glory, that you bear much fruit, showing yourselves to be my disciples" (John 15:8).

Fruit-bearing is the result of remaining in Christ, according to the earlier context of the passage. To remain in Christ means that we are ever growing to become like him, and certainly if we are like him, we will have his heart to "seek and to save what was lost" (Luke 19:10). Clearly, if we abide in Christ, we will bear fruit, and if we do not bear fruit, then we are no longer abiding in him. But what is the "fruit" under consideration?

Through the years, I have heard some very interesting discussions about whether the fruit here was the "fruit of the Spirit" mentioned in Galatians 5:22-23 or the fruit of evangelism. In one sense, the answer is simply yes. If we abide in Christ, we will certainly have both types. As I have listened to these discussions about John 15, it seemed as if some people thought that interpreting the fruit as being *only* the fruit of the Spirit would somehow excuse them from being evangelistic! I do not need to be convinced either way from John 15 to know that a failure to share Christ is sin. The law of love is about all we need to reach that conclusion: How could we love people the way Christ does and not do everything possible to help them be saved? His love drove him to die for them; are we to feel comfortable if we are not even willing to share our faith with them?

The book of John uses this word *karpos* ("fruit" in Greek) several times. (The New American Standard translation is used for the following two quotes since it consistently translates *karpos* as "fruit.") In John 4:36 the fruit is definitely the fruit of evangelism:

> "Already he who reaps is receiving wages, and is gathering fruit for life eternal; that he who sows and he who reaps may rejoice together."

John 12:24 perhaps could be taken either way, although I am inclined to view it as evangelistic fruit:

> "Truly, truly, I say to you, unless a grain of wheat falls into the earth and dies, it remains by itself alone; but if it dies, it bears much fruit."

In context, Jesus is looking forward to the result of his death, which is the salvation of souls.

In John 15:1-8 the term "fruit" is used six times and then it is used twice more in 15:16. Notice what is said in the latter verse:

> "You did not choose me, but I chose you and appointed you to go and bear fruit—fruit that will last. Then the Father will give you whatever you ask in my name."

The similarity of this verse to the Great Commission seems obvious. First, the apostles were chosen by Christ. If we look back to the choosing process of Mark 1:14-18, learning to fish for men was to be a part of their calling. Second, they were appointed for the purpose of going out to bear fruit. The wording of Mark 3:14 springs into the memory:

> He appointed twelve—designating them apostles—that they might be with him and that he might send them out to preach.

Third, the fruit they bore was to last, which is only possible if it comes to maturity, and such maturity is produced by "teaching them to obey everything," as commanded by Jesus in Matthew 28:19-20. Fourth, the context immediately following discusses persecution, which is instigated by the preaching of the Word:

> "Remember the words I spoke to you: 'No servant is greater than his master.' If they persecuted me, they will persecute you also. If they obeyed my teaching, they will obey yours also" (John 15:20).

My conclusion is that the "fruit" of John 15 includes evangelistic fruit, but even if it did not, the necessity of sharing our faith would not be decreased in the least.

Thus, to be a disciple of Jesus, according to the definitions in John's Gospel, we must be totally committed to relationships: a relationship with Jesus based on holding to his teaching by learning and obeying it; a relationship with others in the kingdom which far surpasses love in the world, hurdling all barriers known to mankind; and a relationship with the world as we harvest them for Christ. Therefore, to be discipled means that we are going to be fully trained to be like Jesus in these fundamental areas.

Defining Commitment

Just as John was concerned with defining relationships in the disciple's life, Luke is concerned with defining the commitment. The focus in each gospel is not surprising, in light of who the writers were. John is known as the "apostle of love," making it natural that he would focus on relationships. Luke was a Gentile physician, writing to a Gentile audience whose biggest challenge was repentance. Therefore, it was perfectly natural that he would focus on commitment. Luke's record of the Great Commission (Luke 24:44-49) does not even mention faith or baptism, but only repentance and forgiveness. (Of course, faith and baptism were both presupposed, and Luke emphasizes them both in the Book of Acts.) Luke was emphasizing what would be the greatest need for his intended audience.

In Luke 9:22 Jesus warned his apostles that he was going to be killed and then rise from the dead. From other accounts, we know that the apostles had a difficult time accepting the truth of Jesus' warning. He then proceeded to elaborate about their fate if they continued to follow him, making it clear that these words were not reserved for the apostles, but for any person in any age who would follow him as a disciple:

> Then he said to them all: "If anyone would come after me, he must deny himself and take up his cross daily and follow me. For whoever wants to save his life will lose it, but whoever loses his life for me will save it" (Luke 9:23-24).

What do you think it means "to take up your cross daily"? I think that many of us miss the point here. It certainly does not refer to the troubles in life which are common to man, Christian or non-Christian. I have heard people say, regarding their aches and pains, "This is my cross to bear." Admittedly, their physical challenges may be hard to bear, but this application is not what Jesus had in mind. On the other hand, the spiritual challenges of commitment to the church are not what he referred to either. Some church people seem to think that church attendance, spiritual group meetings, giving, and sharing their faith are to be equated with "cross bearing." Not true. Those activities are a privilege, and if they seem a burden to you, then you are treading on thin ice and need to repent of a lack of gratitude.

Cross bearing meant to Jesus the biggest spiritual challenge he could possibly face. Yes, the cross meant persecution, and it meant death. But it was more than those things to him, because it carried the spiritual implications of his bearing the sins of the world. The challenge was so overwhelming that in anticipation of it, he agonized to the point of sweating blood (Luke 22:44). While it is true that the cross always includes "death to self," it places before us our most formidable challenge. And it must be remembered that not bearing it is not an option, no matter how daunting the challenge. The rich young ruler (Luke 18:18-25) was called to face his highest hurdle, a love for money. Whenever any of us draws a line and says in effect to God, "This far and no further," God is going to introduce him to a cross with that very issue emblazoned at the top of it.

Where have you drawn lines in your life? For many, it is a love for money and materialism. Being called to give liberally on a weekly basis or to sacrifice for special contributions exposes hearts, and many fail the test. They may stay in the visible church, but they do not stay in the invisible one (the spiritually saved). For others it is a certain job, or a relationship in their family or with a member of the opposite sex, or some hobby or entertainment, or any one of many other allurements of the world.

One of the most serious challenges to carrying the cross of Christ is to get out of our comfort zones. To say, "I can't do that," or "I would never do that," or "I would never go there or live there" is to guarantee that Jesus is going to come after you on that very point. Bearing a cross daily must mean that we will draw no lines anywhere in our lives. Although the threat of persecution is a scary one, fear cannot be allowed to determine our level of discipleship. It is total commitment or nothing (in God's eyes). He is either Lord of all, or Lord not at all. The commitment of a disciple demands no less.

The well-known passage in Luke 14:25-33 is perhaps the most lucid regarding the commitment of being a disciple.[1] Here Jesus begins by reiterating the demand to carry our cross, but moves quickly to saying that we must "hate" our families. Of course Jesus is not speaking literally here. The man who called us to love our enemies does not want us to do the opposite to our families. He is using hyperbole to get our attention. Whatever may be said about his statements here, no disciple can allow family to determine what he does as a disciple. If we love family, even mother or father, more than we love Jesus, we are not worthy of him (Matthew 10:37).

I received a letter recently from a woman whose husband is not a disciple. He was giving her a difficult time about her commitment and was working hard to get her to make compromises. He wanted her to go to a traditional-type church with him, which does not practice discipleship, and leave the discipling ministry she was in. I tried explaining to her the difference in making concessions and compromises. Compromises are concerned with going against strong convictions in the more significant areas (like hers), while concessions concern the smaller issues of preference. Compromises encourage those with whom they are made to seek even more compromises. Concessions tend to build appreciation and bridges of further communication and understanding. I have seen many family members turn from being persecutors of disciples and become disciples themselves, but I have never seen this happen when compromise was made by the disciple—never, not even once!

Certainly most of us do not want to hurt our families or disappoint them or go against what they want for us. But we often have no choice in the matter, if they are insisting on compromise of convictions. Jesus' words here and in similar passages admit no other interpretation. Besides that, showing compromise and sentimentality toward family is the worst thing possible for them. Just think about how Jesus dealt with his family before they became his disciples. As recorded in Mark 3:20-21, we find that his family came to "take charge of him, for they said, 'He is out of his mind.'" Do you understand the situation here? Jesus' mother, Mary, and his brothers thought that he was *insane!* I know that he loved them intensely and wanted them to see the truth that he was preaching. So how did he show his love and his desire for their salvation? We find out a few verses later:

> Then Jesus' mother and brothers arrived. Standing outside, they sent someone in to call him. A crowd was sitting around him, and they told him, "Your mother and brothers are outside looking for you."

> "Who are my mother and my brothers?" he asked.
> Then he looked at those seated in a circle around him and
> said, "Here are my mother and my brothers! Whoever
> does God's will is my brother and sister and mother" (Mark
> 3:31-35).

Just picture this occasion—the family arrives to get Jesus, but
are too embarrassed by what they think of him to even go inside
after him. They think he has gone crazy and is inside indoctrinat-
ing a little cult group. Upon being told that his family is outside,
Jesus makes his point about who his real family is (and it was not
them!). He would not even go outside and try to placate them in
the least. As far as the text is concerned, he just kept teaching
those who had a heart to learn and left his family outside until
they decided to leave or until he was quite through with what he
came to do.

Can you imagine what must have been going through the
minds of Mary, James, Joseph, Judas and Simon? (His brother's
names can be found in Mark 6:3.) If they thought Jesus was crazy
before they arrived, just what were they thinking after this little
confrontation? The point is clear—disciples are those who make
Jesus their master and will not compromise their convictions for
anyone, even the closest of family.

In our Luke 14 passage, Jesus says three times that unless we
meet certain conditions, we "cannot be his disciple." The first
two instances are in verse 26 concerning cross bearing and in
verse 27 concerning "hating" family. The third instance is in verse
33, which says "In the same way, any of you who does not give up
everything he has cannot be my disciple." The NASV translates it
"give up all his own possessions." Whatever we have ultimately
belongs to God, even the money he gives us to manage. How we
view money and possessions is one of the best possible indicators
of our discipleship.

Years ago, I remember asking a brother in the church to rent
out the house he owned and move to another area of the city to
lead a house church group of about forty people. He was not on
the ministry staff of the church, but was what in many religious
circles would be called a "lay" leader. My father was in town

visiting our family and was in church when I announced that Jim and Lynn were going to move and assume leadership of that group. My dad was shocked that church leaders would ask a man and his family to do what we asked Jim and his wife to do. Well, *they* were not shocked. When asked initially, they simply responded by saying, "However we can best serve, we are ready to do it." How would you describe this couple? I would just say they are disciples. They understood and accepted Luke 14:33. (I will add that some time later they became ministry staff and have become great leaders in the kingdom.)

As I wrote this account, I remembered a couple in Boston who had done much the same thing. They were not (and are not) on the ministry staff, but in order to meet leadership needs of small groups, they were asked to move twice in a very short time, which they did. The financial counsel they received was likely not the best, and they lost nearly $2,000 in the process. Even though it took them a good while to work out of the debt, they kept a spiritual perspective and trusted God to meet their needs. They are one of the most spiritual families I know, and Jesus will not allow their sacrifice to go unnoticed. How do stories like these hit your heart? Do you find yourself saying, "That's not fair," or "That's not right"? If so, you do not understand Luke 14:33.

Once I received advice about dealing with my possessions that cost me far more than the amount mentioned above. The advice was not good, as it turned out, and some things were not handled well in the whole situation. But I opted to drop it fairly quickly, in the tenor of 1 Corinthians 6:7, "Why not rather be wronged?" To be candid, the situation really challenged my heart— for a while. But Luke 14:33 stayed before my eyes, and I couldn't rationalize around it. I had to reach the point where two basic truths settled my mind once for all. One, I knew I had some greed in my heart, and although I could have defended my actions in a reasonable manner, I knew deep down that greed was not absent. Two, I knew that God was in control and that if I needed the money, he could figure out any number of ways to get it back to me. Looking back to that time, I am "richer" for the experience. I grew in my trust in God and in forgiveness for men, and lost a large amount of greed in the process.

The fact that scares me is that some people would leave God if they lost the $2,000—let alone the larger amount I lost. Therefore, they have just established the price of their soul at somewhere between $2,000 and the amount I lost! What a horrible thought—to sell a soul for a mere pittance of money! The issue here is not money—it is priorities and loving God and the kingdom of God.

As I wrote this chapter, I stopped and called the couple who had lost the $2,000, in order to make sure of the details. The brother expressed a concern which gives you an idea of their grasp of discipleship. He observed that people who have received advice that is not the best often lose their trust in other people. He and his wife have not. They ask for advice all of the time and follow it, and if you could spend an hour with them and their children, you would see how God has abundantly blessed their humble hearts. Similarly, my wife and I have not grown mistrustful. God has continually put people in our lives who have counseled and advised us, and he has poured out blessings on top of blessings. He promised to work all things together for good (Romans 8:28), which would include mistakes made by disciplers. Where is your trust? Where is your humility? Are you willing to get your heart tested by God through men? Are you a disciple or not? The answer is determined by how you are living out the definitions found in John and the commitment found in Luke.

To Follow for Training

"Take my yoke upon you and learn from me, for I am gentle and humble in heart, and you will find rest for your souls" (Matthew 11:29). Following Jesus has as its goal our training to become more and more like him. The apostles understood this principle, which made them eager (at times) to learn. As they watched his life unfold before them on a daily basis, they were anxious to grasp all of the lessons he modeled. They observed his remarkable prayer life, and they said "Lord, teach us to pray, just as John taught his disciples" (Luke 11:1). "Lord, teach us!" That is the cry of a true disciple. We do not follow him merely to end up in heaven with him; we follow him in order to learn everything we can about carrying out his mission on earth. And for the accomplishment of his mission, we must be trained via the discipling process.

Most of this chapter has dealt with the vertical aspect of discipleship (our commitment to Christ). We have taken that path for two basic reasons, one biblical and one practical. The biblical issue is that the terminology relating to discipleship is primarily directed at the vertical relationship. The practical issue is founded on that biblical emphasis: Without first having a sound vertical relationship, the horizontal relationships, in which discipling occurs, cannot function effectively. In a word, we must really want to be discipled. A child who has been coerced into taking piano lessons will be a poor student, regardless of the quality of the music teacher. On the other hand, a willing child will learn quickly, even from an inexperienced teacher. It is a question of motivation, isn't it? Similarly, if a person wants to be as much like Jesus as possible, discipling-partner relationships will be very welcome.

The discipling process is vital in training people in everything from how to pray, to how to study, to how to live a disciplined life, to how to deal *biblically* with issues never mentioned specifically in the Bible (and there are several!). However, we will never be thus trained unless we desire to be trained. About a year ago, I was unexpectedly treated to a golf lesson by a Christian golf professional who taught in one of the country's premier golf schools. He pointed out many things that I was doing wrong, and even videotaped my swing to prove his point. I was fired-up for such an opportunity! He discipled me as a golfer for three hours, and I was overjoyed. Why? Because I love golf, and I would do nearly anything to improve my game. Did I mind being critiqued? No, I loved it because my purpose was to improve. Just imagine what would happen if all disciples were as excited as that to improve as disciples in order to accomplish their purpose for Christ! They would welcome critique and absolutely love discipling—being trained to be their best for God! How do you feel about being discipled? Are you more fired-up about improving something like a golf swing than you are about improving as a representative of Jesus Christ?

Unless and until we have made a disciple's commitment to God, like the one described in this chapter, discipling by the people God puts into our lives will be a burden and not a blessing. Without total commitment to Christ as disciples, we will not seek the training we need, we will not grow and the world will not be won. It is an all-or-nothing proposition. Easy fixes and shortcuts cannot work in life's most important endeavor. It must be done Christ's way. We must become disciples in commitment before we are in a position to be "taught to obey" all that he commanded. But then we must be trained to practice all he taught.

I learned most of these lessons the hard way. As I was learning the principles of discipleship, I was trying very hard to put them into practice in my life and trying to encourage others in the traditional church for which I preached to do the same. As I stated earlier in the book, I was amazed (*flabbergasted* would be a better term) at the lack of cooperation I received from the members. I then went outside the church to find people with hearts to be true disciples. I taught and baptized a number who were absolutely "sold out" for Christ. Then another surprise came my way— they started becoming like the older ones. I discovered that all groups have personalities, and those assimilated into them tend strongly to become like the rest of the group.

When those young members first came into the church fellowship, they asked some very hard questions. "Why aren't most of the members involved in evangelism?" "Why do large numbers come on Sunday morning, fewer on Sunday night, and still fewer to the mid-week service?" I began by telling them that many older members were weak and just needed to be encouraged by our example of being committed and zealous. After the newer ones started becoming like the older ones, I changed my answers to those questions. I told them that the others were, in biblical terms, lukewarm and losers of their first love (Revelation 2:4; 3:15-17). And further, if they did not repent, then they would not be saved. But alas, nothing could turn the tide, and they still became like the larger group. I was preaching for a church in which the members had not signed up to be disciples, and nothing I did could change that. How we come into the church means everything. If we don't come in with a disciple's repentance, committing to stop sinning and dedicate our entire lives to being disciples, then we will not respond to teaching directed at disciples! And even those who know better will be dragged down by the overall tenor of the congregation.

God trains us, if we will let him, through circumstances, the Bible and the people he puts into our lives. But we must want it and want it badly. What does it mean to be a disciple? It means that we are totally committed to following a leader: Jesus, the master discipler. It means that we know his terms and are willing to follow them no matter what the consequences may be. We will obey and trust him to work out all the details of our lives. We will sign the spiritual blank check and then let him fill in all of the blanks. And finally, being a disciple means that we will love being trained. If we are disciples, we will love being discipled. We will seek it out, submit joyfully to it, and trust God to refine our characters and to supply through others the specifics needed to fully utilize the general principles he has given in his word. Nothing is more practical and helpful than being trained as a disciple. Our joy level is tied inseparably to our growth level. Discipling keeps us growing, and therefore it keeps us excited. We do not have to be saddled with ourselves for the rest of our lives, praise God! We can change more and more into his image, and as we do, we will be both happy and productive. Why be a dull, uninteresting, uninterested pool of mediocrity when you can be discipled to be like Jesus?

6

BEING DISCIPLED
WHY IS IT IMPORTANT?

⚜

Being discipled is important for a number of good biblical and practical reasons. It keeps us focused on life's most essential goal–the pursuit of Jesus. It protects us from Satan in that we become more aware of our own sinful tendencies through the helpful input of others. It builds our character, as spirituality becomes the basis of who we are and not simply what we do. Finally, it makes us successful. If we are focused on Jesus, protected from the onslaughts of Satan, developing a more spiritual character, then success is the inevitable result. Let's examine each of these vital elements involved in being discipled.

Discipling Keeps Us Focused

Staying focused as a disciple is no easy task. In the Parable of the Soils, we find that if we stay faithful to God past the "new Christian" stage, our biggest challenge will then be to avoid getting choked by the cares of this life. These challenges are constant. I have never known any disciple who did not at times lose his focus and have to be called back to "sold out" status once again. Being discipled keeps us from wandering far, and it keeps us from staying out of focus for long periods. But when there are so many things that we need to do, what is the key focus needed in our lives as disciples? The answer for me is twofold: The first is to become more and more like Jesus (1 Peter 2:21; 1 John 2:6). The second is to stay focused on his mission for us of seeking and saving the lost (Luke 19:10; Acts 20:24). Just about everything else grows out of these key areas. If I am concentrating on these, life goes well indeed. When I minimize either, my heart begins to harden and my life weakens.

Focused on the Imitation of Jesus

"Whoever claims to live in him must walk as Jesus did" (1 John 2:6). If I could point out one of our most glaring weaknesses in discipling, it would be in imitating Jesus. Hopefully some wonderful exceptions to the general rule exist, but if my experience as a church leader is any indication, we do not understand the significance of imitating Christ. Now, we may use the terminology, but do we really point those whom we are discipling to the specific examples of Jesus on a consistent basis? It is far easier to find a verse condemning an evil practice and/or calling for a good one. The "Thou Shalt Not's" and "Thou Shalt's" are handy for our "quick-fix" American mentality. To spend the time studying deeply the lessons underlying Jesus' behavior and interactions is demanding—but it changes us like nothing else can.

I remember Al Baird telling the story of a man who was studying to become a Christian but had difficulty understanding the need to stop smoking. He was told mainly that he should not do anything to harm his body, which was to be a temple of the Holy Spirit (1 Corinthians 6:19-20). However, he had cut down to one cigarette per day, and his doctor had assured him that such usage would not be harmful. The study had reached an impasse until Al entered the scene, and he asked the man one question: "Would Jesus smoke one cigarette per day?" The man thought for just a minute and said no. The battle was over. He vowed to quit immediately and was baptized soon afterwards.

In my own life I recently saw a similar result. For months I had been struggling with subtle (and not so subtle) attitudes toward someone who had hurt me. Even though the person wasn't a disciple, I tried to bring some resolution to the situation, but they persisted in doing things that hurt me. I found myself nursing some bitterness, in spite of trying to repent of it through prayer. My wife pointed out what she was seeing in me, which was mainly holding back my heart from the person in order to limit additional pain. Although I knew deep down that I was wrong, I was rationalizing that I had good reason to feel as I did. Therefore, nothing really changed, in spite of my guilty conscience and prayers.

But then, something happened that brought an amazing reversal in my thinking. I read one of the daily studies from the book *Jesus with the People.*[1] This article was by Tammy Fleming, and it was about Jesus and Judas. She pointed out how much Jesus must have agonized in prayer daily to keep giving all of his heart to Judas, knowing that it would be he who betrayed him. As Tammy shared honestly about her own struggles to love in this manner, she made the relevant passages about Jesus come alive. I felt a very deep sense of conviction, followed by an immediate repentance. I shared my convictions with others and a weight lifted from my heart. I felt entirely different about the person who had hurt me. I thank God for using Tammy's insights and honesty to bring me back to the example of Jesus.

We have four Gospel accounts in the Bible for a reason: God wanted us to see in Jesus' life the demonstration of other biblical teachings. Again, it is seeing teachings lived out in "flesh and blood" that helps us to learn the most effectively. I have a very strong conviction after my recent experience that all of us need to study the life of Jesus much more than we do. I also have a strong concern that much of our studying of his life is reserved mostly for individual "quiet time" study rather than with one another in our discipling relationships. We simply must spend the time thinking about how to apply Jesus' example to real-life situations in a way which makes the biblical accounts come alive. These types of questions must become much more a part of our discipling times: "What would Jesus do in your situation?" "Why do you think so?" "Which example from Jesus' life most relates to your current problem?" There may be times when we are able to avoid the full impact of challenging biblical commands because of a hardness of heart, but if we have any softness left, the example of Jesus will melt us.

John, the beloved apostle who walked closely with Jesus, left us with this charge:

> But if anyone obeys his word, God's love is truly made complete in him. This is how we know we are in him: Whoever claims to live in him must walk as Jesus did (1 John 2:5-6).

Without focused study, we cannot know how Jesus walked, much less imitate him. I remember a time when I came to some conclusions about the need to preach more about Jesus, at which time I jotted down some ideas about his life which would be food for thought and research. The list I came up with was nothing exhaustive, nor could it be since in him "are hidden all the treasures of wisdom and knowledge" (Colossians 2:3). However, you will find my list below. I am including it here in hopes that you will study these (and other similar topics) and use what you find in your discipling times with others.

- Assurances of Jesus ("Do not be afraid")
- Humility of Jesus
- Prayers of Jesus
- How Jesus Handled Interruptions
- Those Whom Jesus Touched
- Jesus' Intolerance of Hypocrisy
- What If Jesus Had Never Come?
- Titles and Names of Jesus in Scripture
- What Made Jesus Frustrated?
- How Did Jesus Deal with Disappointments?
- Jesus As the Door–As the Vine–As the Light–As the Teacher– As the Lamb of God (many similar others)
- The Magnetism of Jesus
- Unexpected Reactions of Jesus
- Different Reactions to Jesus
- How He Related to: Children, Older People, Women, the Pharisees, the Pagans, the Poor, the Physically Challenged, etc.
- Things that Amazed Jesus
- Jesus As High Priest
- What Made Jesus Joyful?
- What Made Jesus Angry?
- Jesus As Possessor of the Best Masculine Qualities
- Jesus As Possessor of the Best Feminine Qualities
- Jesus As a Disciple to the Father
- The Humanity of Jesus
- The Divinity of Jesus
- Those Whom Jesus Served

The most compelling reason to do anything is because Jesus would have done it. His heart is extensively revealed in the Gospels in ways that can change and direct our lives, but all of us are going to have to dig in much deeper than most of us are accustomed to doing. This digging should take place in our individual study and in our teaching, preaching and discipling of others. The more we use Scripture as we advise other people, the more impact for good it will have; and the more Jesus' example is our scriptural focus, the greater the heart changes thus produced.

Focused on the Mission of Jesus

Many directives are given to disciples, but none is more important than the command to go make more disciples and bring them to God. Jesus came into the world, carried out his ministry and ultimately died on the cross to seek and to save the lost. He woke up every morning thinking about this mission and shut his eyes at night with prayers for this mission controlling his heart. The Great Commission (or the Great Imperative) was the last thing which came from his lips before he ascended back to heaven. We must daily imitate this heart and life. We are in a quest for souls, a battle with Satanic forces for the eternal destiny of countless millions.

As a minister prior to my discipling days, I at least paid homage to the concept that the Great Commission was indeed one of the most fundamental responsibilities we have on planet Earth. But I did not get the big picture until I saw in action those who practiced discipling. Before that, I always seemed to have plenty of people with whom to study, but most of them were funneled to me by others in the church. For special events, I sometimes knocked doors and invited people, but the first time I heard people talking about going out to public places for the express purpose of sharing their faith with strangers, I was a bit threatened by their example. At the same time, I was not comfortable with the concept of building relationships with all kinds of people with one goal in mind—reaching them for Jesus. However, I knew what the Bible said about evangelism and could not argue with the need to be radical in getting out of my comfort zone to reach people.

After I became a part of a church where discipleship and discipling were the norm, I needed much help learning to become a better fisher of men. Most of that help came from people who were much younger than I (physically), but I loved learning from them. I have become much more effective through the years, and I am still trying to learn all I can about affecting people like Jesus did. Much of what I need now is accountability—the kind one finds in good discipling. People in most religious circles are not accustomed to any kind of spiritual accountability and might even be offended by the word. However, properly understood, the concept is biblical and its practice very beneficial.

Jesus sent out the Twelve and the seventy-two on their missions, and then had them report back to him for a "debriefing" of sorts. He wanted to make sure their attitudes were in the right place and that they had learned the lessons he intended for them to learn. Reporting in was a part of their training.

There is really nothing here that is surprising. Can you imagine any business in the world without some form of accountability? Can you imagine any school without it, or any family? In areas *outside of religion,* accountability is absolutely expected.

What determines the need for and the level of accountability in such life situations? The *importance* of the assigned task, pure and simple. What does the lack of accountability in most religious circles say about those groups? They do not view what they do as fundamentally important. However, disciples must view their work as radically important. Remember, we are imitating Jesus.

For disciples, accountability is designed simply to help us follow through with what we are already committed to doing. It should never be seen as a tool to make us do what we do not want to do. If we don't want to do what disciples are biblically mandated to do, then we have a heart problem and accountability is not going to help us until we have a change of heart. But I need accountability in evangelism. I wish that I had the same drive and focus Jesus had, but I do not always have it. I need brothers with whom I can talk and plan as we "spur one another on to love and good deeds." Knowing that others are going to ask me about my evangelism is very good—it spurs me on to do what my spirit wants to do, even when my flesh is weak.

In many churches, leaders are those who tell others what they should be doing, while they are not personally involved in the battle. I am so grateful that I am in a church where leaders are expected to lead the charge, especially in evangelism. As a leader, I am called to be "out there" with the people just as Jesus was. I am grateful to be in a church where others help me to remember that I do not fulfill my mission just by writing books and teaching lessons.

Discipling helps keep us on track in following Jesus as we are his co-workers to save the lost. Is discipling important? Absolutely, for without it, we strongly tend to lose our focus, and Jesus' prime directive falls by the wayside. Be a disciple, be discipled, and stay focused!

Discipling Protects Us from Satan

"But encourage one another daily, as long as it is called To-day, so that none of you may be hardened by sin's deceitfulness" (Hebrews 3:13). One clear purpose of discipling is to assist each other in resisting Satan. When I first was visiting churches that practiced discipling, I met a man in a controversial congregation who was writing a book defending the practice. He gave me a copy of the manuscript, which I took back home with me. A few days later, I started reading it and was shaken to my roots. I honestly don't remember too many details in the material, but I do remember what he said about discipling's potential to stop sin at the temptation level. For three days I read the manuscript, and literally could not sleep at night! My mind would not quit racing and my heart would not stop pounding.

I thought of friends and family members whose lives had been devastated by sin and realized what being discipled could have done to stem the awful tide. One religious relative had become close to a friend at church and had become immoral with the person. They both ended up divorcing their mates and marrying each other, leaving mates and children to wash up on the shores of pain and devastation. I kept thinking, *What if they had been in a group following the Bible's admonitions about discipling? What if they had been open at the temptation level?* I knew in my heart of hearts that the damage could have been averted and lives spared some of the worst pain possible. I could not get the horrors out of my mind, and I could not quit thinking about what might have been if biblical discipling had been part of their lives.

I cried all my tears out in those sleepless nights. And I vowed to God that I would begin obeying his teaching about discipleship and learn as much about it as possible. I knew that in order to do these two things, I would have to accept the controversial nature of the subject and follow God rather than men. I made the decision to follow the Bible and its clear teaching about discipleship and discipling and let the chips fall where they would. Praise God, for my life has never been the same since. Only God knows how much sin and pain have been averted in my family by our dealing with sin at the temptation level.

Those who are not being open about their temptations are playing with spiritual dynamite. Every time I am open with another person about my sins and temptations to sin, my heart breathes a sigh of relief. Delivered again, praise Jesus! Satan then has to retreat into his vile darkness and look for other souls to deceive. But he will be back, tempting me to cover up the garbage in my heart. If I listen to him, he will have the opportunity to get a foothold in my soul. If I listen to God and obey his directives for discipleship, victory is assured. The whole issue is really quite simple, although not always easy. But I would not trade anything for the light flooding my life through discipling. Get open, get help, get healed and get victorious! It is God's plan.

Discipling Builds Our Character

Those who follow Jesus are called to make major changes in their lives. Paul put it this way in Ephesians 4:22-24:

> You were taught, with regard to your former way of life, to put off your old self, which is being corrupted by its deceitful desires; to be made new in the attitude of your minds; and to put on the new self, created to be like God in true righteousness and holiness.

Such a statement sounds great and what is described here is great, but anyone who has worked with people knows that such changes are not easily made. Paul is talking here about major character change, not just redecorating the exterior. Certainly, the Bible teaches that the Holy Spirit is involved in helping us make these changes (2 Corinthians 3:18), but it is clear from the sheer volume of "one another" texts (discussed in Chapter Two) that we are to play a key role in each other's lives. A close look reveals that the Holy Spirit works through our relationships to help us make character changes we could not and would not make on our own (see, for example, 1 Corinthians 12).

We become the way we are in two basic ways: First, we are born with certain qualities or certain tendencies in many areas of both capability and character. (While inheritance is not the total issue, nor the final word in who we become, it unquestionably is a factor.) Second, we are molded by our environment, particularly our closest relationships in that environment, like our family situations. Many possible combinations of inheritance and environment work together to make us who we are at any given point.

Our basic tendencies, which are inborn, can be good or bad. Our outside influences can be good or bad. In between the two extremes, neutral tendencies and influences are possible, but the extremes are the most important in understanding why we are as we are.

If I am born with a "bent" toward a given quality or ability, my "discipling" (atmosphere, influences) can alter it in a major way. Suppose I have a bent toward mathematics. An atmosphere, provided by parents or teachers, supportive of mathematics will most likely produce a highly skillful mathematician. On the other hand, an atmosphere negative toward math can stifle the bent almost entirely. With a neutral atmosphere, the outcome is more unpredictable.

The same principle holds true with a positive character tendency. If I have an inborn tendency for being an unselfish servant (and there are people like this), the "discipling" I receive will affect me significantly. If I have parents who are themselves unselfish and who actively direct me toward serving, I will likely end up as an unselfish person. On the other hand, if my parents are selfish and train me in selfishness (consciously or unconsciously), they can stifle the positive natural bent in my character.

But how does this work when someone lacks certain abilities? Someone without aptitude for math will never develop math abilities in an atmosphere negative toward math. However, an atmosphere highly positive toward math can significantly improve the person's ability to do well in the subject.

Coming back to the more important topic of character development, suppose that I am born with very few tendencies toward unselfishness. A selfish environment will do nothing but make me more selfish. Clearly, two negatives do not a make a positive! However, a positive atmosphere of discipling (parents' example plus their training of the child) can significantly alter the natural tendency toward selfishness. Even with a natural inclination toward selfishness, I can become more unselfish and giving.

We were all born with a variety of strengths and weaknesses, and we have all been exposed to environments that have influenced those in various ways. But the Bible says, in so many words, that "even the best of us is a mess" (Romans 3:23). When we become disciples, we make a conscious decision to put ourselves in an environment where the sinful tendencies will be discouraged and the godly tendencies will be encouraged, and we should welcome any relationship that contributes to this environment. Satan is strong, sin is real and we cannot develop righteousness without a serious commitment to it. Success in making changes will never be permanent by accident: It takes planning and perseverance.

We can change. God is in the changing business. Change may not be easy, but "all things are possible with God"! (Mark 10:27). A child with positive tendencies needs mostly direction to channel and develop the tendencies. A child with negative tendencies, needs a balance of *correction* and *direction*. His natural direction must be continually corrected and changed into the right direction. When this approach is applied frequently and consistently, the changes will occur at some point.

In many ways we are all children who still need to change. Jesus calls us to become like a child (Matthew 18:1-4) and accept the needed direction and correction from God through his Word and through his people (see 2 Timothy 3:16-4:2). In some areas we need the help of others who will provide direction. In other areas we need the help of others who will provide correction. But the bottom line is: We need each other in order to make lasting character changes.

The conclusion of the matter is that all of us need to develop an accurate view of our weaknesses, develop long-range and short-range plans for change, and put the plans into effect *daily*. Disciplers are invaluable in helping us see our weaknesses accurately, formulating practical plans on a weekly basis, and following through on a daily basis. If we have deep convictions about our weaknesses, a deep desire to change, a plan which includes discipling to help us change behavior, and a strong prayer life to allow God to change our hearts, we will change both character and actions. We will become more and more like Jesus.

One of the most practical definitions of discipling I ever heard came from my friend Douglas Arthur. He said "Discipling is gentle pressure—relentlessly applied!" Discipling involves pressure, but it is the welcome, gentle pressure of one who loves us and genuinely wants us to be our best for God. To achieve that lofty goal, the loving pressure must be applied consistently and without exception. Just think of how this approach relates to training children. If parents follow it, blessed indeed will be their children. And if discipleship partners follow it with each other, blessed will be our lives as we become more and more like our Pattern.

Discipling Makes Us Successful

We all want to succeed. No one likes failure. Doing things God's way brings encouraging results into our lives—and doing things his way includes being discipled to grow and change. Being discipled brings such positive benefits, and blessed are those who view it in this way. They cannot fail in their spiritual life. Those who want to be discipled show humility, and God always blesses humility. Those who see it as a burden, a duty or an intrusion into their privacy are headed for heartache.

Success for the Master should be the preeminent goal in our lives. Everything that relates to our being effective for him must become an issue of discipling, including personality, people skills, verbal skills, reliability, dress, habits, etc. If our goal is to win as many as possible, we are going to have to relate well to as many

as possible. And we are going to have to concentrate on remov-
ing anything "unrelatable" from our lives and personalities. Paul
summarized his soul quest in these words: "I have become all
things to all men so that by all possible means I might save some"
(1 Corinthians 9:22b). Dare we do less?

Certainly one of the issues we face as disciples is our use of
time and resources for God. Priorities have to be constantly ex-
amined and decisions made which reflect our calling. Just as none
of our possessions really belongs to us (Luke 14:33), neither does
our time. Just about now, some of us start feeling a tightening in
our chest, don't we? We like to think of "our" time and having
"our" space. Frankly, we are selfish far beyond our understanding. Paul often talked of being a slave (*doulos* in Greek) of Christ.
This is not the word of a household servant, but of one who is
someone else's property. Slaves have no rights whatsoever, only
privileges. Praise God that we have the best Slave-owner in the
universe and that he grants us many exalted privileges! But we
are still slaves, responsible for pleasing the Master at all costs.
Are we willing to pay the price?[2]

Some years ago, Nick and Debbie Young moved to Boston
for further training as they prepared to lead a church planting to
Dallas. We were privileged to be able to disciple them for the
months they were here. Although we were acquainted, we did
not know each other well. However, that was destined to change
quickly. The first time they came to our house for a discipling
time, Nick jumped right in to tell us about a marriage "bump"
they had just experienced. He and Debbie said that they wanted
us to know as much about them as quickly as possible in order to
gain the most from our discipling relationship. Some time later, I
heard Nick soundly condemn what he called "battleship" discipleship. If you are familiar with the game, the players try to guess
the location of the other player's ships and then sink them. In
discipling terms, it means that we don't volunteer much unless
our discipler "hits" our sin exactly, and then we confess it. Nick
and Debbie never played those games with us because they really
believe in discipleship.

Once they asked us to come to their house for dinner and a
family devotional with their two young children. Specifically, they

asked that we observe them and evaluate their parenting. After doing exactly that, I learned a couple of lessons. One, if we spend time with a family for the purpose of evaluating them, we notice much more than we would otherwise. Usually we notice only the blatant things, but if we are trying to see anything which might be improved, we will definitely see more. Two, disciples who are serious about their roles in life will not only welcome input, they will seek ways to get it. No battleship discipleship!

Would it surprise you to know that the Youngs have been amazingly successful in ministry and family? From that first discipling time with them, I expected nothing less. They had the same religious background that Theresa and I had, and they knew what life was like without discipleship. They, and we, have sought it, learned and grown from it, and experienced successes beyond anything we ever asked or imagined. It is the way of Christ, and it cannot be improved upon. Let your independent pride and self-ishness run rampant, and both you and your family will be cursed. Humble yourself and determine to get all the help you can to become like Jesus in every area of your life, and you will experience success consistently. It cannot be otherwise, for it is written into the laws of the universe by the Universe Maker himself!

7

BEING DISCIPLED
THE KEYS TO SUCCESS

⁑

Being disciped is the close involvement of another person of the same sex in our lives for the purpose of helping us to become more like Jesus. It encompasses every aspect of life, that we might be well-rounded and mature. The more mature we become, the stronger influence we will exert in the lives of our brothers and sisters in Christ and in the lives of those who are not yet a part of his kingdom. But what are the keys? Which key qualities do we especially need if we are to gain everything possible from discipling and become mature as disciples? Let's spend some time looking at the basic qualities essential to the most consistent growth possible. If the following "keys" are in your life, discipling will work for you.

The Key of Openness

There are three basic levels of communication: the cliché (weather, sports, clothes, etc.); the opinion level, when we venture out a little more with definite opinions; and the emotional level, which is obviously the most vulnerable. Learning to open up at the emotional level was one of the most difficult hurdles I have ever crossed. Men in our culture have what appears to be a natural aversion to this level of communication. However, women are much more comfortable with it, and most wives deeply desire to experience this kind of communication with their husbands.

When we read through the Bible looking for openness at the feeling level, we will be impressed. God sets the pace, as might be expected! He lays his heart out time after time. Jesus did the same, as did many other biblical characters. Especially revealing is a study of Paul's life. Try reading the book of 2 Corinthians with the purpose of studying Paul's levels of communication. His openness about his struggles and the terms of endearment he used toward others definitely call us men much higher in being expressive and vulnerable.[1]

It was a marriage enrichment seminar that I attended before I became a disciple that convinced me to begin opening up with my feelings. Just prior to that time, I had received a year-end evaluation by the elders of the little church I preached for, and I reacted very negatively to it (due to pride and insecurity). One of the statements I clearly remember was that their wives thought I was aloof and arrogant. I actually argued with them about the opinion of their wives and assured them that it wasn't true! My response proved their point precisely!

In those days the preacher was usually responsible for teaching what we called "the ladies' Bible class." My class included these wives. After the marriage seminar I decided to try a novel approach. My lecture format in the church auditorium was about to give way to something much more inviting. First, I had a friend at church change the drab fellowship hall into a bright room with blue carpet and blue wall covering. Then the women and I began sitting in a circle for a discussion-group format. I chose topics requiring more openness generally, and I forced myself to personally get vulnerable with them. I told them that I knew some of them considered me to be prideful and aloof, and although I was sure I put up that front, it was only a cover for my insecurity. In fact, I went on to inform them, I was especially insecure around women! After that bold admission, the change in the dynamic was dramatic. They were now very anxious to make me feel accepted and approved!

The lesson wasn't lost on me. Suddenly I found that openness paid amazing dividends. First, people are drawn to you as a person. They will never see your humility unless they first see your humanity. And when you open the curtains of your heart and let them in, they will be attracted greatly. Second, they will be encouraged to begin opening up themselves. Third, you will grow emotionally and spiritually. The more vulnerable you are, the faster you grow. Did you get that? Let me say it again. *The more vulnerable you are, the faster you grow!* A minister friend heard me speak on this subject in a traditional church when I was first learning to be open, and he made a statement to his congregation that I've never forgotten: "We come to church hiding behind our little shells of protection, and about all we do together is bump shells and go home." We desperately need to get out of our shells and enjoy the growth that is ours for the taking!

What does all of this have to do with discipling? Everything! Discipling relationships are designed by God to meet our need to be open with our feelings. We humans are such people pleasers and conflict avoiders that we have "stuffed" tons of attitudes inside, to our detriment. Our need to be open at the feeling level can hardly be overstated. Such vulnerability blesses us in two ways. First, it can strengthen our self image and confidence. Second, it limits the effects of sin, which when locked up inside, destroys our souls.

As stated earlier, learning to be open was very difficult for me, and at times is still difficult. But I am committed to being open, because the results are highly beneficial. I can remember a number of specific times when my attitudes were terrible and my mood horrible and the thought of opening up was painful. Yet, after fighting through and doing it, I felt on top of the world in a very short time. Prior to getting it all out, Satan caused my imagination to go wild. *If I let others know what I am really like, then they won't like me (or respect me, or love me). In fact, I'll probably be asked to leave the ministry!* Of course, none of these things happened. Actually, it was quite the opposite, as people responded to my openness (and confession of sin) with love and grace. No wonder Satan hates our openness! Clearing out our hearts has an unbelievable effect on our moods and attitudes.

But keep in mind the main purpose of openness. It is designed to bring our hearts out in the open, so that our discipleship partners can help to spiritually tune us up. Sometimes after opening up with bad attitudes and getting corrected, some think or say, "Well, at least I was open. I don't see why you are on my case now!" Openness with attitudes doesn't make them correct. Being honest is absolutely essential, true enough, but essential because our hearts can be seen clearly and then helped.

Once I attended a Marriage Encounter and heard a certain statement repeated over and over. It went something like this: "Feelings are not right or wrong; they just are." I appreciate the emphasis on being open with feelings, but attitudes behind feelings certainly are right or wrong. If right, they need to be shared and commended, and if wrong, they need to be shared and corrected. The fact is, until we think biblically about something, we will not really feel good about it. Hence the need to be open in order to find out what is inside us, that we might be helped to align attitudes and feelings with biblical teaching. If you are not now totally committed to being open with your life—victories and defeats, dreams and fears, temptations and sins then please repent and make that commitment now. You will never be a happy and successful disciple without it.

The Key of Seeking Advice

Seeking advice is one of the greatest needs and blessings in a disciple's life. Outside the kingdom, just where would you go to receive good advice about life? The last time I looked, I did not notice many truly successful people out there (at least not successful in the areas that are most important to me!). But praise God that in the kingdom great advice abounds. Many scriptures point out the tremendous value of seeking godly advice. Here are but a few, all from the book of Proverbs:[2]

- The way of a fool seems right to him,
    but a wise man listens to advice (12:15).

- Pride only breeds quarrels,
    but wisdom is found in those who take advice
    (13:10).

- Plans fail for lack of counsel,
    but with many advisers they succeed (15:22).

- Listen to advice and accept instruction,
    and in the end you will be wise (19:20).

- Make plans by seeking advice;
    if you wage war, obtain guidance (20:18).

- Perfume and incense bring joy to the heart,
   and the pleasantness of one's friend springs from
   his earnest counsel (27:9).

The last one in the list is especially appropriate in describing the relationship between discipling partners. Our counsel for one another grows out of a loving friendship and an earnest desire to help each other grow and experience joy. I don't know about you, but I have already made enough mistakes in my life. Seeking advice has spared me much heartache. Often our decisions may not have earth-shaking consequences, but in being followers of Jesus (who did everything well: Mark 7:37), we should want to make the very best choices. In fact, once we gain a reasonable amount of spiritual perspective, most of our choices will not be between good and bad, but between good, better and best. Paul described this truth in these words:

> And this is my prayer: that your love may abound more and more in knowledge and depth of insight, so that you may be able to discern what is best and may be pure and blameless until the day of Christ (Philippians 1:9-10).

Several practical suggestions are in order here to help you obtain and use advice in the best way. First, pray that God will really work through those from whom you are going to seek advice, that he will give you and them wisdom. Second, seek advice in all areas of life, especially if you are a newer disciple. Get advice about priorities, time usage, spending time with old friends, evangelism, entertainment options, finances and the like. In doing this, you will learn the areas in which your judgment is best and worst. In the areas where your judgment is weakest, you will know to make sure to seek plenty of advice in the future. It is difficult to conceive of getting too much advice, so tend to seek much, not little. Third, the weightier the consequences of your decisions, the more advice you should seek. However, when seeking counsel from a number of people, be careful not to just keep asking additional people until you hear what you want to hear! It is normal to enter the decision-making mode with some preconceived ideas, but our hearts must be open in order to really consider what others say. If I receive conflicting advice, I go back to the parties who differ and attempt to find a way for us all to end up on the same page. Certainly, you should give much heavier weight to the mature disciples in your life who know you the best.

Fourth, keep your heart open to the advice of others, but don't glibly accept it if your heart isn't there. On one occasion, I remember seeking some very important advice from a very mature leader. Although I did not feel settled about going the route he suggested, in the guise of being a "good disciple," I followed the advice. The results were not good. Later I mentioned the outcome to him and confessed that I had not felt comfortable with his advice and told him why. He responded by saying that if I had given him the benefit of hearing those reasons earlier, his advice would have been different. Good point. From this I learned to keep talking until I feel settled and both of us end up in agreement, if at all possible (and just about always, it is). And I have also learned that to keep praying for wisdom throughout the whole process helps me to get settled out emotionally and in touch with what may be keeping me from being comfortable with the advice.

The Key of a Submissive Spirit

To possess a submissive spirit is to possess a very spiritual quality, but since it is spiritual, it is also unnatural. We tend to grow up trusting no one nearly as much as we trust ourselves. We think we are the center of the universe, and we like being in control. If we have been hurt significantly by authority figures in our lives, submission is all the harder. In any event, one of our most pervasive sins is pride, and pride and submission are most unwelcome partners. The antidote is obviously a good dose of humility.

Do you want to be a wise person in the sight of God? Then develop a submissive spirit, as James tells us:

> But the wisdom that comes from heaven is first of all pure; then peace-loving, considerate, submissive, full of mercy and good fruit, impartial and sincere (James 3:17).

This development is based on accepting at the emotional level what is taught in 1 Peter 2:18-3:8. As the account begins, slaves are given a startling command: "Slaves, submit yourselves to your masters with all respect, not only to those who are good and considerate, but also to those who are harsh" (1 Peter 2:18). Our human nature cries out against God's teaching here, as we say, "Wait a minute—submitting to a good master who deserves respect may be all right, but this business of respecting a harsh one doesn't make any sense at all!"

However, the disciple doesn't practice submission simply because it makes worldly sense. We do it not because of who the master is, but because of who the Master is! We do it because of *whose* we are and *who* we are. How are we able to do such a challenging thing? As we continue reading the passage, we find the answer: Imitate Christ. He did not retaliate when mistreated because he had entrusted himself to God, really believing that God was in control and would work out everything for his good. (Romans 8:28 does say that, doesn't it?) The same principle was next applied to women and their need to submit to their husband's leadership (1 Peter 3:1-6); then to husbands who needed to submit to their wife's needs (1 Peter 3:7); and finally to each other in the church (1 Peter 3:8). The latter verse puts it this way:

> Finally, all of you, live in harmony with one another; be sympathetic, love as brothers, be compassionate and humble.

You see, the submissive spirit is the umbrella under which we will be protected and led by God.

Biblically, we are obligated to practice submission in all kinds of relationships in the world (bosses, law officers and other public officials, teachers, etc.). If this submission to worldly authority is to be carried out with "all respect," then how much more should we have submissive spirits toward those in the church—especially if they are in some way directly responsible for our well-being, as is a discipleship partner? Remember that being discipled keeps us in a humble mode, and God will always bless humility.

When I first heard of discipling partners, I thought it sounded pretty good—as an older leader, I could disciple younger leaders in the kingdom. When I put two and two together and realized that I would also need to be discipled, then my pride rose up a bit! However, once I started receiving the blessings of having a submissive spirit in this relationship and in relationships in the kingdom generally, I felt tremendously better.

A most important passage for understanding this need for submission is 1 Peter 5:5-6:

> Young men, in the same way be submissive to those who are older. All of you, clothe yourselves with humility toward one another, because,

> "God opposes the proud
>   but gives grace to the humble."

> Humble yourselves, therefore, under God's mighty hand, that he may lift you up in due time.

Several lessons stand out in these verses. First, younger men need to have submissive spirits toward older men, and it makes sense that this principle applies to both chronological and spiritual age. Second, we all should be clothed with humility toward one another, regardless of age and maturity distinctions. Third, humbling ourselves under God's mighty hand is done by practicing humility with one another. (The "therefore" makes this point clear.) Fourth, we will be lifted up at the proper time by God. He always blesses humility, and humility is demonstrated almost exclusively by how we relate to other human beings. Be submissive to those in your life, trusting that God will work through them (and if need be, in spite of them!). And get ready to receive blessings like never before!

The Key of Imitation

One evidence of being humble is the desire to imitate Christ in others. Imitation is without question the fastest way to learn how to do something, be it a golf swing or a culinary procedure.

A number of years ago, I taught in a ministers' training school. In a preaching class, I assigned topics for speeches of different types and lengths. Once, in delivering a full-length sermon, a student preached a sermon that he and most of the students had heard me preach about the second coming of Christ. That student imitated my preaching very closely in both content and delivery. In the critique session afterwards, one of his fellow students was very critical of his imitating of me. Personally, I thought he was a very wise student because Jesus himself said, "A student is not above his teacher, but everyone who is fully trained will be like his teacher" (Luke 6:40). Maybe you would think it coincidental, but the imitator in this story, Joe Fields, has gone on to become a very successful evangelist in the kingdom of God, and the critic has been through divorce and many other rough times. The issue is pride and humility, wouldn't you think?

When I first started preaching, my name might well have been "Gordon Hood," for I was a great thief in my imitation of others! One of my mentors took me along with him when he preached and taught in personal evangelism workshops. I taped every lesson he did, and when he started asking me to preach in one of the slots in the workshop, I delivered his lesson as exactly as I could—with him in the audience listening! I changed nothing except the personal illustrations which didn't fit my life, but even then, I tried to find my own which were as parallel to his as possible. It never would have dawned on me that by imitating so precisely I "wasn't my own man," or "wasn't being true to myself." It all seemed pretty simple to me: He was the better preacher, and the fastest way to become better myself was to imitate him. The fact that I became viewed as a very good speaker very quickly was no accident. I just imitated and grew fast.

If we trust that God has put us with discipleship partners in order to help us grow, then we will want to learn from them by imitating. The Bible amply emphasizes the need to learn from one another via the imitation process. Imitating another disciple takes humility, and since pride can cause us to shy away from imitation, I am including a number of passages to help us get the picture.

- "Come, follow me," Jesus said, "and I will make you fishers of men" (Jesus, Mark 1:17).

- "I tell you the truth, anyone who has faith in me will do what I have been doing" (Jesus, John 14:12b).

- "My sheep listen to my voice; I know them, and they follow me" (Jesus, John 10:27).

- Therefore I urge you to imitate me (Paul, 1 Corinthians 4:16).

- Follow my example, as I follow the example of Christ (Paul, 1 Corinthians 11:1).

- Join with others in following my example, brothers, and take note of those who live according to the pattern we gave you (Paul, Philippians 3:17).

- You became imitators of us and of the Lord; in spite of severe suffering, you welcomed the message with the joy given by the Holy Spirit (Paul, 1 Thessalonians 1:6).

- For you yourselves know how you ought to follow our example. We were not idle when we were with you (Paul, 2 Thessalonians 3:7).

- Remember your leaders, who spoke the word of God to you. Consider the outcome of their way of life and imitate their faith (Hebrews 13:7).

Certainly we are not to imitate in another's life that which is not Christlike, but we are to learn as much as possible from them. Much of what we learn will be along very practical lines. Perhaps we need a better sense of humor or a better sense of soberness. Maybe they have more Bible knowledge than we, or if less, more practical wisdom about how to apply it. Mark it down: You are teamed up with your discipleship partner for God's reasons, and you need to trust that fact and learn everything possible. Without humility, you are going to miss out on learning some very valuable lessons.

Years back, Al Baird discipled me for a time. I had just been appointed as an elder and evangelist, while he had served in both roles for a while. During the time he discipled me, I was prideful.

(I thought of nicer ways to describe my problem here, but I need to practice the vulnerability I've been preaching, don't I?!). I am an emotionally based person, and he is not. I thought that he wouldn't be able to really understand me, and therefore, wasn't the right one to be discipling me. God (or someone) had clearly made a mistake in putting us together. Looking back, I realize how prideful and stupid I was! I was too emotional and needed to imitate Al in how he practiced self-control as he dealt with emotionally charged situations.

Through the intervening years, I have seen Al dismantle "bombs" that a more emotionally based person would have exploded. Just about every time I talk with Al now, which is fairly often, I tell him that he is my hero—and he is. I just wish I had been humble enough much earlier in our relationship to have let him be the hero and role model that he is to me now. I would have learned much more from him, and he would have enjoyed discipling me much more. I give you my permission not to imitate my poor example in this case; it definitely was not a spiritual example. Don't waste valuable opportunities! Imitate, learn quickly and be blessed powerfully by God.

The Key of Reliability

Reliability is one of the most important evidences of the disciplined life, without which we cannot be effective disciples. In an earlier chapter, we used 2 Timothy 2:1-7 to show that the discipling process is more than a good idea—it is a biblical mandate. The passage has more to teach us, especially in defining the quality of reliability. Read it carefully, and then we will think through the pertinent points together.

> [1]You then, my son, be strong in the grace that is in Christ Jesus. [2]And the things you have heard me say in the presence of many witnesses entrust to reliable men who will also be qualified to teach others. [3]Endure hardship with us like a good soldier of Christ Jesus. [4]No one serving as a soldier gets involved in civilian affairs—he wants to please his commanding officer. [5]Similarly, if anyone competes as an athlete, he does not receive the victor's crown unless

he competes according to the rules. ⁶The hardworking farmer should be the first to receive a share of the crops. ⁷Reflect on what I am saying, for the Lord will give you insight into all this.

The entire population of God's kingdom falls under the challenges enjoined here, for we either fit into the category of "reliable men" or in that of "others." Therefore, what does the passage teach us about being disciplined and trustworthy? Beginning with verse 1, we find that our necessary foundation is an understanding of God's grace. The balance between law and grace, faith and works, performance and merit is difficult to keep sorted out in our lives at times. We tend to feel great when we have performed well and terrible when things have gone badly. And if we are feeling great because of successful performance, we are prone to slack off and become (at least for a time) unreliable. If we are feeling terrible because our performance is flawed, then we may well lose motivation and reliability along with it. Jesus warned his servants not to rejoice because of a spiritually successful performance, but because of their salvation (Luke 10:20). As servants of God, we cannot go emotionally up and down as if we were riding a roller coaster, and the only way to avoid this is to find security in understanding and accepting the grace of God. ³ We will still have good days and bad, but disciples have God in either case.

In verses 3-4, we find that a disciple is to be like a soldier. Incidentally, these illustrations are going to tell us a lot about the overall atmosphere of the church. Some denominations tend to have the atmosphere of a country club, while others seem like a hospital (full of sick folk), but Christ's church must be more like a spiritual *boot camp!* The soldier/disciple endures hardship, and he does not become focused on "civilian" (non-kingdom) pursuits. His prime objective in life is to please Jesus, his commanding officer. What are civilian pursuits? You fill in the blank. (It's not hard to do, is it?) Entertainment, possessions, careers, even family relationships can easily become worldly in their impact on us. I have seen many single disciples who were remarkably focused on things of the kingdom, but after marriage their hearts turned to houses, careers, how to spend "spare" time and even family issues. Honestly, we need more discipling the more responsibilities we have—more than most of us dream! Priorities get cloudy fast, and without others in our life calling us back to our first love for Jesus, we will lose our focus on the mission.

In verse 5, we are called to enroll in the training camp of an athlete. We are competing daily for the souls of men. Serious athletes pay some very high physical, emotional and financial prices to become outstanding in their sport. It is no less true for us as disciples of Jesus and of one another. In my flesh, I'm lazy— and I think most of us are. We may apply ourselves diligently in the areas we find easiest and most enjoyable, but to be God's athlete, we are going to have to deny self to do the difficult training and to submit to coaching. No athlete gets to the Olympics without self denial in some rather extreme ways and getting input, motivation and direction from a coach. Can we as disciples do less? Is our Cause less important than theirs? Many of us act like it is, don't we? Without discipling or coaching, we will not end up with the crown of victory for ourselves and for others. Do you see the seriousness of being discipled and being a discipler?

In verse 6, we are to be hardworking farmers in the harvest field for Christ. Farmers do not sleep in, nor do they work short hours. I remember spending time at my uncle's when he was only a part-time farmer, and we daily arose at 4:00 A.M. to begin the day of hard work. Now that's serious! After I became a part of a discipling church, my nights became shorter and longer: The working time was much longer, and the sleeping time was definitely shorter. A preacher friend, watching me from afar, once asked in all seriousness what I thought of "exhaustion theology"! I simply told him that I didn't preach it (as theology), but I often seemed to practice it. Someone once made the observation that disciples will probably live shorter lives because of their work level and sleep loss. Maybe so, but what of it? I did not come into the world to set a record for longevity. I came into the world to burn my candle out for Christ, at both ends when necessary. Of course, I am not saying that we should not take care of our physical bodies. But I am going to say exactly what Paul did in 1 Timothy 4:8, namely that "physical training is of some value, but godliness has value for all things, holding promise for both the present life and the life to come."

The point of these illustrations in reference to discipling relationships is that biblical reliability goes against the grain of our sinful nature. It demands that we deny self, stay focused, work hard, train well and teach others to do the same. How many people would live such a life of self denial for God without help from other people? That's easy to answer—just look at churches who don't put discipling-partner relationships into practice. How many athletes have the discipline to achieve excellence as a one-man show? How many soldiers do? Maybe the farmers do better at self-motivation, but on the other hand, they starve if they don't work hard! Without question, the second law of thermodynamics affects our levels of spirituality and effectiveness unless we have people in our lives to encourage and spur us on. I desperately need to be discipled! And so do you! We need to commit ourselves to being discipled into reliability in all situations and to disciple others to be the same. The reliability of a disciplined character is an integral part of being a follower of Jesus.

In this chapter I have given you the keys to being successfully discipled. Focus on these. Go after your weaknesses. Bring your attitudes into line with the things I have described here, and you will be blessed. Do not look at the problems your discipler has. Do not blame him or her for your condition. Listen to what God is calling you to, and take hold of these keys with all your heart. You will be amazed at how God will work in your discipling relationship to transform your life.

8

BEING DISCIPLED THE PRACTICALS

✠

Being discipled is all about attitude. Those who have a great attitude are grateful for discipling; they grow from discipling; they see their lives and their relationships blessed. The five keys we just looked at in the last chapter could be called attitude keys. Wander from them, and it will not be long before you are spiritually weakened. Stay with them, and you will experience the power of God. But now that we have looked at the crucial attitudes, it is time to examine some practicals that will enable God to further bless your discipling relationships.

Appreciate Organization

Everyone's business ends up being no one's business. Occasionally some of us react negatively to the organizing and scheduling of spiritual activities, reasoning that relationships should just happen naturally. In our hectic society, nothing good seems to just "happen." For the most part, I find that times with my wife for dating or talking through issues must be planned. Oh sure, sometimes we have a good talk on the spur of the moment, but if we left it up to happenstance, it would not occur nearly often enough. My phone calls to our children and other close relatives don't seem to just "happen." Let's face it—we live in a world of overflowing schedules, and we are going to have to organize if we are to make the best use of our time.

In order to encourage discipleship, it is normal to organize so that everyone has a discipling partner. Those of us in churches where this is done need to be grateful that someone cares enough to make it happen. Several factors are considered by the leaders who are organizing discipling relationships: geography (allowing the discipleship partners to get time together more easily); ministry group; age and maturity (chronological and spiritual); marital status (marrieds need to be paired up with marrieds when possible); leadership roles and potential; special needs (transportation, physical challenges, family challenges, etc.); and perhaps others. Consideration is given in pairing people up who can really help one another grow. Of course, those inclined to be negative about such arrangements would say, "You can't legislate friendships!" True enough, but disciples can be organized in a way that affords powerful, spiritual friendships the opportunity to develop. A part of the problem reflected in the previous negative comment is worldly thinking: "Who am I naturally drawn to?" But in the kingdom, we are all brothers and sisters and need to learn to be a close family. The relationships which at first seem unnatural are likely the ones in which we grow most!

Biblically, the necessity for organization is quite clear. In Exodus 18, Moses' father-in-law, Jethro, pointed out the dire need to organize the Israelites. On his advice, Moses appointed leaders of thousands, hundreds, fifties and tens. Probably some in the nation were saying, "You can't legislate these relationships," but neither God nor Moses listened to them!

In Acts 6, the apostles appointed seven men to oversee the distribution of food to the Grecian widows. Note the *attitudes* present in that pristine early church:

> In those days when the number of disciples was increasing, the Grecian Jews among them complained against the Hebraic Jews because their widows were being overlooked in the daily distribution of food (Acts 6:1).

However, once the apostles organized, everyone was happy with the arrangement (Acts 6:5). Were we not informed of their satisfaction, we might assume that at least someone would have been saying, "We shouldn't have to organize to take care of our own widows—it should just happen naturally, out of the overflow of our hearts." Other passages could be included, but these are sufficient to demonstrate what logic already demands: Organization is always

needed to make any group function effectively. So appreciate organization in the church; God is behind it.

Think Friendship

Discipleship partners should be or should become great
friends. Some come into the kingdom with mistaken attitudes
about close relationships. They think that they can only have one
best friend at a time and that being close to one person rules out
other close relationships. Our model for loving is God, who loves
everyone incredibly more than they can imagine! Therefore, as
we imitate him, we will learn to love more and more people more
and more deeply. But we must begin with the few, and in this
case, the one.

Worldly friendships are formed almost solely on the basis of
sharing things in common. In other words, if you can really identify with a person, then (and only then) do you have a foundation
for developing a really close relationship. However, when we come
into the kingdom, we find ourselves in a "melting pot" of diverse
people and personality types. We then begin to learn how to relate to all different kinds, many of whom would never have been
our close friends outside of Christ—which is the beauty of being
in the kingdom! Our relational abilities will be nurtured and re-
fined in some amazing ways.

One of those ways will be by working through relationship
differences. The two types of people who offer us the most challenge are those most unlike us and those most like us. The latter
situation occurs when someone with our same weaknesses offers
a flesh-and-blood example of what we do not like about ourselves.
Can you recall certain people "getting under your skin" simply
because they reminded you of what you dislike in yourself? Sometimes we call that the "Laban principle," named after Jacob's father-in-law (Genesis 28-31). Jacob was a real schemer and trick-
ster, but he was a mere novice compared to Laban. His "school
of discipleship" was a hard one, but in the end Jacob developed
into a much more spiritual man!

When God puts us with discipleship partners who have our
same weaknesses, our patience gets sorely tested. But, we often come to some strong convictions about changing, plus we

are in a great position to understand and help the other person who shares our same problems. When we are teamed up with such a person, we had better develop a sense of humor quickly if we don't have one, and we had better recognize that God certainly has one!

Then sometimes God puts us with spiritual buddies who are very unlike us, which ushers in different, but no less severe, challenges. I have been told that the Boston church, of which I am a part, has represented in its membership at least eighty different nations, not to mention the myriad of other differences. Learning to relate to all of those variations is not easy, but it is character building and highly rewarding. If Paul was set on becoming all things to all men to save some, then we should be set on becoming all things to all disciples to help mature them in Christ.

How do we develop best-friend spiritual relationships? We start with the determination to do it, regardless of the challenges involved. Then, we begin developing the friendship by sharing our lives in at least these four ways: (1) opening up our hearts to one another, (2) serving together, (3) praying together and (4) playing together.

Direct, open communication, including confession of temptations and sins, is key. Openness makes it all come together—heart to heart and soul to soul. Working side by side in the kingdom in studying with non-Christians or counseling or serving others will draw you close. Praying together is a good beginning step in learning what is in each other's heart. We have a hard time faking where or who we are when we are talking to God. Playing together is an essential part of the bonding process. Loosen up and have fun doing something both of you enjoy. I love getting out on the golf course with a discipleship partner or playing Hearts (the card game) together. Being competitive, I often have to repent of something before the round or game is over, but that's a part of spiritual male bonding!

In general, forget the idea that friendship must come naturally or it is not real. Friendships that we work to build can become some of the most special ones in our lives. When for organizational and ministry reasons, you have to change discipling relationships, don't lose the friendship you have built. You will not get as much time with a person who moves on to become someone else's discipling partner, but keep them in your heart. Call them, write them and stay in touch.

Keep Expectations Reasonable

One of the most consistent challenges in relationships revolves around expectations. It doesn't matter whether we are talking about relationships between marriage partners or between parent and child or between any other two people, expectations are a *huge* issue. Often we don't even know what our expectations are until someone doesn't meet them. (If you are married, you need no further convincing of this!) In discipleship partners, certain unrealistic expectations can creep in and induce needless pain.

The first of those is the expectation that my discipling partner be a miracle worker in helping my character to change! Habits are not so difficult that they cannot be broken; avoiding something for about thirty days may loosen the grip of even a seriously bad habit. But character changes are on a different scale. Our characters have been formed over many years and resist being reformed. In an earlier chapter, we talked about how the discipling process is necessary to making these deep-rooted changes. But even with help, it takes firm convictions and decisions on our part to see our characters change permanently. Discipleship partners are indispensable to making these changes, but they are only tools and surely not the total cure.

The Hebrew writer gave us a most helpful insight as he described why some don't change.

> We have much to say about this, but it is hard to explain because you are slow to learn. In fact, though by this time you ought to be teachers, you need someone to teach you the elementary truths of God's word all over again. You need milk, not solid food! Anyone who lives on milk, being still an infant, is not acquainted with the teaching about righteousness. But solid food is for the mature, who by constant use have trained themselves to distinguish good from evil (Hebrews 5:11-14).

If we are slow in our character growth, it is our own fault. We can't blame our discipleship partners. Take charge of your life and constantly practice righteousness until you become mature. No person *can* do those things for you, and God *will* not. We want to be "zapped" into immediate easy change, but it does not work that way!

Once our son, Bryan, was assigned a project in school and procrastinated until the night before it was due. He then came asking for my help, basically hoping that I would mostly do it for him. I told him to stay up and work on it during the night (while I slept), and if he reached a certain stipulated point, then I would get up early the following morning and help him finish. No way was I going to do for him what he could do for himself! I was willing to help him with the part he could not do, but that was all I was willing to do. It clearly was an issue of character development.

God is the same kind of father. He absolutely will not do for us what we can do for ourselves. Thankfully, our extremity is his opportunity, and he will help in the situations that we cannot handle. But he expects us to take responsibility for who and where we are. Our victim mentalities are emotionally and spiritually debilitating. Our environments may have been poor as we grew up, and our gene pools limited, but we are who we are spiritually because of our own choices. The sooner we take responsibility for ourselves and start "training ourselves" to distinguish between the good and the bad, the sooner our characters will change. Expect more of yourself, and be realistic about what a discipling partner can contribute to the process of your maturation in Christ.

Other expectations can also damage our relationships. We can expect our discipler to be too much like us. I spoke earlier of how my own sinful expectations along these lines hurt my relationship with Al Baird. Instead of rejoicing over the differences in our emotional make-ups and learning from them, I jumped to some *convulsions* and limited what might otherwise have been learned! In a similar vein, we can expect our discipler to be perfect. Only one Discipler is perfect, and his name is Jesus. The human channels through which he disciples us are certainly imperfect and sinful creatures, although they are striving to be righteous. All humans have flaws. Even my angelic wife has some *minor* flaws—minor

compared to her husband's! What would happen if I always focused on those flaws? Soon I would see nothing else! The same
principle is true in all other relationships, including those with
discipling partners. Deal with your own flaws, and let your love for
your discipleship buddy cover over a multitude of sins (1 Peter 4:8).

Another unreasonable expectation can be looking for too much
time and attention from those who already have packed lives. In
the final section of this chapter we will examine scheduling and
make suggestions about maintaining the right balance and perspective, but suffice it to say here that we have to practice the
Golden Rule and not make demands of others that we would
have great difficulty meeting were we in their shoes. Be full of
grace and be appreciative, not demanding and disappointed.

There are other unrealistic expectations to deal with in
discipling relationships, but these should help us develop a feel
for what works and what doesn't. We cannot be spoiled spiritual
children who are never satisfied because our expectations are too
high. We need to concentrate on being givers who bring joy into
the lives of our disciplers.

Value Accountability

As mentioned in an earlier chapter, accountability is designed
only to help us follow through with what we are already committed to doing. It should never be viewed as added pressure to make
us do what we don't want to do. I want to have "quiet times" with
God daily, share my faith daily and do many spiritual activities
consistently. I appreciate my brothers and sisters in Christ asking
me how I am doing in these areas. Even at the age of fifty-four, as
a mature person who wears many "hats" of leadership, I need
accountability—and I always will.

Recently in a discipleship time with Randy McKean, the two
of us talked for a long while about personal discipline, specifically about the area of food intake. He has been dieting and has
lost significant weight. His example convicted and motivated me
to make a decision to imitate him. I committed to begin a new
approach the next day and shared with him my weak areas in
controlling my eating, requesting that he ask me about how I am
doing in those areas. He agreed, but had me agree to provide

him with a specific plan for losing the weight. When we met the next week I gave him a computerized chart showing my exact target weights for the next twelve weeks. Making myself accountable to Randy is no burden. Even if he had brought up the subject originally, I would still be appreciative. I need to lose the weight, and I need help in doing it.

Our view of accountability reflects our view of demands and commands generally. Think about the following carefully, and make the needed application to your heart. In essence, the laws of God are directives containing at least some built-in accountability. If we want to be our best for him, we appreciate those directives and warnings. If we do not have a heart to please him at all costs, we will find ourselves resenting his "intrusion" into our lives. One person looks at the sign which says "Keep Off the Grass," and he is grateful that someone is trying to preserve the beauty of that environment. Another person looks at the same sign and feels a strong urge to stomp on the grass. It is a question of heart and focus.

Our view of accountability, whether from God's expressed principles or those we formulate to carry them out, reveals our hearts and our true motivations. If you do not like accountability, you have a spiritual problem, period. Repent and learn to embrace every form of help available to promote your growth, especially accountability through those God has put in your life!

Schedule for Success

It takes time and scheduling to develop great discipling relationships. Jesus called his disciples to be with him (Mark 3:14). Daily contact is more than a good idea—it is in the Bible (Hebrews 3:13). We are out and about in the sinful world all day, which takes courage out of us. Thus we need a brother or sister to put courage back *in* (encourage) us daily! The length of our phone conversations or visits will vary depending on the needs we have and the time we have available, but the contact itself is a blessing from God. Besides the daily contact, a *weekly* discipleship time is a reasonable expectation for all of us. Just to maintain our spiritual equilibrium, these weekly and daily settings are vital; without them the opportunity for growth is severely limited. I talk with many disciples, especially those who are married and have families, who describe serious challenges in working out consistent time with their discipling partners. I know there are difficulties, but my conviction is that God will always help us find a way to work his plan. I suspect that in many of these situations two of the basics of discipleship are being neglected: namely, advice and accountability. If you are not dealing well with the challenge of scheduling, get advice; set up a plan, and then be accountable to someone for following through. If there is not love, you will find an excuse. If there is love, you will find a way.

Not only do we need to schedule a discipleship time together, we also need to have a format to gain the most from it. Such times should include at least several things from the following possibilities:

- Sharing victories, struggles, sins, dreams, plans and anything else on our hearts about our lives.

- Opening the Bible for insights and answers to the above needs. (My fear is that for some of us who have been in discipling relationships for a number of years, this has become something we do far too infrequently.)

- Sharing about exciting quiet times (another good reason to open the Word together).

- Praying together—a constant need (and once again, something I believe few of us do enough of). Discipleship partners should always be prayer partners.

- Asking advice in many areas. (We should be tired of making mistakes by now and want to get the best input possible on a consistent basis. Proverbs 12:15 states, "The way of a fool seems right to him, but a wise man listens to advice.")

- Obtaining input and direction for the upcoming week in our mission for Christ (and in related areas).

- Getting advice and direction regarding those you are discipling.

- Asking for loving accountability about the directions we received the past week (Luke 9:10).

- Going out to share our faith and serve others who need help.

Other good things could be added to the list, but the main emphasis is that the times should be scheduled, consistent, planned and spiritual. As I have already said, play and recreation should be a part of our friendships; however, if all we do is shoot hoops, watch sports or catch movies together, we will not help each other to grow continually stronger.

A special and very important word is in order regarding long-distance discipling relationships between ministry leaders. If you are discipled by a leader in another city or discipling someone in this situation, you must pay careful attention to ensure that the discipling times occur consistently. This means that you as a disciple must really go after being discipled, and as a discipler, you must schedule and keep a weekly time to talk. Since this limited contact will mainly provide ministry direction, a disciple *must* seek input for his or her personal life from mature disciples in the local ministry. Considering the number of leaders who are discipled in this long-distance fashion, we cannot overstate the importance of following these suggestions!

The practicals of discipleship will unquestionably work in your life if you appreciate the need for organization, think in terms of friendship, keep your expectations reasonable, value accountability and schedule for success. Be a disciple, be discipled and be happy!

Part 3

BEING A DISCIPLER FOR JESUS

Being a discipler for Jesus is a privilege and a significant challenge. It demands that we are be continually growing disciples ourselves, seeking to call others higher by our example as well as by our words. Nothing provides a greater sense of satisfaction than helping another person become more and more like Jesus. When we are being disciples, making disciples and maturing disciples, we are most like the One whose name we wear. Effectiveness in discipling others is well within our grasp if we simply follow his example of loving leadership. The principles in this section of the book will significantly improve all our interpersonal relationships, but especially those involving the discipling of others for Jesus.

9

BE A RELATIONSHIP BUILDER

⁜

To disciple another person for Jesus is a weighty responsibility and a precious opportunity. Fundamentally, this means being a spiritual friend, and in most cases, an older brother or sister spiritually. I once heard the chain of discipling relationships in the church described something like this: As we are trying to grow in Christ, we reach up to join hands with someone who is more mature spiritually than we are and who can pull us higher; as we are being helped to grow, we then reach down to someone somewhat less mature spiritually than we are and pull them higher; Jesus is at the top of this discipling chain reeling us all in! This little illustration helps us to see how all of us fit in to the process of discipling as we help each grow and mature. Of course, sometimes discipleship partners may be on the same plane of maturity and would relate more equally to one another. But, even then, you still have a spiritual buddy to help you grow.

If you are the discipler and the more mature person in the relationship, your leadership must be spiritual. The most important distinction between worldly leadership and spiritual leadership concerns the issue of relationship. Leaders in the kingdom are "servant leaders" (Matthew 20:25-28), not "bosses," at every level, and especially in the leadership exercised as a discipler. I cannot say this strongly enough. Jesus was emphatic on this point. All of our influence with a discipleship partner should be through the relationship (i.e. friendship) itself, not through a "positional authority" mind-set.

Generally, there are three kinds of authority found in relationships: *relational* authority exerted by a trusted friend; *knowledge* authority such as that of a doctor or other expert; *positional* authority such as the boss with an employee. More will be said in Chapter Thirteen to clarify the different types of authority in the kingdom, but suffice it to say, discipling is characterized by relational authority and knowledge authority almost entirely. Thus, the person being discipled should have a humble and submissive spirit, but so should the discipler.

The Apostle Paul was a master at leading others through relationships, and this truth is perhaps illustrated best in his interaction with the very young church at Thessalonica. Tremendous lessons may be gleaned from 1 Thessalonians in studying how he worked through relationships to keep those disciples strong and growing even though he had only been with them physically for about three weeks. If we put into practice the principles found in this short letter, our relational skills will soar and our discipling relationships will yield blessings beyond our imagination. Let's search for Paul's relationship building "gems" as we strive to imitate his heart and effectiveness. (The impact here will be much greater if you keep your Bible open to the passages and read them before reading the comments about them.)

Start a Smile and Compliment Club (1:2-9)

As you read this passage, you should be impressed with Paul's expressions of appreciation both for the relationship he enjoyed with the Thessalonian disciples and for their hard work. His gratitude for them was continual and his encouraging comments about them surely made them feel like they were very special to Paul and to God. Paul was a charter member of the "Smile and Compliment Club." Are you? He went on to challenge them in a number of ways, but the foundation he used for those challenges was positive reinforcement. It is often said that we need to hear ten positives about ourselves in order to handle one negative. I would think the number is even higher than that! The strongest of us has some fragile areas in our ego. We all need to be built up, and some of us need it much more than others. A good friend and discipler figures out what helps us to keep our emotional and spiritual equilibrium and tries to meet those needs.

Some of us, because of the poor parenting received when we

were children, seem always to have to follow up any positive comment we make with an offsetting negative. "Well, yes, what you did there was good, *but...*" (followed by comments about how to make it better). If you attach a "but" to all of the positive comments you make to others, you are setting up a situation in which the person you are trying to help feels like they never measure up. Do you feel like that about your own life? If your parents took that sort of approach, then your answer is likely "yes."

I remember a dear sister in the Lord recalling her days as a child bringing home report cards. One particularly painful memory was when she worked as hard as she could, and received all *A's* except for one *B*. Guess which part her dad focused on? You guessed it. In her little heart, she felt that perfection was all that would please her dad. And some of us feel that way about our spiritual Dad in heaven. If so, we pass that same spiritual insecurity on to those whom we disciple, and in spite of progress they make, it will feel to them like it is never enough.

Obviously, we need to call others continually higher, but the issue is how to do that while helping them to build a good self-image and security in the relationship. Paul made his brothers and sisters feel like they were awesome in his sight and in God's. Then when the challenges came, they were fired-up to meet them. They felt like they were already on top of the world and determined to soar to the heavens, rather than feeling like they were in the pits trying to climb up to the top of the hole. Don't miss this important difference as you seek to build godly relationships. It is fundamental to developing happy, productive disciples.

Explain Your Motives (2:1-6a)

Paul neither demanded trust nor assumed it—he *built* it! The principal way he built trust was by explaining his motives. Some people seem to have a knack of making others feel uncomfortable in conversations. They tend to ask questions and make comments in a way that puts others on the spot or leaves them feeling apprehensive, wondering where the conversation is leading. We often make people ill at ease by not adequately explaining what our goals are with them.

For purposes of illustration, think about the visitors who attend the services of a biblical church for the first time. They arrive with significant apprehension, just as we did the first time. The apprehension is heightened by observing the expressive fellowship and the animated atmosphere. Then they hear the most challenging sermon they have ever heard in their lives, at the conclusion of which the preacher may say something along these lines: "We want to study the Bible with you. Ask the person who invited you to set up a study time." Have you ever stopped to think how such an invitation might be perceived? Of course we know *exactly* what we mean by "studying the Bible" with someone, but they don't have a clue. Wouldn't it be much better to explain the details involved in such a study? Once they understand what you are asking, they will be much more at ease and much more likely to agree to a study.

The same principle is involved in relationships generally and certainly in close ones which have some built-in expectations as a part of them. I do not like having the feeling that another person in a conversation with me has a hidden agenda. I appreciate someone telling me up front what they have in mind, then working through the discussion and ending by evaluating how well they think we covered the intended agenda. This business of being up front and open in conversing is terribly important.

Even when the conversation has nothing to do with a concern for the other person, directness is appreciated. Think about phone calls you have received, informing you that the caller wants to get together for a talk. If they don't tell you why, what starts happening in your mind? You begin building imaginary scenarios, most of which have fearful components to them. Do you enjoy getting such calls, and then being filled with apprehension until the time of the appointment arrives? Certainly not. So don't treat other people that way! Obviously, there are legitimate situations when the nature of the discussion must wait until you are together. But unless the situation demands it, just practice the Golden Rule and treat others with respect and sensitivity.

Paul didn't have to contend with the blessings and curses of a telephone, but if he had, he would have been careful to explain motives and use direct conversation. It puts people at ease. Imitate him.

Love Like a Mother (2:6b-9)

Paul was a good imitator of Jesus, who possessed the positive qualities normally identified as masculine and as feminine. Jesus was the perfect human, and as such, he embodied every positive quality of humanity. Paul's love for people made him a good "mom" and a good "dad," as we will discover in chapter 2 of 1 Thessalonians. To begin with, notice how he described himself as showing a mother's love.

First, Paul was gentle. Picture a mother holding her newborn baby—talk about gentle and unintimidating! If you recall, gentleness is one of the Spirit's fruits (Galatians 5:23). I can remember a time when I was afraid others would think I was not "hard line" in my leadership. Thankfully, I figured out that being "hard line" has much more to do with directness in speech than with demeanor. Speaking the truth in love (Ephesians 4:15) is all about honesty, not about decibels or facial expressions. Some of the most heart-piercing challenges I have ever received have been delivered in the most gentle fashion. Occasionally, I have needed to receive a challenge with a stronger delivery style, but usually, the right content alone will open my heart to hearing and heeding needed changes. (I am talking here about more personal times with others. When preaching, there is certainly the time and place for speaking with "a loud voice." See Jesus' example in John 7:37.)

Second, Paul was "delighted" to share not only the message but his life. This is truly a mother's heart. This is real family. Just how well do the people you disciple know you? The answer: only as well as you help them to know you! The need for openness in relationships cannot be overstated. Close spiritual relationships cannot be built without it. When I begin discipling a person, I want to find out all about their lives, and I want them to know everything about mine. I love taking long walks with a new spiritual friend and sharing all about our early years, our dreams and fears, our successes and failures—everything that makes us who we are. Bonding with one another in such ways knits our hearts and prepares us to really help the other person.

I am viewed as a very helpful counselor. For those skills, I have many to thank, for many have had a part in training me. If I had to identify only one counseling skill that is most important in my helping others, the choice would be simple to make. Without question, it is my use of personal example. My adage is "Never waste an experience, even a sinful one." When helping others work through their problems, I can nearly always find something from my own life with which they can identify. If I succeeded in a situation, they are encouraged by my example of success. If I failed in a situation, they are encouraged by my perseverance and repentance. I can remember trying to build relationships with people, even reasonably spiritual ones, when their lack of openness left me feeling that I still did not know the real person. (Note that I said "reasonably" spiritual, because any person who does not share his life like Paul did is limited spiritually by either pride or fear or both.) Be like Paul, then those in your life will be drawn to your genuineness, and your subsequent relationship will build a security in them with both you and with God.

Third, he worked "night and day" in order to benefit them most. I remember many a night when Theresa willingly sacrificed sleep to care for our children when they were sick. I have discovered that losing sleep or otherwise being inconvenienced for someone has a profound effect on them. Are you willing to sacrifice in loving a spiritual brother or sister? Are you willing to really work hard to serve them?

Of course, working hard for others is one thing; working hard happily and gratefully is yet another thing! Some of us work hard, but then we play the martyr, or something akin to it! In Matthew 6:1-18, Jesus spoke of working hard by giving, praying and fasting, but he said to do it without informing others of what a spiritual person you are! His message was to do those things in secret and let God reward you. Of course, Paul did mention his hard work in our text, but you can be assured he did it only to make those in his reading audience feel loved, not to induce pity for himself. And you can further be assured that his manner of life when with them was not one of calling attention to himself. He always pointed people to Jesus, not to himself.

Yes, Paul was a loving "mom," pouring out his life for his children. Mothers are not driven by duty, but by desire; not by their personal need, but by their children's; not by a seeking of recognition and approval, but by a longing to bless and serve the objects of their love. Do you love your discipling partners with a mother's love?

Love Like a Father (2:10-12)

Paul described his leadership of the church in "fatherly" terms. He led as a father leads his family. His main focus was his personal example of righteousness. ("You are witnesses, and so is God, of how holy, righteous and blameless we were among you who believed.") He understood that first and foremost a father must be an example to those he leads. Unless we as spiritual leaders and disciplers are truly righteous, we have neither the right nor the power to lead. The importance of being stellar examples to those whom we lead cannot be overstated.

One of discipling's scariest principles is that those whom we lead tend to dilute our strengths and maximize our weaknesses. This means that often our disciples will not equal our strengths, but will surpass our weaknesses. In one way, the principle makes sense, because we are the leaders and should be setting the pace and the example for those who follow. In another way, it is a sobering thought and should motivate us to minimize our weaknesses and to further increase our strengths. None of us is perfect, nor will we be this side of eternity. But are we *trying* to be? Several concerns along these lines come to my mind, and I implore you veterans to pay close attention.

First, I do not see us continuing to change significantly after we have been disciples for a while. We expect and see amazing changes in people as they study the Bible and enter the kingdom. However, as time passes we seem to develop a different attitude toward change in ourselves. Why is that?

Some would argue that we change in the big areas in the early days and are thus more mature and in need of less change after a while. There is some truth to that argument, to be sure, but it contains one fatal flaw: We reach this conclusion because we are comparing ourselves to each other rather than to Jesus. Compared to others, I am mature and spiritual and have ceased to practice the bad habits which once plagued my life. Certainly I have grown and grown a lot—praise God! But when I quit comparing myself to what I used to be like or to what others are like, and start comparing myself to Jesus, my urgency to grow and change goes through the roof. Far too many of us "spiritually mature" types are being duped by Satan into being far too accepting of the status quo of our spirituality. This gives us one more reason to study the life of Jesus much more diligently than we normally do.

Second, I see us excusing ourselves for "just being this way." I know that many personality differences existed between Paul and Peter, and John and Andrew. But those were differences in personality, not in weak character maintained through complacency! Their greatest desire was to imitate their Master, and they did not excuse laziness and unrepentant hearts by saying, "That's just me!" I find myself getting a bit heated up as I write this because too many of us who have been in the kingdom rationalize our lack of continual growth much better than we continue to seek that growth. And we need to repent. I appreciate our willingness to confess our character sins when they arise, but I think God would appreciate our having enough conviction to deal with these sins and change them. Paul often spoke of having a clear conscience before God and men. A Bible study of these phrases would help you gain conviction. Paul could easily say "Imitate me," because of his conviction and the growth which it produced. Can you do the same?

Third, I do not see us calling each other higher in the same way we did when we were younger disciples. The main difference between the church I am in, and the one in which I once was in, is discipleship, plain and simple. But if we quit discipling one another (calling each other to become more and more like Jesus), we will cease to be the church of the Bible (and it could happen). I need people in my life to help me grow in every way a person can be helped to grow. I have not outgrown that need at age fifty-four, nor will I if I live to be ninety-four! We need to be disciples, which is tantamount to saying that we need to be discipled. Then, and only then, will we be the "fatherly" examples other disciples need.

Paul goes on to show what qualities we need to be fatherly. Note the words Paul uses: "...as a father deals with his own children, encouraging, comforting and urging you to live lives worthy of God..." Fathers are the bottom-line sort of people who do not let sentimentality overrule reality! Mothers often are too governed by their emotional attachments, which is why God planned for babies to have both fathers and mothers. Yet, Paul's example is that all of us, regardless of our gender, are to be completely loving.

Close emotional attachment and challenge must go together if we are to elicit the most profound growth in those whom we disciple or otherwise lead. If fathers are only known as disciplinarians to their children, the children's view of authority, including God's authority, will be warped. If disciplers are known only for their urging, and not their encouraging and comforting, those whom they disciple will definitely suffer ill effects. Be a good mother and be a good father. Paul was; imitate him as he imitated Jesus.

Feel What They Feel (2:14; 3:2-5)

It is true that a *sentimental* leader is not very helpful in the long run, but neither is an *unsympathetic* one. We must learn to feel with other people, especially the ones we are most responsible for helping to grow. Trying to motivate those who do not think you really understand their struggles is a difficult task indeed. Sometimes "hard liners" think that recognizing the pain of others encourages them to wallow in their misery. Undoubtedly, this can be true with some people, and those kinds need to be discipled about that tendency. But just because someone might abuse the situation does not change what humans need from one another, and it certainly doesn't change what the Bible teaches.

There are several words in the Greek New Testament that can be translated "compassion." One is a long word *(splagchnizesthai)* that is used only of God and Jesus. The literal meaning conveys the idea of being so carried away with another's pain that your heart feels like it is being drawn out of your body toward him. Read the following passages with that definition in mind: Matthew 9:36; 14:14; 15:32; 18:27; 20:34. If you are one of those afraid of being too sympathetic or too feeling-oriented, you need a dose of Jesus! Surely you don't think that he felt his whole body drawn into feeling the pain of others without ever expressing it to them.

When someone is hurting, they need to talk it out. Once they are able to let the pain out, then they will be in a position to hear and accept the needed direction to deal with what is causing the pain. Failing to listen sympathetically is failing to love. But after we do listen, we must be sensitive in giving direction. Telling someone "You shouldn't feel that way" is insensitive at best and devastating at worst! As disciplers, we need to learn to view their situation from God's perspective, combined with the love we offer them by feeling their pain. Don't be afraid to love, to listen and to direct your friend back to biblical thinking. Just keep it all in the proper order as you do it.

Insist on Righteousness (4:1-8)

Paul demanded righteous living. As is often the case today, he dealt with the area of sexuality and sexual temptations. We live in a wicked, immoral world, and none of us is immune to its influence on our thinking. Pornography has long been a temptation, but it has never been more available and accessible than today. Cable television delivers it right to your home with the press of a button. Video stores are located on every corner, filled with R-rated and X-rated flicks to stir our lustful imaginations. Nearly every time I go on-line via my computer, I am besieged with advertisements for pornographic yet "safe" (as far as privacy goes) viewing of just about every sexual act imaginable. The web sites for these sensuous adventures are spelled out quite clearly. Many, including spiritual leaders, have succumbed to such offers.

I ask those whom I disciple the hard questions about their personal righteousness, including (and perhaps *especially*) their sexuality. Lust and masturbation are often some of the greatest temptations men face, and many women struggle with them as well. If we are going to deal with Satan effectively, no subject should be off-limits between discipleship partners. This kind of openness necessitates that discipling relationships be of the same gender. Paul did not think any subject taboo or otherwise off-limits. Of course, dozens of other temptations and sins beside sexual ones need to be dealt with openly and frankly as well. If we value relationships as much as he did, we must also address issues frankly. Demand personal righteousness of those whom you love God does.

Teach Them to Love Each Other (4:9-10)

Since Jesus taught that love between disciples is the primary badge demonstrating to the world that we are his, we must all constantly teach others how to love more and more. Paul did precisely that in this passage. He commended them for loving, but urged them to practice it in increasing measure. The world understands the concept of the friendship *(phileo)* type of love, but knows little of God's kind *(agape)*. The first is often based on common interests, the latter is an unconditional commitment. Although the Bible is full of teachings about how to love, certain texts stand out (for example, 1 Corinthians 13:4-8) and should be studied deeply and applied often in our discipling relationships. We have to learn to love our families with this kind of love also. In Titus 2:3-5, Paul taught that the older women should teach the younger women to love their husbands and children. We think that family love is a type of automatic, natural thing, but it isn't.

Years ago, I was trying to help a new member of the church to be a better parent. His young son, about five years old at the time, was clearly in need of some discipline. I asked him about how he disciplined his son, and quickly found out that he was like most parents in our society these days—he practiced little or no discipline. I shared a few passages about the biblical admonition to use applied psychology on the lower half of the anatomy (a spanking, in other words). His eyes opened wide in horror as he exclaimed, "I love my son too much to do that!" I had to teach him how to love his son, for he had not a clue about how to do it. I simply turned to Proverbs 13:24 and had him read it: "He who spares the rod hates his son, but he who loves him is careful to discipline him." Then we talked specifically about how to apply this type of disciplinary action and other types as well. The point is that if people don't know how to love even their families, then they certainly are going to need a lot of help in learning to love one another in the kingdom of God. Let's teach our discipling buddies to imitate God by learning how to love more and more people, more and more deeply.

Don't Forget Eternity (4:13-5:11)

I am very thankful to be part of a fellowship in which the everyday life of a disciple is dealt with consistently. It has been said that some religious people are so heavenly minded that they are no earthly good! That is certainly an extreme, to be sure. But I think we often go to the other extreme. We do not think enough about the next life to keep our perspective about this one. I love being a disciple. Every day can be an adventure when we spend it hand in hand with God, doing his bidding. But some days are not like that for me, and assuming you are human, not for you either. A popular bumper sticker says, "Life is tough and then you die." Even in that cynical comment there's truth to be found. The popular idea spread by certain "televangelists" that life will always be a bowl of cherries is false doctrine.

Paul, in his vulnerable way, said that he, at points, despaired even of life (2 Corinthians 1:8). In Romans 8:22-25, he wrote that disciples "groan inwardly" in this life. Life on earth, at its best, is still not heaven. And God never intended that all of our deepest longings be met here, even in the church! Heaven beckons, and we will never find our ultimate fulfillment until we enter its gates. When I read passages outlining Paul's suffering and mistreatment, such as 2 Corinthians 11:23-29, I find myself wondering how he stayed faithful in the battle. Not to wonder—he told us earlier in the same book:

> Therefore we do not lose heart. Though outwardly we are wasting away, yet inwardly we are being renewed day by day. For our light and momentary troubles are achieving for us an eternal glory that far outweighs them all. So we fix our eyes not on what is seen, but on what is unseen. For what is seen is temporary, but what is unseen is eternal (2 Corinthians 4:16-18).

Paul was enabled to endure all that he suffered by keeping his focus on the next life. The issues of this life are sometimes extremely burdensome, and the only way to deal with those issues and those difficult times is to keep an eternal perspective.

My concern really should be how I am going to feel about my difficulties a hundred years from now (as men count time), or a thousand years from now or five trillion! In our Thessalonians text, Paul strove to keep his readers focused on heaven (4:13-18), and he also warned them of Judgment (5:1-11). Yes, most of our emphasis in discipling must be on the needs of the day, for even Jesus warned about living in tomorrow before it becomes today (Matthew 6:34); but if you teach your disciples to keep an eternal perspective of both heaven and hell, they will rise up and call you blessed!

Deal Constantly with the Heart (5:12-28)

My biggest mistake as a young parent was in dealing much more with behavior than attitudes. It is easier and quicker to follow that approach, and it seems to work in the early years of children's lives. However, it is not really working, for all behavior must spring from the heart, and thus all work to effect behavioral change must be an "inside-out" job. The Jews whom Jesus confronted in the first century looked religiously great on the outside, but inwardly were full of "dead men's bones and everything unclean" (Matthew 23:27). Discipling of behavior must be done by first discipling the heart, which then will change the behavior. This is a time-consuming and energy-draining process, but all short-cuts will lead to horrible spiritual maladies.

You must learn to find out what is in the heart and then deal with it appropriately. Ask how the other person is feeling about what they did. Ask the kinds of questions that force them to look inside and to face up to what is really there. We are sometimes such Pharisees that we have a hard time admitting even to ourselves that we feel hate toward someone, or envy or jealousy or lust or any one of a long list of "religiously unacceptable" sins. Discipler, the only way to help your disciple open up is to be the model of how to do it. Be open in a graphic and pointed way. Be painfully open. Then the one whom you are helping can get his heart out on the table and you can help him identify the specific sins, repent and change. Deal with the heart—beginning with your own.

In verse 14 Paul helps us see that not everyone we disciple needs the same things. "Different strokes for different folks" is a wise saying. As Paul puts it, "warn those who are idle, encourage the timid, help the weak, be patient with everyone." What is good for the idle, may crush the timid. While the timid may need support, the weak may need direction.[1]

One attitude Paul dealt with in this passage concerned their need to appreciate their leaders. It is misplaced humility for a leader to shy away from teaching on this subject. The very nature of leadership means that we are the very ones who must teach such appreciation. If we are teaching it in order to direct appreciation toward ourselves, we have a problem. But if we stress the honor of being servant leaders in God's kingdom, everyone will end up blessed (including us). Since Satan is always seeking to erode trust in leaders, we would do well indeed to fill our conversations with the names of leaders and the respect and appreciation we have for them. People come into the kingdom trained by the world in quite the opposite way, and they need much help in learning to honor leaders in the proper way.

The concluding part of 1 Thessalonians contains three of my favorite verses about attitudes. These three succinct commands in 5:16-18, if followed seriously, would change any person's life overnight! He simply writes:

> Be joyful always; pray continually; give thanks in all circumstances, for this is God's will for you in Christ Jesus.

Isn't that what discipleship is all about—helping your friend to be happy, prayerful and thankful in any and every situation? When we change hearts, we change lives. No blessing, other than salvation, could be greater than learning to think and feel like Jesus.

Discipling another person is not about shaping up someone else. It is about building a relationship that will inspire, motivate and guide. The practical relationship "gems" in this brief letter will change your life and that of your discipleship partner, as you learn from Paul, the "unlikely" relationship expert whose view of relationships was dramatically changed by Jesus.

10

BE A PATIENT TRAINER

✠

The time and effort required to build something varies according to its value. If it can be done easily and quickly, it likely will not be worth much to us or anyone else. Certainly this principle holds true when we are talking about building character. People who are past their childhood years have characters that are well established, for good or bad. Changing them into the image of Christ will take time and energy, and will require the help of others. The effective discipler needs a number of qualities and attitudes, none more important than patience. The training process is neither quick nor easy, but the rewards of helping someone become spiritually mature are eternally satisfying.

Train Disciples to Think

We have much the same goal with our disciples that parents have with their children—teaching them to think correctly. In the case of discipling, we need to teach others to think spiritually. Occasionally I hear concerns expressed about the possibility of someone's mind being controlled by a discipler. If it weren't such a serious charge, it would be absolutely laughable. I discovered rather quickly when my children were small that the little critters were not going to be controlled by me or their mom without some serious effort. Controlling another person's mind seems to me impossible, but I would not want to do that even if I thought I could. The goal of discipling is to teach another person to think for himself, and yet to think like Jesus. *He* does want to control our minds.

From God's perspective, our minds are going to be controlled either by him or by Satan. Those who think they are in control of their own minds are thoroughly deceived by the devil.

> The god of this age has blinded the minds of unbelievers, so that they cannot see the light of the gospel of the glory of Christ, who is the image of God (2 Corinthians 4:4).

Paul spoke of the right kind of biblical "mind-control" in a number of passages. In 2 Corinthians 10:5, he wrote: "We take captive every thought to make it obedient to Christ." In Romans 8:5-6, we read

> Those who live according to the sinful nature have their minds set on what that nature desires; but those who live in accordance with the Spirit have their minds set on what the Spirit desires. The mind of sinful man is death, but the mind controlled by the spirit is life and peace.

A few chapters later, he added,

> Do not conform any longer to the pattern of this world, but be transformed by the renewing of your mind. Then you will be able to test and approve what God's will is—his good, pleasing and perfect will (Romans 12:2).

Other applicable passages could be included, but the point is that we either learn to think spiritually and be controlled by God, or we continue with worldly thinking and are controlled by Satan. A good discipler helps us do the former.

However, learning how to think spiritually after we have been so thoroughly trained to think unspiritually is a challenge. It takes much time and much help to rewrite bad programming. As disciplers of those trying to learn the new way of Christ, we are going to have to exercise much patience. But if we are excited about Jesus and the spiritual realm, we will be excited to train others. Now that I have become computer literate, I love teaching my friends what I have learned. When they learn a new and helpful hardware or software solution, their faces light up. Their appreciative response lights up my heart. That is the mind-set to keep when discipling about weightier matters. We are sharing with friends the most exciting things in our lives. It is not coincidental that Jesus spoke of sharing his joy with his disciples in the same context in which he spoke of them being his friends because he had shared the Father's business with them (John 15:10-15). It all ties in together. Sharing the most important things in life yields close friendship and great joy!

Keep these principles in mind when those whom you disciple are struggling with learning to think spiritually. They will slip and fall and get back up over and over again. You have one of several choices when they are struggling. One, you can be impatient with them, which will result in shutting down their openness. Then they will not share the troubles plaguing their hearts and will likely go downhill from that point. Impatience does more damage than most of us realize. Two, you can get overly concerned and "heavy" in spirit, which also shuts them down. At an earlier time in my life, I allowed struggles in the life of someone I was trying to convert or disciple to put me in a somber mood. Being sober is good, because sin is real, but being somber helps no one. Three, obviously the best choice is to stay full of faith, which helps you to keep upbeat and lighthearted. Just think: God has chosen you to help change someone's destiny in both time and eternity. Keep perspective and stay joyful.

While writing this chapter I had a phone conversation with my first cousin and his wife who became disciples a couple of months ago. When we started talking, they shared that the week had been a struggle for them. I shared spiritual principles and stories from my own life which helped them immensely. I was neither impatient nor heavy-spirited. I was full of faith about them and fired-up about God and the Bible, which I shared with them, and when they hung up, they were fired-up too! Amen! They will struggle while they are growing as disciples. Surprise, surprise! Don't you? We all do. But I have many solutions to what they are facing, and I believe with all my heart that they are going to let their hearts and lives continue to be molded by God's answers. And they are going to sense my spirit in the matter and will be influenced by it. Negativity is contagious, but so is enthusiasm. Stay excited and faithful.

From one perspective, the fact that newer Christians are struggling is a very good sign. At least they are now fighting back! Before they were Christians they just went the way of the flesh, but now they are facing off with the forces of evil and fighting back. Helping them to understand that principle will encourage them. It takes time to build spiritual understanding in people, so be patient. Just continue to share the Bible and how God has helped you to deal with challenges, while keeping an upbeat, faithful spirit. Your patient training of others will not only help them; they will be repeating your solutions to others as time goes by, and those others will eventually be doing the same with yet others. Discipling works. Persevere and you will be amazed at how people will change. Hang in there, and enjoy the ride as you do.

Train Righteously

Leading others in any capacity, including discipling, must be governed by righteousness. The Golden Rule is golden, and it must rule relationships in the kingdom. One of the most damaging aspects of poor leadership is harshness. I came to the conclusion long ago that God will not ultimately tolerate harshness at any level of leadership. I have seen leaders with the tendency to be harsh who repented and changed, and I have seen God deal very strongly with those who did not repent. But a word of caution is in order here. I have also heard the charge of harshness used by those trying to avoid the challenges to change given by a discipleship partner or other leader.

In our society, most churches and church leaders have been anything but directive in the lives of their members. Most preachers and other leaders have mastered the fine art of almost saying something! To state that they are not much like Jesus and the leaders in the early church is to be guilty of understatement to the nth degree. But this kind of wishy-washy, wimpy leadership is the stuff of which modern religion is made. Therefore, when people start attending services or become members of a true biblical church, they are going to feel some pressure when being taught to "obey everything" Jesus commanded (Matthew 28:20). If their hearts are set on becoming like Jesus, the pressure will be welcomed and very helpful. If their hearts are beginning to harden, they are going to react with resistance and will often cry, "Harshness!" Between the extremes of no direction and harsh direction lies the truth of how leaders are to lead. One extreme is no less sinful than the other, although we are inclined to think that harshness is worse. Lack of leadership is just as bad, especially when we see its ultimate consequences. Yet, harshness can never be excused. It is unloving and ungodly.

When I first became a part of a discipling church, I had already heard quite a few stories about alleged harshness. Within weeks of joining the church, our son (a teen at the time) began claiming that the teen leaders were being heavy-handed with him. His story sounded very plausible, and parents have a way of being sentimental with their own children. I was tempted to be that way in this case, but I remembered Proverbs 18:17, which states: "The first to present his case seems right, till another comes forward and questions him." I talked to the youth leaders, who very candidly suggested that our son was trying to avoid dealing with sin in his life. We went back to our son and told him what the teen leaders had said, and further, that we believed their side of the story was much more probable than his. The result was that within a couple of weeks he came to us, confessing some hidden sin and repenting. He went on to become a disciple and now as an adult is doing great. Praise God for the discipling he received, which was direct but certainly not harsh.

During those early days in that congregation, other disciples came to me complaining of harshness from disciplers or other leaders. Without exception, I practiced Proverbs 18:17 and got both parties together. I was actually quite surprised at how little true harshness I discovered. Nearly always, it was a case of someone not being willing to deal with the unrighteousness in his or her life. And in those situations, we nearly always resolved it with repentance and a renewal of the discipling relationship. The point I want to make is that the directness of speaking the truth in love (Ephesians 4:15) is so out of the ordinary in the typical church that some are going to have to develop an understanding of, and an appreciation for, discipling. Therefore don't be harsh, but don't avoid dealing with the life of the one whom you disciple. It is a wonderful aid in producing holy living.

Another area in which leaders must remain righteous is in keeping confidences. Disciplers are going to know much about the ones they disciple, which is only right, but discretion in handling that knowledge is of paramount importance. For designated church leaders, confidentiality has potential legal implications. Laws are not only quite specific in this area; they are also quite varied from state to state. Such laws do apply to leaders within all types of organizations, whether religious or business. Therefore, the scope and purpose of our study is not such that we should or could deal with this topic from the standpoint of leadership and legalities.

However, considering our biblical responsibilities as individual disciples, some basic observations are certainly in order. Sharing something about one person with another person, whether the information falls into the area of confidentiality or not, should be done with care. A good place to begin is with a consideration of the Golden Rule—if the situation were reversed, would you want the same things said about you?

The biblical admonitions which forbid gossip and slander clearly apply. In Proverbs 11:13 a "gossip" is defined as one who betrays a confidence. The *intent* of the one talking is not at issue in the passage—only the *result* is! In Ephesians 4:29, all unwholesome talk is forbidden and is then contrasted with talk which is helpful for building others up and for benefiting those who listen. In 1 Peter 2:1, every kind of slander is forbidden. If you are not sure if something is slander or not, assume that it has that potential and take the cautious route. Apply the Golden Rule and the principles of these two passages to help you decide.

If you are thinking about sharing details about another person's life in a potentially sensitive area without their knowledge, ask yourself the following questions:

1. *Why* am I thinking about sharing these things?
2. Will my sharing benefit the one about whom I am sharing?

3. Will my sharing benefit the one with whom I am sharing?
4. In the reverse situation, would I want the same things shared about me?

As we grow as Christians, we understand more about the grace and forgiveness of God, and are much less self-conscious about our weaknesses. I have often said that it is a great comfort to know that I could not be blackmailed in any way regarding my past, because I have been very open publicly about it. (This book is good evidence of that point.) Since Satan works best in the dark (John 3:19-21), being open with our sins is a major way to keep him from controlling us. This is why James 5:16 ("confess your sins to one another") is in the Bible. Therefore, all of us as disciples need to cultivate openness about our own lives, and to eliminate the pride which produces self-consciousness. However, our openness about another person's life is a different issue and needs to be handled with the care discussed in the above section. When you do feel that a third party is needed to assist with a discipling situation of a more sensitive nature or when confidentiality has been specifically requested, you should get the permission of the person you are discipling before talking with another person. Even then it is sometimes best to describe the situation in generic terms without giving the person's name. Overall, most of us need to deepen our convictions and heighten our sensitivity in this area.

One final observation is needed on the subject. When sin in a disciple's life has become such that church discipline has to be exercised (see Matthew 18:15-17), the person and at least the general nature of his or her sin will be made public within the group with whom they are most closely associated. In the event that someone has become a public enemy of the church, the church must be publicly warned for their own spiritual protection. Along these lines, consider the mention of a number of such enemies by name in the New Testament (1 Timothy 1:20; 2 Timothy 1:15; 2:17; 4:10,14; 3 John 9-10).

Once again, as in all other areas of life, one of the greatest guides for relationships is the one Jesus gave in Luke 6:31: "Do to others as you would have them do to you." As a discipler, train *in* righteousness by treating your discipling partner *with* righteousness.

Leave Room for God

When we do all that we can as a discipler to train patiently with a righteous approach, one need remains: Leave room for God, for this is the finest demonstration of godly patience. One of my favorite passages regarding the dynamics of relationships is found in 2 Timothy 2:23-26. Because of its importance to the subject of being a patient trainer, I will quote it and explain its principles carefully.

> Don't have anything to do with foolish and stupid arguments, because you know they produce quarrels. And the Lord's servant must not quarrel; instead, he must be kind to everyone, able to teach, not resentful. Those who oppose him he must gently instruct, in the hope that God will grant them repentance leading them to a knowledge of the truth, and that they will come to their senses and escape from the trap of the devil, who has taken them captive to do his will.

Arguments are nearly always foolish and stupid, and they lead to quarrels and wars. A patient trainer of others is the Lord's servant, and the Lord's servant must not quarrel. He must figure out how to disciple others without having an argumentative nature himself or being pulled in by someone who does. Arguments always shed much more heat than light. What is the antidote for these kinds of impatient interactions with our fellow disciples? A number of components must be included in the cure.

One, refuse to quarrel. It is forbidden, and therefore to do it is sin. Self control is available to us as a part of the fruit of the Holy Spirit (Galatians 5:23). We have the choice of quarreling or not. Don't do it. Avoid this relationship-damaging sin.

Two, be kind, for kindness is also a part of the Spirit's fruit (Galatians 5:22). Kindness introduced into a potentially explosive situation does wonders. Note the words of Proverbs 25:21-22:

If your enemy is hungry, give him food to eat;
    if he is thirsty, give him water to drink.
In doing this, you will heap burning coals on his head,
    and the LORD will reward you.

If kind actions will melt an enemy in due time, we can expect kindness to melt an emotionally aroused disciple much quicker. Stay calm and be kind—to *everyone*. The "everyone" includes your mate, your relatives, your children and your disciples. Sometimes we are most impatient with those whom we love most. It is an issue of pride. We might be willing to take much time carefully reasoning with someone else, but with those who are closer emotionally, we can take it personally if they do not capitulate to our ideas immediately. In this case, we are being prideful, insensitive and unreasonable. Be gentle, and be gentle to everyone.

Three, keep teaching biblical principles in a calm spirit. I can remember many occasions when I dismantled bombs by patiently pointing people to the words of Scripture and having them read it for themselves. If we simply refer to it or state the principle in it or even quote it, they may still remain irate. However, when they read it aloud themselves, something happens. We leave room for God, and he works. Keep the Bible open and keep teaching.

Four, we must not become resentful. What does that mean in this context? It means that we avoid taking the words of the one opposing us in too personal a way. If they are saying untrue things about us or saying it in a bad manner, they are out of control, not us. Don't take it personally; it's really their problem unless you make it yours. Admittedly, great self-control is needed when being verbally attacked by another, especially someone emotionally close to you. But by God's Spirit, self-control is available for the asking.

An understanding of the spiritual dynamics at work will help you to stay in control without being deeply hurt. As you read 2 Timothy 2:26, you find that a person who has lost his temper is actually out of his senses and at that point, taken captive by Satan. How do you relate to a person who is out of his senses on drugs or alcohol? You take what they say with a "grain of salt" and are not hurt by them as you calmly try to reason with them in hopes of helping them sober up. You must learn to do the same with someone who is out of control of their temper. In either case, Satan has captured them, and it is your job to carefully and lovingly try to get them back. You are God's gentle tool to accomplish this important task. You cannot *make* them do anything. Even God is not going to force them, so why should you try? Calmly and gently instruct with biblical principles, leaving room for God.

Communication in discipling is highly important, and we must learn to follow the above principles if we are to communicate effectively. In a practical sense, I often describe the communication process as having three "gears." Gear one is the nice conversational tone in which we talk much of the time, which is neither very direct nor confrontational. Gear three is very confrontational, but is mostly misused. We stay in gear one as conflict avoiders until we cannot hold it in any longer, and then we shift to gear three and blow up and blow people away! In the kingdom, we need to function most of the time in gear two—that mode of directness and honesty which addresses the issues straight on in a calm, reasonable manner.

In any kind of corrective mode, we have to choose how much of the correction comes in manner of presentation and how much in the content presented. Almost always in any kind of one-on-one relationship, the emphasis should come from the content itself and not from its presentation. In other words, loud volume and animated body demeanor are not appropriate! Although there may be occasions when extra firmness is in order, this approach will be not be the norm. If a person in a higher level of leadership deems that a strong manner is necessary, it should be controlled and purposely used to help people come to convictions and repentance when no other approach has worked. Of course, disciplers who lose control, become harsh, sarcastic or the like must do the same thing parents often have to do: confess their sin and ask for forgiveness. Rare will be the discipler who does not need to do this at some point in a relationship.

I have met a few people who seem to think that when teaching Bible studies for those coming to Christ initially or discipling those in Christ, they need to "push" the emotional "buttons" of the one being addressed. I think more insult than instruction occurs when we are trying to force the issues and the heart. If something needs to be pushed to the surface, let God and the Bible do it. Leave room for God. Teach and apply biblical principles, but do it with a calm, reasoned approach. Discipling will at times have its moments when the sparks do fly, as iron sharpens iron (Proverbs 27:17). But let the sparks come from a heart being confronted lovingly with the Bible in hand. When the emotions do calm down, the heart will be ready to receive direction and correction in a unique way. Satan will have been resisted and repelled, leaving a pliable and appreciative heart in the person being discipled. Follow the above principles and make the most of every opportunity.

Patience is a virtue whose value is at its height when exercised to help another person become more like Jesus. Train patiently, train righteously and train without any hint of an argumentative spirit. In essence, just think of how physical children best respond to training and use a very similar approach in training spiritual children. Do your best, pray about the rest and above all, leave room for God to mold the heart by using you as a tool.

11

BE A HUMBLE ADVISOR

✠

One of the greatest blessings in the kingdom is being able to obtain good biblical counsel, and as a discipler, to provide it for others. The Scriptures contain an abundance of wisdom to guide us in this vital area. However, because we are dealing with the crucial issues in people's lives and not all matters are clear cut, giving biblical advice requires great care.

The Nature of Biblical Advice

Just how do we determine what advice should be given in areas involving application of biblical principles? The Bible gives us the principles we need to live a life pleasing to God (2 Timothy 3:16-17; 2 Peter 1:3-4). However, it doesn't give us all details we might wish to know. In many cases, God states some things in very direct terms, which we call *explicit* teaching. In some cases, a biblical teaching is *implicit*, in that a certain truth is implied but not expressly stated. The degree of certainty we can have about implicit teachings can vary. Some things are very clearly implied. Others may tend toward the "opinion" area we will look at more closely at the end of this chapter. Establishing guidelines for Christian conduct often is rightly done by using biblical implications, but we need to be sure these are the ones about which we can have great certainty.

For example, what do you think the Bible has to say about a Christian marrying a non-Christian? It does not explicitly address the issue, but the implications are quite compelling. In 2 Corinthians 6:14-16, we find that we should not be "unequally yoked together" with unbelievers. The yoke here is not specifically applied to marriage, but no yoke in life has more far-reaching consequences than marriage. In 1 Corinthians 9:5, Paul argued that he had the right to take a "believing wife" along with him, just as did Peter, the Lord's brothers and the rest of the apostles. Then, 1 Corinthians 7:39 says that a widow is free to remarry "anyone she wishes, but he must belong to the Lord." If a widow who had already perhaps lived most of her life was bound to marry only a Christian, then how much more important would it be for someone with most of his or her life yet in front of them to do the same? When you deal with a number of verses that relate to a given subject, the evidence can become very compelling in a certain direction. I have no question that the issue of Christians marrying only Christians falls into this category.

Out of such implied, but definite, teaching comes further applications to dating practices of single disciples. These guidelines would include Christians dating only Christians, since in Western culture, we marry someone we date. Other strongly suggested practices in dating would be the wisdom of double dating or group dating. The Bible insists on purity of both life and example. Paul gave the following warning:

> But among you there must not be even a hint of sexual immorality, or of any kind of impurity, or of greed, because these are improper for God's holy people (Ephesians 5:3).

In our society, impurity and immorality are often assumed to be a part of any dating relationship. Therefore, to protect our purity and example, dating practices need to be very different from those in the world.

When I was a dating single, I would have been far better off following these types of guidelines. As it was, I was guilty of the sexual sins more openly accepted now but still commonly practiced decades ago. Frankly, one of the things most appealing to me as a father about the discipling churches was the dating guidelines. My children knew better than to complain about the guidelines, because their parents praised God for them! At their recent weddings, as they stood before me with their chosen partners for life, having been pure in their dating relationships, we all praised Jesus together! And now they are enjoying their sexual relationship without the guilt of sinful memories. Thank the Lord for righteous guidelines.

I have noticed that specific advice on such things as dating sometimes differs slightly from church to church, even when all involved are radical disciples. That is not surprising. When we are working with implicit teaching, the further an issue takes us away from a clear biblical principle the more room for differences there will be. However, the important thing may not be so much the actual decision made or the actual advice given, but the attitude that we have through the whole process. Once again our point is: God blesses humility.

Our giving of biblical advice often is no more than simply sharing a passage that directly addresses the issue under consideration. At other times, we are dealing with implications which are derived by looking at a number of passages which relate directly or by principle to the topic of concern. Sometimes we may be looking at areas involving only judgment, which is based solely on experiences of disciples and what seems to have worked best. Regardless of which route we are following to determine the advice, we are seeking only what is going to bless the one whom we are advising. It may involve a choice of right or wrong, or it may involve choices of good, better and best. In all cases, we need to remain biblically grounded, practical and humble in advice giving. It will be well worth the time and effort required in teaching the other person to think and act biblically.

Sometimes people get the idea that seeking advice means asking for permission. If that is the way those you disciple think, you should help them correct their view. A discipler is not someone who gives another permission to do anything. A discipler is one who offers counsel based on his or her knowledge of the Scriptures, the people involved and the circumstances. It is up to the disciple to consider that input, be prayerful and make a decision out of his or her own convictions. Those who think in terms of getting permission not only view the situation wrongly, but they may tend to blame the advisor if things do not go well.

Faith or Opinion?

In giving advice, we must be able to distinguish whether we are dealing with an area of biblical faith or an area of opinion. Unless the Scriptures clearly settle an issue, we must realize that advice is only advice, even though we are trying to base it on biblical principles. The less specifically a topic is covered in the Bible, the more room for variations in its interpretation. Most of us would probably be more comfortable with all of the "gray" areas eliminated, leaving everyone in perfect agreement on every possible topic. However, God did not think that best—probably to make us less dogmatic and keep us humble.

Thankfully, we do have many areas of "black and white" in the Bible. Sin lists, like those in 1 Corinthians 6:9-10, Galatians 5:19-21 and 2 Timothy 3:1-5 do not leave much room for variations in interpretation. Certain things are always right, and certain things are always wrong. None of us has to seek advice about whether to lie or steal, for these practices are categorically wrong. But many other avenues open to us are not directly addressed in the Bible, and decisions about them fall more into the realm of judgment or opinion. As those who advise others, we will quite often share our opinions and the spiritual reasoning behind them, but be compelled to leave room for alternate opinions. Raising doubts about the right or wrong of biblically clear teaching is bad, but so is binding others by your opinions in areas where the Bible has not clearly taught the point in question.

Romans 14 is a key passage about the reality of gray areas, where the issues are truly matters of opinion and therefore viewed differently by different brothers. In Romans 14:1-8, Paul's point is that we have room in the kingdom for these kinds of differences. In such areas, we need to live by our own consciences and avoid dogmatism. Specifically, he addresses the eating of certain foods and the observance of certain days. Jews and Gentiles had very different backgrounds and were comfortable with different practices in these areas. Without dealing with the specifics involved, since that is not our purpose, we can say that all of us are not going to have the same consciences in these opinion areas. Therefore, we had better be careful about binding our opinions as law. What seems perfectly clear to us may still be only an opinion.

One thing that helps me identify whether or not we are dealing with matters of opinion is knowing that strong brothers have different views of a given practice. For example, some disciples drink alcohol and others choose not to drink. Those with alcohol abuse in their backgrounds are going to have more sensitive consciences than those who don't. We must first of all make sure that none of us "goes over the line" in drinking to excess. Mike Leatherwood recently has written a book about overcoming addictions, entitled *Some Sat in Darkness.*[1] Frankly, some things he wrote about observing the misuse of alcohol by those in the kingdom, including leaders, was highly disturbing to me. I do not think the Bible forbids all drinking, but we had better be very careful about what we choose to do in this area. However, we also are going to have to be careful not to bind what the Lord has not bound. We might be able to make a good case for abstaining from everything that could possibly lead to abuse, but we would end up with just that—a good case, and not necessarily a biblical case.

Another practice about which disciples have come to differing conclusions regards the type of movies we are comfortable watching. The last movie I saw left me disturbed. I went to it because it was highly acclaimed for its realism and quality of acting, but once I had seen it I was left with a very strong feeling that Jesus would neither have attended this movie nor many similar ones that most of us watch. Certain scriptures do come to mind when I think about the kinds of things we see portrayed on the big screen and our TV screens.

> Have nothing to do with the fruitless deeds of darkness, but rather expose them. For it is shameful even to mention what the disobedient do in secret (Ephesians 5:11-12).

I have difficulty reasoning that it is shameful to even *mention* sinful worldly activities, but somehow okay to watch them take place on a movie screen. I also have difficulty with the apparent double standard of condemning the sinful practices of Romans 1 in a Sunday morning sermon and then paying good money to watch the same sins acted out in a Sunday night movie. Although I have growing convictions about what I am going to subject my eyes and ears (and heart) to in the future, I know that I will have to be careful not to legislate in this area. But I will not hesitate to point out passages like the one above and ask disciples whether they think Jesus would watch what they watch.

I have seen some disciples who were trained in certain areas who came very close to the line of binding opinions in their area of expertise. If their specialty is noise pollution, they might be offended by a sound system at church which cranked out the decibels. If their specialty is nutrition, they might be agitated in the presence of sweet eaters and of those who relished foods with higher fat contents. Still others might be overly sensitized to the use of any type of prescription drugs, feeling deeply that the natural herb route is the only way to treat the body's ills. Still others are conditioned to disdain hunting or the wearing of furs, and some are so "into" recycling that they are horrified by those who throw their newspapers, bottles and cans in the trash. Many other things could be added to the list, because whatever we think we know most about, we become most attached to emotionally. Tolerance is a tough thing for all of us in certain areas, but as advice givers, we must keep taking good doses of humility and not start playing God.

In Romans 14:9-12, Paul makes the case that there simply is no room in the kingdom for judgmental attitudes toward one another. Narrow-mindedness and self-righteousness are condemned strongly by Jesus. We must keep our hearts knit together in spite of differences of opinion in certain areas and the tensions which may be thus aroused. When the Bible specifically teaches something, it is binding and must be followed. On the other hand, advice for individuals in areas of opinion is not in the same category. However, our attitudes must lead us strongly toward the seeking of agreement, not toward relishing differences—it is an issue of heart and unity.

Paul moves on in Romans 14:13-23 to argue against setting examples which destroy our brothers. We should not exercise our liberty in a way that causes a weaker brother to stumble. Nor should we ever violate our own consciences. Lest we interpret this section in a manner that contradicts the earlier sections of the chapter, note that causing a brother to "stumble" is equivalent to causing him to "fall" or "be destroyed." In my distant past when I was in a legalistic church, I often heard some argue that if a person did something that merely disturbed someone else, then the person should stop doing it. But the text doesn't say that you have to stop doing anything that might cause a cranky person to "grumble"! The word used is "stumble"! However, the point should be clear in reading Romans 14 that we have to maintain humility in giving advice and not bind or loose where God has not.

Seeking a Second Opinion

As disciplers giving advice, we need to know our limitations and learn to get plenty of collaborative advice. In other words, when giving advice, if you have any questions at all about what might be best, seek further advice from a mature spiritual person (keeping in mind what we have already said about confidentiality). The more significant the consequences of decisions being sought, the more need to get this collaborative advice. As an elder of a very large church, I am asked to give much advice about very weighty issues. But, few actually seek more advice than I do, even when I have a good idea about the best route to follow. If the consequences of a decision are serious, I want to make doubly sure that the advice given is the best possible. Serendipitous in this case is the rapid growth in wisdom gained by seeking secondary advice. *A humble discipler or other leader at any level must be a serious seeker of advice himself.*

As one being discipled, we should be anxious to seek advice and then to follow it. However, as mentioned in an earlier chapter, we cannot glibly follow it, especially if we have any qualms or questions of conscience. None of us should ever feel "trapped" as a disciple, nor should a discipler want to ever allow such a dynamic to evolve in a discipling relationship. Humility is required on both sides. Consider the following questions in being prepared to lead and follow in a spiritual manner:

- In giving advice and direction, is your approach to teach the other person *how* to think, or to do their thinking *for* them?

- How can someone not follow advice without being independent and/or rebellious?

- What is your response when the advice you give is not followed?

- Are you comfortable letting someone you disciple know that you are open to bringing someone else in if they have trouble with your advice?

- What is the correct way to handle such an appeal as the one leading? As the one being led?

Your answers to these questions will tell you a great deal about your leadership, your followership and your heart! Don't take them lightly!

What should be done when one being discipled cannot agree with the advice given by his discipler? No one should ever be, or even feel, boxed in. Our loyalty and allegiance is first and foremost to God. The right to get more input from a leader with more responsibility should be a component understood by both people in a discipling relationship. Interestingly, some have had a rather strange idea of loyalty in this arena.

When I first came to Boston, I discipled a brother who was mature chronologically (about forty years old), but who misunderstood loyalty. He reached an impasse in his discipling relationship with another brother who was about his same age and needed some help. Neither was on the ministry staff, but both were leaders of small groups. I arranged a session for the three of us, heard them both out and then discipled them both in the areas where they were wrong. After the third brother left, my discipleship partner was livid with me for the way I had handled the session. He argued that I should have taken his side against the other brother, simply because he was the leader. I was amazed at his reaction. He asked why I had not supported him as the leader, and the question was easy to answer. "Because you were wrong," I answered. The issue is never *who* is right; the issue is only *what* is right. He then said (of the former leader of his ministry), "John (not his real name) would never have done what you did!" I replied, "Then he would have been wrong too, and if you are correct about him, I pray that he learns quickly what you both need to learn."

The above situation did not come to a complete resolution that day, but since God has a sense of humor, it was resolved in a (now) funny way. This brother and I reached our own impasse some weeks or months later. He was starting to feel trapped with me as his discipler, which I certainly did not want. So, I had an opportunity to practice what I preached. I asked the brother who discipled me (Wyndham Shaw) to get us together and help us resolve our differences. Wyndham did exactly with the two of us what I had done earlier with him and the other brother. We each shared our side of the story, and then Wyndham definitely "came forward and questioned" both of us! (Proverbs 18:17). We each had fault in the situation, and we both were treated directly and impartially. After that session, the brother rejected his misguided "leader loyalty" doctrine!

My pride flared up a bit in the time together, but it was dealt with and humility reigned. I truly believe that God and Scriptures are more important than even personal relationships. I want to be the best people-helper I can possibly be, and when I am wrong, I want to repent and change. Frankly, I don't care who it is who points out my sin and thus helps me to change. My wife probably gives me the best input. My children, even when much younger, discipled me from time to time when I wasn't leading the right way. As long as their attitudes were respectful, I not only responded humbly to it, I appreciated it and respected them for both their convictions and courage. Whether disciple or discipler, we are all works in progress. Perhaps you have seen the lapel button that reads "PBPGINFWMY!" ("Please be patient—God is not finished with me yet!") Be a humble disciple, and be a humble discipler. Clothe yourself with humility (Colossians 3:12) and you will be a well-dressed advisor to those whom you disciple.

12

BE A GRACEFUL LEADER

One of the most precious aspects of God's nature is his strong urge to lavish grace on mankind (see Ephesians 1:7-8). Nothing motivates us better or longer than grace. When we really grasp what God is offering us, then we allow him to grasp our hearts and souls in a permanent way. My favorite book in the Bible is Romans because its main subject is grace. As has often been said, "If you get Romans, God gets you." When people leave God, I am convinced that something in their understanding of his graceful nature must be deficient. But if understanding and teaching grace is important, *treating* others with grace is more important. The means of motivating those under our leadership is absolutely a crucial issue, and nothing will suffice except motivating as God does. What are the keys to leading with godly motivation?

Acceptance

The foundation of our salvation is that God accepts us because of Christ, not because of our performance. Ephesians 2:8-9 says:

> For it is by grace you have been saved, through faith—and this not from yourselves, it is the gift of God—not by works, so that no one can boast.

Since man does have a part in his own salvation, in that he must choose it, we can develop an erroneous attitude about our part in the process. We are tempted to say that God's part *plus* man's part equals salvation. Stated another way, God's grace *plus* man's faith equals salvation. The problem here is the implication that our part is on an equal or near equal plane with God's part.

A much more accurate way to describe the "grace through faith" salvation process is to say that faith *relying* on grace secures salvation. We, in no sense, earn redemption—we merely accept the work of God based on the cross of Christ. A spiritual song expresses it in this way: "He paid a debt he did not owe; I owed a debt I could not pay."

You may be wondering what all of this has to do with our discipling of other people. Actually, quite a lot if we are to lead and motivate like God does. He never says, "Measure up and I'll accept you." He accepts us in Christ and then works to help us live in a righteous manner. In fact, immediately after the verses quoted above, Ephesians 2:10 goes on to say,

> For we are God's workmanship, created in Christ Jesus to do good works, which God prepared in advance for us to do.

Works are a part of the plan, but we work because we *are* saved, not to *be* saved. Godly discipling follows the same principles, as we accept those whom we lead without putting them on the performance treadmill.

For the most part, we live in a world based on performance. Our neurotic society did not become such without cause. Even most of our families emphasized performance far more than they realized. Parents, even with good intentions, made us feel that their acceptance was conditional in many ways. They likely were trying to keep us reaching higher, but although this type of motivation might promote achievement, it also fosters insecurity. We simply must break the "perform to be accepted" mentality in all righteous relationships—between God and man, and between man and man.

My children are my children during all kinds of times, including the good, the bad and the ugly. In their growing-up years, I loved them when they were bad and when they were good. In fact, I probably felt more loving concern for them when they were not doing well. God is the same way as a father. Think of passages like Romans 5:8: "While we were still sinners, Christ died for us." When we are doing terribly, his heart reaches out to us incredibly. We simply must learn to treat one another in the same way, regardless of whether we are dealing with physical children or spiritual children. We can never emotionally "shut out" someone when they have disappointed us.

Friendship is the basis of discipling, as it was with Jesus and his disciples (John 15:15). Real friends stick with us through thick and thin. We cannot resort to "doghouse" discipleship, by distancing ourselves emotionally from someone who has not measured up to our expectations. Many families have this dynamic as a fundamental part of their relationships. Once a disruption occurs, the "silent treatment" is administered until a certain amount of time has passed. The disruption is not discussed, but at the point that the supposed time requirement has been met, life resumes as if nothing had happened. The emotional disapproval, with its inherent punishment, has run its course, and life returns to normal. Did you have a family like that, or at least a relationship within the family that followed this pattern? It is very common in families where conflict avoidance reigns. Some are "one day" families, some are "two day" families—or worse!

The "doghouse" approach to dealing with sin or disappointments in relationships is void of understanding the biblical approach to resolving conflict in relationships. When wrongs have been committed, we are to call each other to repentance, not penance. The former focuses on God in seeking pardon, and the latter on self, in attempting to "work off" sins. The primary difference in "godly" and "worldly" sorrow (2 Corinthians 7:8-11) is whether we look up to God for help to change or look down on ourselves in self-pity. Repentance produces a recognition of guilt and deals with it righteously by turning to God for forgiveness and the strength to change. Penance produces a guilt trip and attempts to earn forgiveness in some fashion. Guilt is real, and its purpose is to produce godly sorrow; but guilt trips are satanic to the core. God has absolutely no desire that anyone be put on a guilt trip.

One of the worst ways to motivate children is to put them on a guilt trip, chaining them emotionally to the "doghouse." It does more emotional damage than we can imagine. When children disobey, they need to be helped to face the wrong and repent, and the quicker the process can be accomplished, the better. I remember watching Kip McKean discipline his children when they were younger. He confronted their wrong behavior in a very direct (but not harsh) manner, which led them to repent quickly. They confessed, apologized and prayed for God's forgiveness. Then Kip usually made time to play basketball or relate to them in a fun way, and it was as if the "carefrontation" was immediately forgotten—and it was. The child had learned the lesson and was able to go on with life.

When God forgives, he forgets, and we must do the same. I remember watching Kip and the kids playing after one of these times of correction and wishing I had been as godly with my own children when they were the same age. Before I became a true disciple and began being discipled, I made the mistake of using some of the doghouse techniques. Don't do it with your children or with God's children as you disciple them.

Sometimes parents become overly conscious of how their children's behavior reflects on them as parents. They become reactionary and self-focused rather than concentrating on how to train their kids. As spiritual leaders at any level, we can make the same mistake. If we do, we have stopped loving those whom we lead and are now using them to make ourselves look good (or at least to keep us from looking bad). Disciplers must learn to look to the needs of their disciples, especially when they have messed up, and not start worrying about how they now appear as a leader. It is a matter of acceptance in either case—of our disciples and of ourselves. We are all sinners, and as such, we are going to make mistakes even though our goal is to not sin. Since God accepts us sinners in Christ, we are going to have to learn to accept ourselves and each other when we sin.

Freedom

The principle of accepting each other in Christ sets the atmosphere for enjoying freedom in our relationships. Many Bible-readers have marveled at how often the apostle Peter made mistakes. I marvel at the freedom Jesus gave him in which to make them! Righteous relationships are characterized by the freedom to be who we are while we become who we are meant to be. Read that sentence again, for much hangs in the balance here.

I once heard about a rather widespread survey of college students, in which their emotional stability and maturity were measured as a means of determining the effectiveness of parenting styles. The different parenting styles were distilled down into four basic types. One was the *authoritarian* style, in which the parents (usually the dad) ran the family like a drill sergeant. "Do what I say when I say it, and don't talk back." Another style was the *authoritative*, where the parents were definitely in charge as the leaders, but were not "control freaks." A third style was the *permissive* and a fourth, the *indifferent*. The permissive parents allowed their children to mostly do just what they wanted, being afraid to lead more strongly. The indifferent were very uninvolved with their offspring, letting them go their own way almost entirely.

Which of the four styles do you think produced the most emotionally stable and mature young adults? The most effective leadership style was judged to be the authoritative, and the authoritarian was dead last. Is that what you were thinking? Effectiveness is tied to the quality of relationship. The authoritative parent loved enough to be involved and to set guidelines. The permissive parents were concerned but weak in leadership because of giving in too often. The indifferent parent had little or no relationship with his children, but the authoritarian parent had a bad relationship, and not surprisingly, one which produced by far the most rebellion.

Jesus is unquestionably an authoritative leader. He is in charge, make no mistake about it, but he never tries to force us to do anything. That would be contrary to his purpose of developing a close relationship with us. He leads us, but he doesn't force us. He provides direction, advice and motivation, but he allows us the freedom to choose. He wants us to freely choose him and the righteous life that he offers. Is that how you see God? Is that how you see yourself as a leader? Which parenting style most closely correlates to your style of parenting (if you have children) and to your style of discipling others in the kingdom? We have stressed repeatedly that our purpose as disciplers is not to think for other people, but to train them to think righteously. I have seen some whose grasp of human nature was so highly flawed that their concept of leading seemed to be "Why think, when you can be discipled?" Not only is such a concept unbiblical, it is stupid. A "good disciple" is not simply one who does what he is told; he is one who learns the biblical and practical foundations for thinking spiritually and making right decisions.

Now back to Peter. Why did he seem to make more mistakes than the other apostles? Remember that John called himself "the disciple whom Jesus loved"? Jesus loved all of them more than any of them could possibly grasp, but John appeared to have a greater capacity to accept it. In a similar way, I think Peter grasped his freedom in Christ better than the rest did. He made some pretty serious blunders, one of which caused Jesus to call him "Satan," but he felt free to be himself. The result was that he was discipled over and over and then emerged as the key speaker on Pentecost (Acts 2) and one of the two most influential apostles on earth. (Of course, Paul was the other.) Judas obviously did not utilize his freedom to be himself, and his heart was not discipled as a result. Both Judas and Peter had the freedom, but one used it and was exalted by God, while the other did not use it, and literally destroyed himself.

As disciplers, we are not simply trying to produce "a good Christian performance" in those we disciple. We are trying to set up the atmosphere of freedom, in which honesty and openness can flourish. Then a disciple learns to be more and more effective for God. If we do not make people feel free to be real, their hearts will not come out and therefore cannot be properly discipled. Discipling is focused on making spiritual progress rather than on trying to look good for the moment. Paul's observation in Philippians 3:15-16 is classic:

> All of us who are mature should take such a view of things. And if on some point you think differently, that too God will make clear to you. Only let us live up to what we have already attained.

Mature disciples have mature views. Immature disciples think differently on some points, but Paul is not alarmed by that fact of life. He simply says that God will make it clear to the immature at some point if they just do their best in their present understanding. Paul saw discipleship as developing, but developing toward a destination he knew none of us would ever reach—the perfection of Christ. However, the trip is a wonderful experience in which growth and progress are guaranteed if we stay close to God and get discipled.

Expectations

People respond incredibly to what others expect of them, especially to the expectations of those with whom they have the most significant relationships. I learned the rather remarkable power of expectations in a very unusual way many years ago. At the time, I had recently graduated from college and was serving as a band director in a junior high school. From conversations in the teachers' lounge, I gathered that nearly all teachers were having a different experience from me in one specific area. They seemed to hate teaching on Fridays, claiming that the kids were restless and difficult to control as they looked forward to the weekends. However, I loved teaching on Fridays, especially the last class period of the day. My concert band met on that period each day, and since they were my top group, I enjoyed them most. They seemed to be at the peak of their performance on what other teachers referred to as "dreaded Friday sixth period."

It took me about a year to figure out why my experiences on Fridays differed so sharply from those of my fellow teachers. Most of them came in on Mondays rested up and ready to start their weeks. By the end of the week, they were worn out. On the other hand, I came to school on Mondays, feeling like all of the weekend was not out of me yet. I hated Mondays like the others hated Fridays. By midweek, I was more in gear and by Friday, my juices were flowing and my adrenaline cranking! Are you starting to get the picture? Because the other teachers were worn out on Fridays and dreading teaching then, their students were "climbing the walls." However, I was in fifth gear by Friday and my students rose to my expectations and overcame their natural tendencies. Is that not *amazing*—the power of expectations in the lives of those whom we lead?

I had another experience in that band room which reinforced the same lesson. As a newer teacher, I was still pretty idealistic and had not learned all of our limitations yet. I decided to pass out a high school level march (by John Philip Sousa, in case you are an old band member) and have the students both learn and memorize it for the upcoming parade of marching bands. I knew it would be difficult for my students to learn, since most of them had only been playing instruments for a year or two. But I passed it out, explained it and brought my baton down for them to begin. As I expected, they did abysmally at the outset. But I didn't tell them I expected them to do poorly at first. In fact, I told them in no uncertain terms that I expected far better! (I know—I lied. But I wasn't a Christian in those days, and I was trying to pull off a bluff!) The second time I started them off on the march, they played it amazingly well and went straight through without stopping. I was *shocked!* How did they do it? In a nutshell, they responded to the expectations of their teacher and played far beyond their level of training. At the parade later that spring, they almost blew the walls of the downtown buildings back as they proudly marched down those streets in front of the onlooking crowds. Needless to say, I almost popped my buttons off my shirt! And I learned that most of our limitations are in our minds. Do you believe that?

How do you tend to view people in general: positively or negatively? Your answer will tell you much about yourself. If you understand the nature of the world and its sin, you see the world as a messed-up place. As Paul said in Titus 3:3,

> At one time we too were foolish, disobedient, deceived and enslaved by all kinds of passions and pleasures. We lived in malice and envy, being hated and hating one another.

Hardly a pretty picture, is it? On the other hand, if you understand the kingdom of God and the righteousness he provides, you will feel quite another way about disciples. Paul also had a word to say about this side of the coin.

> I myself am convinced, my brothers, that you yourselves are full of goodness, complete in knowledge and competent to instruct one another (Romans 15:14).

Of what are *you* convinced about those in the kingdom—especially those whom you disciple? Your expectations of them will have an amazing influence on what they will become.

Have Expectations

In the first place, you must *have* expectations in the relationship. Discipleship times are not simply cake and coffee times; they are times for discipling. Find out how your spiritual friend is doing in the most important areas of life. One way to cover these bases is to ask how they are doing in the four key areas of relationships: relationship with God; with family (if single, this includes relationships with roommates and with the opposite sex); with disciples; and with the world (evangelism, and any problem relationships which might exist). If we cover these four basic areas, we will likely have dealt with the most pertinent issues in their lives.

Not only should your discipling time cover these areas in discussion, but also goals for each should be set. Just think of how discussing these four areas could yield fruitful results in each area. Pick out what needs to be changed or done in each, write it down and then share how things are progressing each week. If we have nothing to shoot at, we will hit the target with deadly accuracy, which means that we will be growing and changing very little. What are the long range and short range goals for your life? What are they in the lives of those whom you disciple? Do you have expectations for yourself? For others? Goals and accountability are the stuff of which progress is made. Set some (very specific goals) and make some (progress, that is). Care enough to have expectations, to help others set goals, and then to hold them accountable for following through.

Have Reasonable Expectations

Our expectations in discipling should be reasonable in several ways. One, they should be individualized. We are all born with different capacities and we have had different influences in our lives shaping those capacities. We have different needs and respond differently to events in our lives, to failures and to correction. Disciplers have to learn what each person he disciples needs and figure out what motivates him best. Some of us work great with certain types of people and don't have a clue about how to work with other types. The best leader is the one who can work with the most types of people. Study the example of Jesus on this point. Pay the price of learning how to disciple all kinds—then you can be like Jesus.

Having expectations which "stretch" our disciples is vital, but if we expect too much too soon, the faith of the person we are trying to help can be damaged, to say nothing of their self-esteem. We speak often of the need to have kingdom dreams, which is true, but disciples need input in developing those dreams. I can remember people who initially had dreams about being on the ministry staff who did not have the necessary abilities to serve in that capacity. Some of them did not diligently pursue a career track as soon as they should have, because they were waiting for an opportunity that never came. Other disciples had kingdom dreams to go out on a church-planting team, but again, did not have the needed abilities or training to see the dream realized. Some of these became disillusioned to the point that they fell away or are now afraid to formulate dreams for the future.

Disciples really need to get advice before setting their hearts on their dreams, and we as disciplers need to be honest, yet sensitive, in advising them. As an elder and full-time minister, if I think a person has virtually no chance of being on the ministry staff, I feel compelled to express my judgment, the reasoning behind it and to provide ideas for other dreams which are more suited to their talents, abilities and faith. If I think they have at least some possibility of fulfilling the ministry dream, I need to express it as only a possibility and give them good input about how to develop toward that goal. If they seem ideal for ministry, I also tell them that, complete with input about continuing to grow into it. Since I am only human, I have to be careful about being too definite in any direction. I could be wrong, and I also tell them that. (Major decisions about one's future in the ministry should not be made without consulting ministry leaders or elders.)

All disciples should be encouraged to have kingdom dreams, and there are many possibilities and fulfilling ways to serve. Needs abound in the kingdom in areas such as administration, children's ministry, special ministries, benevolent service, and arts and entertainment. Keep in mind that a failure to reach any dream carries the potential for disappointment. Often, I appeal to what I call the "Joseph principle." Joseph was a biblical character of amazing convictions and spiritual credentials in the midst of some very difficult circumstances. (See Genesis 30-50.) He had no idea that he was going to end up as "vice president" of Egypt and actually run the greatest country in the world at that time. But he had a great idea of how to live one day at a time and to be his absolute best for God in that day. In thirteen long years, he went from rejected brother to slave to jailbird. However, he remained faithful to God with no help from any person in the world, and in the end he was greatly exalted by his God. If all of us had the dream of being the best disciple possible every day, God would take care of all of our dreams. When it is not certain what God's specific will is for the future, just follow the Joseph principle. We cannot go wrong with this approach to life—nor can those disciples whom we advise.

Two, our expectations need to be kept reasonable by seeking progress in disciples, not perfection as our goal. That being true, we should be practicing what might be called "situational discipling," allowing their life situations to determine when we deal more heavily with character issues. In other words, we as disciplers should not constantly harp on deeper character weaknesses which will take a long time to change. Sins of choice need immediate attention, but the deeper things are going to change more gradually. Keep in mind Doug Arthur's definition of discipling: "gentle pressure, relentlessly applied." Gentleness and perseverance are great partners in bringing about character change. Surely we need to change those deeper weaknesses, but if that's all we hear about week after week in our discipling times, we will lose our love for discipleship.

The issue is keeping our balance, isn't it? Can you imagine what it would have been like to spend three years in the presence of Jesus if he had pointed out everything he saw in you that needed to change all of the time? Since he read minds, he knew every thought, every attitude, every weakness perfectly. Had he not been a "situational discipler," his apostles would have hated getting up in the morning—every morning! We need to look for growth and progress in those we are discipling. Disciple with that goal in mind, and deal with the deeply rooted character issues as they manifest themselves in life situations. Everyone will stay happier, and the growth will come in God's time.

Three, our expectations should keep us focused on training, not simply correcting. Our terminology at times indicates attitudes which are not the most helpful. For example, we may say after a strong correction or rebuke, "I really got discipled!" Well, if we needed a rebuke, praise God that we received it. But the way it was described leaves the impression that "getting discipled" applies only to strong, corrective direction, and it can cause younger disciples to fear discipling in general and correction specifically. In a similar vein, the word "discipline" in relation to parenting has to do with training, not simply correcting and punishing. But some parents are too short-sighted and see it in only the latter way, instead of viewing it as an umbrella covering *all* aspects of a child's life-training (most of which certainly shouldn't be corrective).

A good carpenter finishes a table top by sanding and scrutinizing, sanding and scrutinizing, over and over again. He looks at the table in the light to find every little blemish, and sands it away. When he has removed the last imperfection he sees, then he applies the stain and protective coating. If we try to use this approach in discipling people, we are going to be miserable and produce miserable disciples. Deal with one or two big issues at hand, and leave other imperfections for later. If we ask for wisdom, God will make known in time what needs some loving "sanding" (James 1:5). The process of discipling is just that: a process.

Have Great Expectations

Yes, the expectations must be reasonable, but they must be nonetheless great. Perhaps not great in the eyes of men, nor great in comparison to other men, but great in the eyes of God by reaching the true potential he has placed within each of us. I do not have to compare myself to great, respected leaders in God's movement; I simply have to be the best Gordon Ferguson possible. And I have an idea that he can be much greater than he is because God's measure of greatness is servanthood (Matthew 20:25-28), and I have yet much improvement to make in that area! But whatever I am at any one point, it is mostly because of the faith others have expressed in me. Certain statements made about my potential have given me the faith to move in those directions. How much faith do you express in your disciples?

Just think of how Cephas must have felt when Jesus called him "Rocky!" (John 1:42). And of how John must have felt to be invited into the Master's inner circle, even though he was almost certainly only a teenager. Jesus chose apostles who were the brunt of jokes and jeers as they formed the little ragtag group who followed him around. They looked common, they smelled common, they acted common and they spoke with funny accents. But Jesus believed in them, and that was enough for them. His faith lifted them above the taunts and mockery which followed them all the days of their lives. And they became among the most influential men the world has ever known. The glory of the *ordinary* was that they became the *extraordinary*. Had we seen them in the early days of their apostleship, we would likely have joined in the joking. But Jesus believed in the power of discipling to change lives in a way the world could not believe.

The Apostles did not miss Jesus' point when they became the kingdom's leading disciplers. Paul took his *Timothys*, with their weak stomachs and timid personalities, and molded them into earth-shaking evangelists. Barnabas took Saul under his wing when the other apostles were all afraid of him and helped him change from a rabid radical into a minister of mercy. Barnabas stuck with John Mark, even when his weak character caused Paul to refuse to take him back on another missionary journey. The price tag for Barnabas was high in this case, for it cost him his position as Paul's right-hand partner in the mission field. You could clearly argue, as some have, that Paul made the better choice at the time, not letting sentimentality interfere with the mission at hand. However, I am more drawn to Barnabas than to Paul in this case!

Paul grew to appreciate the man Mark eventually became, asking for him when in prison during his final days (2 Timothy 4:11).

Learning to be a graceful leader is a lifetime project, but the dividends paid will be far more valuable than almost any other adventure on which you could embark. Learn what these three words are all about: acceptance, freedom and expectation. Then on the Great Day when we all stand before God, many people in that vast throng will rise up and call you "blessed" for having given the kind of discipling that changed the course of their lives forevermore! Praise God!

Part 4

ISSUES, CHALLENGES AND OPPORTUNITIES

Discipling others to Christ is neither simple nor easy. When we undertake this challenge, issues are raised, challenges surface and new opportunities are afforded. In this final section, we will look at some of these matters, attempting to tie up some loose ends and hopefully address questions that our earlier discussions may have raised.

13

WHO HAS AUTHORITY?

In this chapter, we want to examine the subject of authority in the church from a broad perspective, not just from the perspective of leadership in discipling relationships. It is hard to exaggerate the importance of authority in our world and in the church. Satan's hatred for authority tells us a great deal. He evidently became who he is through rebellion against the authority of God. Everything we are told about him makes it clear that he will do all within his power (which is considerable) to destroy authority and respect for it. As humans, we are never more satanic than when despising authority and encouraging others to do the same (2 Peter 2:10).

The Bible wastes no time in showing us Satan's hatred of authority and his devious way of undermining it. He approached Eve (Genesis 3) by saying that God had forbidden her and Adam to eat from *every* tree in the Garden. Eve responded by essentially saying "No, it was really only *one* tree, but if we eat from it we will die." Satan pretty much replied, "Not true—God is lying to you because he doesn't want you to gain his knowledge." What was Satan doing here? Undermining trust in the authority of God. He has not changed his approach one iota in the thousands of years since Eve ate the forbidden fruit. He hates every form of authority (except his own) and will continue his attempts to tear it down in every nation, society, family and certainly in the church of the Almighty God!

Search the pages of sacred history and you will find the same story repeated over and over. Moses, one of God's greatest leaders and the most humble one on earth (Numbers 12:3), had to deal incessantly with rebellion against his leadership. Even his own brother and sister rose up to question him. Just listen to their envious pettiness:

"Has the LORD spoken only through Moses?" they asked.
"Hasn't he also spoken through us?" And the LORD heard
this (Numbers 12:2).

The root of rebellion against authority is pride and envy, pure
and simple, whether by Satan, Aaron and Miriam—or you and
me! But mark it down: God is listening, and he does not take
rebellion lightly. Just read the rest of the account in Numbers 12
and see what happened to big sister. Since she was the one most
directly punished, we can surmise that she was a true daughter of
Eve and instigated the rebellion.

What do we find in the New Testament about this subject?
As the only sinless man ever to live went about loving and serving perfectly, the supposedly spiritual folk were continually asking, "By what authority are you doing these things?" (See Matthew 21:23, Mark 11:28, Luke 20:2 and John 2:18.) Their little
positions of worldly authority were being threatened by true spiritual leadership, and they were listening very attentively as Satan
whispered his lies and distortions in their ears. Paul, proclaimer
of grace and model of humility, constantly had to defend his
authority, much to his embarrassment. Reading 2 Corinthians
10-13 with this thought in mind shows us this point clearly. What
we need to understand is that God always has leaders through
whom he works, and Satan and his demons always incite rebellion against those leaders by filling men's hearts with pride, envy
and distrust.

One additional note is needed before we move to specific
biblical teaching about authority. When leaders or "would-be"
leaders rebel against true authority, they usually do so because of
pride and envy. It is sometimes the case that people resist authority because of fear and mistrust, developed by having endured
ungodly leadership. Such resistance is still viewed by God as rebellion, but the root cause is somewhat different. The seriousness of rebellion is obvious, but leaders who tempt followers to
resist by leading in an unrighteous manner are just as guilty. On
both sides of the coin we must be extremely careful. Godly leadership is absolutely essential, and godly followership is just as
essential. God will not tolerate less.

The Provision for Authority

The need for authority exists in every group who has any purpose to accomplish. Without leadership and the authority inherent in it, no group can possibly achieve its purposes. In America (along with most of the rest of the world), society is bordering on chaos because of a breakdown of authority. The deterioration of homes and schools, former bastions for developing respect for authority, is nothing short of amazing. However, no organization can survive and flourish without authority. God's groups through the centuries required leadership and authority but did not always have the right kind of it. Without proper authority, God's nation suffered greatly (Judges 21:25). Moses could not lead the nation without the support of many other leaders exercising authority (Exodus 18:13-26). God placed leadership in the church in order to lead his people to maturity and productivity (Ephesians 4:11-16).

As mentioned in an earlier chapter, authority is exercised in several basic ways. Relational authority occurs when a family member or trusted friend has some influence on our decisions. Knowledge authority is present when we allow people with training and experience to exercise the influence of their expertise. Positional authority is that exerted by a designated official, such as an officer in the military or a manager in the workplace. He or she leads perhaps with all three types, but in any case, has the third type simply on the basis of position.

Which kind of authority should we find in the church? Without a doubt, authority in the kingdom is to be viewed first of all as *relational* in nature. Even though everyone in a congregation cannot know all leaders on an intimate basis, we must see each other as family and work hard to build family. Regarding the authority of *knowledge*, more experienced leadership will exert more influence than the less experienced. In a physical family, the older brothers and sisters teach the younger ones many valuable things. God never intended for the parents to be the sole trainers of the children. Older siblings and extended family members were all to have a part in the task. Surely this design is also a part of his plan for his spiritual family. Discipleship, as described in Matthew 28:19-20, is based on these principles. God is the one with the greatest expertise, but we can and must learn much from others in the kingdom.

But what about positional authority in the church? Do we have that? Because of seeing a wrong exercise of authority, many religious people have concluded that every vestige of positional authority is to be avoided. However, the Bible makes it clear that God has designated authority in several areas, including the church. The broad list would be:

1. Government – Romans 13:1-7; 1 Peter 2:13-17
2. Masters (Employers) – Colossians 3:22-24;
   1 Peter 2:18-20
3. Husbands – Ephesians 5:22-25; 1 Peter 3:1-6
4. Parents – Ephesians 6:1-3
5. Church leaders – 1 Thessalonians 5:12-13
   (and the other passages to follow)

I remember spending hours with a young man in a foreign country discussing these issues. He admitted that positional authority was authorized by God in government, in business, between husband and wife, and between parents and children, but argued emphatically that it is *not* authorized in the church. Do you see the lack of logic in this line of reasoning? According to him, God instituted authority in every realm except the most important one!

Of course, it is true that positional authority does not exist in isolation in the church, without being combined with the other types. However, positional authority definitely has a place in the kingdom.

Key New Testament Texts

To disciples who had a worldly view of authority, Jesus spoke these words:

> Jesus called them together and said, "You know that the rulers of the Gentiles lord it over them, and their high officials exercise authority over them. Not so with you. Instead, whoever wants to become great among you must be your

servant, and whoever wants to be first must be your slave—just as the Son of Man did not come to be served, but to serve, and to give his life as a ransom for many" (Matthew 20:25-28).

The word for "authority" (verse 25) here is from the Greek *exousia*. Does Jesus' statement in this text thus rule out all authority in the church, as some claim? For starters, note that in verse 28, Jesus is using himself as an example of the right kind of leader, a servant leader. Yet, he has all authority (*exousia*) in heaven and on earth (Matthew 28:18). Does his having "all authority" indicate that only he has *exousia*? No, it cannot mean that, for in 2 Corinthians 10:8 and 13:10, Paul claims to have the authority (*exousia*) of an apostle. Since Jesus was given all authority by the Father, he then could imitate the Father by sharing his authority with the leaders he had chosen. Obviously Jesus is not ruling out all authority in the church, but he unquestionably is ruling out *positional-only* authority in which people lord it over others and do not lead with example and relationship. (See 1 Peter 5:1-4 for a similar application.)

To a church where people were apparently becoming independent of leadership, the writer of Hebrews penned these words:

Obey your leaders and submit to their authority. They keep watch over you as men who must give an account. Obey them so that their work will be a joy, not a burden, for that would be of no advantage to you (Hebrews 13:17).

The word "authority" in the NIV is not in the Greek, so the literal translation would be "obey and submit to them" (as leaders). The word "obey" is from the Greek *peitho*, and the literal meaning is "be persuaded." My young friend with the misconception regarding authority, mentioned earlier, argued that the leader has no authority, but only the power of persuasion. While it is true that good leaders need to persuade their people from the Scriptures and with valid reasoning, this passage is not directed at leaders! Followers are commanded to *be persuaded*. Just as no leader can make us submit if we do not have a submissive heart, no leader can persuade anyone who refuses to be persuaded. Even God pleads with us to be persuaded, for it is submission from the heart that he is after!

The same word is found in James 3:3, which reads: "When we put bits into the mouths of horses to make them *obey* us, we can turn the whole animal" (emphasis added). People are not horses and leaders should not use bits, but the usage here shows us that the word is hardly a weak one.

Who are the leaders in Hebrews 13:17? They are recognized congregational leaders with a designated work in the church, for which they will give an account. That is obvious from the context, and besides, who else could they be? What other leaders could he describe in this way? Since they have this role and weighty responsibility, he says make their work a joy! This is a most important passage, but we must be careful how we apply it. To apply it to a six-month-old Christian discipling a two-month-old Christian and to say the six-month-old is the leader being described here would be a misapplication of Scripture and might be hazardous to the spiritual health of both! This does not, however, give the younger disciple license to rebel against the one trying to help him. God blesses humility and opposes pride in all situations. It is just that in such cases we should think more in terms of peer relationships and less about someone being over someone.

To the sometimes rowdy Corinthians, Paul wrote words they no doubt needed:

> You know that the household of Stephanas were the first converts in Achaia, and they have devoted themselves to the service of the saints. I urge you, brothers, to submit to such as these and to everyone who joins in the work, and labors at it (1 Corinthians 16:15).

The word "submit" in verse 16 is from *hupotasso* in the Greek. It is also a strong word, as its usage in James 4:7 would indicate: "*Submit yourselves* then, to God. Resist the devil, and he will flee from you" (emphasis added).

This passage in 1 Corinthians 16 shows the natural ordering of leadership relationships in a developing church. The earlier converts became the early leaders, as would be expected, and should have been submitted to as leaders. Also, all the others who "joined in the work" (almost certainly, *as* leaders, given the meaning of *hupotasso* in Greek) should have been submitted to as well. This pattern is very natural in any organization. Those on the "ground floor" gain the most experience, and naturally lead the less experienced ones who come in later. Levels of leadership develop in this manner, as experience and knowledge dictate who is best equipped to lead.

Some people have tried to escape the clear teaching of this passage by appealing to verse 12 in the same chapter (1 Corinthians 16) regarding the unwillingness of Apollos to follow the urging of Paul. However, any appeal which sets one scripture in contradiction to another is a very suspect appeal to begin with! The issue in this verse was not *whether* Apollos was going to do what Paul asked, but only *when* he was going to do it. We must also keep in mind that we are talking about two very influential leaders with different responsibilities which had to be taken into consideration. Timing in discharging ministry responsibilities is always a big issue. Comparing this situation with submission to leaders in a congregation is comparing apples and oranges. On the other hand, the passage does show the correctness of discussing differing opinions with the right spirit and even working out compromises (on timing, in this case).

A number of passages from letters to evangelists demonstrate that Paul expected them to use authority in leading churches. To give you the flavor of such scriptures, they are included here without comment but with emphasis added:

> As I urged you when I went into Macedonia, stay there in Ephesus so that you may *command* certain men not to teach false doctrines any longer (1 Timothy 1:3).

> *Command and teach* these things. Don't let anyone look down on you because you are young, but set an example for the believers in speech, in life, in love, in faith and in purity (1 Timothy 4:11-12).

> *Command* those who are rich in this present world not to be arrogant nor to put their hope in wealth, which is so

uncertain, but to put their hope in God, who richly provides us with everything for our enjoyment. *Command* them to do good, to be rich in good deeds, and to be generous and willing to share (1 Timothy 6:17-18).

Keep reminding them of these things. *Warn* them before God against quarreling about words; it is of no value, and only ruins those who listen (2 Timothy 2:14).

In the presence of God and of Christ Jesus, who will judge the living and the dead, and in view of his appearing and his kingdom, I give you this charge: Preach the Word; be prepared in season and out of season; *correct, rebuke and encourage*—with great patience and careful instruction. For the time will come when men will not put up with sound doctrine. Instead, to suit their own desires, they will gather around them a great number of teachers to say what their itching ears want to hear. They will turn their ears away from the truth and turn aside to myths. But you, keep your head in all situations, endure hardship, do the work of an evangelist, discharge all the duties of your ministry (2 Timothy 4:1-5).

The reason I left you in Crete was that you might *straighten out* what was left unfinished and appoint elders in every town, as I directed you (Titus 1:5).

For there are many rebellious people, mere talkers and deceivers, especially those of the circumcision group. They *must be silenced*, because they are ruining whole households by teaching things they ought not to teach—and that for the sake of dishonest gain. (Titus 1:10-12).

These, then, are the things you should teach. Encourage and rebuke with *all authority*. Do not let anyone despise you (Titus 2:15).

Even a cursory reading of these passages should convince anyone that authority in the church is established by God.

The Extent of Authority

When Scripture speaks clearly, all of us have the authority to apply *the* Authority (Scripture) to people's lives. The challenges come when Scripture does not speak definitively on some matter, but decisions must be made. Who has the authority; how much do they have, and how should it be used?

Common Sense

Common sense and practical judgment are definitely required when the "book, chapter and verse" method does not provide specific instruction about a topic. In other words, leadership in the church is not only authorized to enforce obedience to specific biblical commands; it is also authorized to designate the practicals required to carry out those commands. Decisions of all sorts have to be made, including when to meet, where to meet, how to organize and other such nonbiblical (but not antibiblical) issues.

Once these decisions are made by leadership, we must follow them. If not, chaos would rule. Therefore, even in these areas of judgment, leaders' decisions should be followed unless one of two conditions exist: one, you are asked to violate Scripture (Acts 5:29); or two, you are asked to violate your conscience (Romans 14:23). However, to appeal to the conscience as a reason for not submitting is a serious matter and cannot be used simply as an excuse to do your own thing!

A related point is that spiritual maturity brings with it a certain authority. A very mature Christian, even at lower levels of leadership, would exert more influence generally than would a young Christian. The reason is obvious: He has more knowledge and expertise to offer. But when we are discussing this type of knowledge authority in lower-level leaders, how binding is it? An important part of the answer concerns the impact made by the response of the follower. Would he be the only one affected by his decisions, or would others be affected as well? If the impact were only on the person making the decision, that is much different than making a decision which affects many people. Therefore, in one case, the input might be viewed by the leader more as advice, while in the other case, he would view it more as a command. Sensitive leadership and humble followership will protect all of us.

A Biblical Precedent

In determining the authority of different levels of leadership in the church, including the possible authority of a discipler, Moses and Jethro have valuable insights which remain helpful to us centuries later. Take your Bible and read carefully Exodus 18:13-26.

Different levels of leadership were appointed by Moses at Jethro's suggestion. If they had different levels of leadership, then by necessity they had different levels of authority. The higher the level of leadership, the higher the level of responsibility; and the higher the level of responsibility, the higher the level of authority. Leaders of tens dealt with their ten, meeting needs and solving every problem they could. If they reached an impasse, they went to the leader over them for help, which would have been a leader of fifty.

If this leader could not solve it, he appealed to a leader of a hundred, and next to a leader of a thousand, and ultimately to Moses. Leaders at lower levels took care of as many situations as possible before appealing to a higher-level leader. The same principle should be applied in the church. The lead evangelist and the elders are not the ones to call first (nor second nor third usually). It is not because they are not concerned, but because ignoring the principle of working through the various levels of leadership has deleterious consequences: It leaves leaders stretched too thin, making them ineffective, and it leaves their followers unsatisfied (or worse). Sheer numbers alone dictate that Jethro's solution is the only one which can possibly work in any larger group. So to complete the thought, a leader of even a small group must be allowed the authority to lead that group. Otherwise, top leaders will be overwhelmed with needs and details.

Present-day Application

What does all of this have to do with the discipling relationship? Using the Exodus 18 model, a leader would have positional authority at the level of leading a group of ten people. (I recognize that this OT example is not technically binding on the church, but it would be foolish for us to ignore the wisdom we can gain from it.) With groups smaller than this, any leadership is exercised through either relational authority or the authority of knowledge (or expertise). Therefore, applying the principle to discipling relationships would mean that no positional authority exists in the typical one-on-one relationship. The influence exerted is of the relational and knowledge types. However, as we have said earlier, on the discipling level, think *friendship*, not authority— but also think submission and humility and enjoy the blessings! Both discipler and disciple should think in this way.

Let me hasten to add that some positional authority does inhere in certain discipling relationships. Those in which a leader of a group of ten or more is the discipler will possess a degree of positional authority, varying according to his or her level of leadership. Thus, as he disciples someone in his group, he has a bit of additional authority because of his leadership position. However, in a one-on-one relationship, he definitely needs to focus on the relational and knowledge influence in his leadership. Thinking very much about positional authority tends to move us in a direction away from humility, as a husband or as a parent or as a leader over thousands. People are always going to be motivated much more righteously through relationship than through anyone's position. That's why positional authority in the church must never be exercised in isolation from the other two types of authority. Even Paul was quite reticent about appealing to his authority as an apostle.

> This is why I write these things when I am absent, that when I come I may not have to be harsh in my use of authority—the authority the Lord gave me for building you up, not for tearing you down (2 Corinthians 13:10).

In the situation where church staff members are discipling other staff members, something of an "employer/employee" relationship is involved. Therefore, some positional authority is included because of that aspect of the relationship. Perhaps we could make a helpful distinction in the cases where some positional authority is inherent. *If the discipling directly relates to the discipler's group leadership, some positional authority would be appropriately exercised.* Otherwise, it would not. In other words, if the group has been asked to do something as a group, then the group leader would have the responsibility and right to deal with that request as the leader, even with individuals in the group. Since his discipleship partner is likely in his group, when addressing the group's assignment, he would be giving direction as the group leader, even in a private setting.

Frankly, I am not interested in trying to settle every possible question in this area, for that would be approaching the subject with a wrong mind-set. The husband who does not lead by love and servanthood, and feels the necessity to cry out, "I'm the boss around here!" has already lost his case. Any church leader who is highly conscious of his "position" is in trouble already. Leaders need to think "role and responsibility," not "position and authority." We must be servant leaders like him who actually possessed all authority. The best counsel for those being discipled is just keep a humble heart and a submissive spirit. Don't start reasoning "If he doesn't have authority, then why should I have a submissive spirit?" Go back and read the earlier chapters of the book. The two apostles who had the most authority of *every* type had a word for all of us, discipler and disciple alike: "Submit to one another out of reverence for Christ" (Ephesians 5:21); "All of you, clothe yourselves with humility toward one another, because, 'God opposes the proud but gives grace to the humble'" (1 Peter 5:5).

Conclusion

In conclusion, since authority in God's kingdom is a part of his plan to save our individual souls and those of the world, let's keep in mind the basics of submission to God-ordained leadership. Submission is *not*:

- Obeying only when you are in agreement with the direction given.
- Obeying only outwardly, without heart involvement and positive attitudes.
- Obeying only when you think the leader has led in just the right manner.

- Obeying without speaking your mind and sharing your viewpoint. Stuffing your feelings is not proper submission (and it gives you spiritual indigestion!).
- Obeying only a part of the directions given (sometimes called "filtering"). This is deceptive and dishonest. If you are having difficulty agreeing with the directions, keep talking until you and the leader are in harmony.
- Continuing to seek advice until you find someone who will say what you want to hear. In such cases, you are likely sharing only the facts in the situation which will help you get your way. You should always be in harmony with everyone who gives you advice, even if you do decide to go in a different direction. Keep talking until everybody involved feels good about the situation.

Submission is:
- A willingness to be persuaded and to be unified with those leading.
- A recognition that submission is a great producer of humility and that God always blesses humility.
- A deep conviction that God leads through the leaders whom he has raised up, and that to follow these leaders, human though they are, is to follow God.

God's provision of leadership is truly a blessing in our lives. The order he has established in the universe and in his church is both logical and powerful. May we trust his authority by trusting the authority he has ordained in his kingdom and may we all, leader and follower alike, remain clothed with humility.

14

THE CHALLENGE
OF CHANGE

✠

Is change a challenge for you? If you think about your answer for a moment, it will probably come back as yes and no. However, my guess is that the majority of us would have an immediate reaction of no, even though we could think of many things we would like to see change. We are at many levels resistant to change. Changes in our hometown neighborhoods, even if under the umbrella of progress, are disappointing to us. Once we have become comfortable with almost anything, we hate to hear the word "change." Admittedly, sometimes change signals bad things. Declining health, downsizing in our companies, divorce, children going through the tough stages, and any one of a number of other things are examples of negative change.

On the other hand, each of us, I'm sure, could probably think of a long list of things we would give almost anything to see changed. A reversal of the few things mentioned above would be good for starters. In between the obviously positive and the obviously negative are the kinds of changes which may strike us as bad, but are really quite good. *Spiritual growth is a positive, but the process through which it comes may seem negative.* Faith is learning to look at life and its challenges with a heavenly perspective, and when it still doesn't make sense, to trust God anyway. Romans 8:28 ("...in all things God works for the good of those who love him and are called according to his purpose") is an oft-quoted verse, but our emotions don't handle it nearly as well as our intellects. However, in it God lays his reputation on the line by saying that he can and will bring good out of every situation.

But the qualifier is that we must keep the faith and keep looking for the good that he promised.

In this chapter, we will examine the challenge of looking at life through the eyes of God, which, as might be suspected, will vary from the way we would naturally look at it. Our seemingly built-in resistance to change, especially changes which make demands on us, must be dealt with if we are to become the disciples and disciplers we were designed to be. As we address the various challenges, we will try to give the spiritual perspectives most typically needed by both disciple and discipler. We need to keep our minds and hearts open—God wants to change them both! Seeing through his eyes will help us be happier and more productive.

Changes in Ministry

When I was growing up, we went to a small neighborhood church which was attended by the same people year in and year out. We didn't grow, and we didn't shrink. (At the size we were, we couldn't have shrunk much anyway!) For the past dozen years, I have been a part of discipling churches in which spiritual and numeric growth make almost constant change necessary. We may change ministry configuration. We may change where we meet on Sundays, since rented facilities are the norm for most of us in discipling ministries. We may change leaders. We may change nomenclature. (Are our groups of twenty to forty now "house churches," "discipleship groups," "family groups," "mission teams" or what?!) Such changes drive some people "up a wall"! How should we feel about all the changes?

The early church provides a dramatic illustration. They grew from 120 to 3,120 in one day! Can you imagine the logistical problems which faced them? They continued to grow rapidly in Jerusalem, and when they did start spreading to other cities, the multiplication of disciples was continuous. (How could it have been otherwise, since they were following the Master's plan of evangelism?) Missionaries like Paul were here, there and everywhere. And in his training of other ministers, they became much like him: "movers and shakers."

Why should we be surprised or upset by the same kinds of ministry changes in our day? It took that to carry out the Great

Commission in the first century, and it will take nothing less to-day. Being a part of a movement committed to reaching the lost at home and abroad will, of necessity, put us all in the middle of fairly constant ministry changes. In the days of the Judges the Israelites wanted a king so they could be like the other nations. I sometimes wonder if those among us who dread changes aren't more influenced by the churches around us, with their apathetic "stability," than they are by the Bible. I do know that there are some downsides to ministry change and that such changes should be made with care, but overall, we can expect to live in a state of flux until we go to heaven. Having been a part of churches for years that didn't change, I am most thankful to be in one which continues to change due to increasing numbers and a plan to evangelize the world. We need to adjust our attitudes if they tend to be negative about ministry changes in general.

But, let's be more specific. When churches reconfigure them-selves, often even the smaller group levels are affected. Changes in discipleship partners can be a part of the package. How do you personally feel about those changes? We should feel some amount of godly regret, for although we should remain very close friends, the amount of contact will in all probability lessen. However, we should also feel excited about the opportunity to develop another very close spiritual relationship with a different person. If we have a worldly view of friendships, we may feel that our new disciple-ship partners can never measure up to our last ones. It is true that the new one can never take the *place* of the old one, just as one child cannot take the place of another child in a family. But a mother can keep loving each new child born to her with a special love that does not reduce the love felt for her previous children. The same principle applies to having a new discipleship partner. Remember, the more we become like God, the more people we are able to love more deeply.

When ministry changes come, even those which affect our discipling relationships, we need to learn to build great relation-ships quickly with the new people in our lives. A wonderful bibli-cal example of how to quickly develop love and loyalty to a new leader is seen in 2 Samuel 15. David and his men were fleeing from Jerusalem at the time of Absalom's rebellion, and some

Gittites were in his company. David gave one of their leaders the opportunity to leave, but he refused. His reply should be an upward call to all of us regarding realigning loyalties to new leadership quickly:

> The king said to Ittai the Gittite, "Why should you come along with us? Go back and stay with King Absalom. You are a foreigner, an exile from your homeland. You came only yesterday. And today shall I make you wander about with us, when I do not know where I am going? Go back, and take your countrymen. May kindness and faithfulness be with you."
>
> But Ittai replied to the king, "As surely as the LORD lives, and as my lord the king lives, wherever my lord the king may be, whether it means life or death, there will your servant be" (2 Samuel 15:19-21).

The end result of that loyalty was that Ittai soon became one of three captains in David's entire army!

> David mustered the men who were with him and appointed over them commanders of thousands and commanders of hundreds. David sent the troops out—a third under the command of Joab, a third under Joab's brother Abishai son of Zeruiah, and a third under Ittai the Gittite. The king told the troops, "I myself will surely march out with you" (2 Samuel 18:1-2).

As I look back on the people I have been discipled by, I see that I learned some invaluable lessons from each. They had different strengths and weaknesses, but I believe that God had important lessons to share with me through them that have changed my life. As I think about those whom I have discipled, I would not take anything for the experiences. I also learned valuable lessons from them, and perhaps more importantly, I learned to love each of them deeply, thus becoming more like God. Some of the changes were hard ones for me emotionally, but looking back, I would have not have grown as I have without the changes, nor would I have developed such a case of "enlargement of the heart"! Don't fear changes in the ministry—embrace them. Trust that God is in control and that he will make it all work together for good.

Perhaps you have experienced ministry changes of another sort. Maybe you were a leader who found your role diminished. How do you deal with such changes, that may cause you to doubt yourself or God or both? I have seen some lose leadership roles, even ministry staff roles, and leave God as a result. How sad! I also have seen many face the changes with faith. As I think about the membership of the Boston church, I can think of many who once were in ministry positions or other leadership roles who are not in them now. I see most of them still faithfully serving God, in spite of changes in their roles. I love and respect them immensely. They are "blooming where they are planted," and doing their best for God. They are imitators of David, who once said, "I would rather be a doorkeeper in the house of my God than dwell in the tents of the wicked" (Psalm 84:10). Is this your attitude?

Why do you serve God? If the answer is anything besides love for him and appreciation for your salvation, you are going to have problems. I love the fellowship of the church and the love of my brothers and sisters, but that is not why I became a part of the kingdom. I am very thankful to be a leader, but that is not why I am in the kingdom. If I had relationship problems in the church, even very serious ones, I wouldn't leave. Nor would I leave if I were relieved of my leadership roles. I signed up with the army of God, led by his Commander, Jesus Christ, and it is a lifetime commitment. Upon enlistment, I made the good confession, "Jesus is Lord." No change nor any amount of change could possibly alter that commitment, for he was the Lord of my life then, he is now and he always will be. Changes will come and changes will go, but disciples must adapt and accept, embrace and enlarge. And we must disciple one another to do this. God will bless us through it all in ways we could never predict!

Aging Gracefully

As one with a "child of the '60s" mind-set, the idea of aging isn't particularly appealing to me. I still think of myself as being about thirty, as difficult as that may be to comprehend. One of the reasons for my reluctance to think of myself as an older man is because I have observed too many people who have developed hardening of the attitudes along with hardening of the arteries. Old age shows the exact direction in which we have been pointing during our earlier years. Most old folks are either really pleasant or really sour. I do not enjoy being around old "grouches," and I definitely don't want to end up as one myself!

Although we are addressing mainly the issue of aging chronologically, aging spiritually often ushers in similar dynamics. Those inclined to be cynical are saying or thinking things similar to these about discipling relationships: "I've heard that before"; "You can't legislate friendships"; or "I've never found those kind of relationships." We simply cannot allow ourselves or those we are discipling to join the "negativizers" in our world and continue in their cynicism.

Having said that, aging is a challenge, and it ushers in some genuine difficulties. I learned some lessons from my father about these difficulties. He was a young thinker and remained very physically active until just before he died. But when others on the job started viewing him as too old to do certain things, it took a toll on his self-esteem. He began to "think old" at that point. After retirement, his finances were more limited and more bothersome to him. At age sixty-five he was diagnosed with cancer, and for the final six years of his life, that battle affected him physically and emotionally in some very sad ways. I hate being sick, and the thought of going through what he went through to die is frightening to me. We must have a really close walk with the Lord to play the "end game" well. And we will need the compassion of Christ to help those who are going through the loop before us. Discipling older people has its special challenges and special opportunities.

To Older Disciples

First, a word to the older ones. If you are being discipled by younger people, it is important to share what is in your heart with them—the aches and pains, the fears and the faith. But two cautions are in order for you as you share. One, don't let yourself become focused on your difficulties. Share how you are feeling, and then move on to the areas in your life over which you still have some control. I have asked some older people the simple question, "How are you today?" and received a long medical report. Some people seem to "enjoy" poor health for years—don't be one of them. Learn how to unload your burdens honestly and quickly, and then turn to conversation which is "helpful for building others up according to their needs, that it may benefit those who listen" (Ephesians 4:29).

Second, don't expect people to fully understand all that you feel and are going through. It won't happen until they get there. A few years back, our "nest" emptied as our children grew up and left home. Most of our closest friends in the ministry are younger than we and did not understand the emotional hit we were facing. Now, as some of them are beginning to reach that stage of life, they are understanding for the first time what it feels like to walk into that freshly vacated bedroom. We all get our turn, don't we? And at times we feel like it's "too soon old and too late smart." When you feel that others just don't understand, you may be quite right. But don't get hurt and embittered—God understands and can help you, in order that you then can help those coming behind you through the doors of middle age and beyond.

One of my favorite biblical characters is Caleb, whose youthful heart rose above the limitations of his body. As he requested the opportunity to fight giants for the mountainous territory, he made this amazing comment:

> "Now then, just as the LORD promised, he has kept me alive for forty-five years since the time he said this to Moses, while Israel moved about in the desert. So here I am today, eighty-five years old! I am still as strong today as the day Moses sent me out; I'm just as vigorous to go out to battle now as I was then" (Joshua 14:10-11).

When we die let us die with the sword of the Spirit (Ephesians 6:17) in our hand. For a soldier in the army of God, there can be no putting us out to pasture. Our retirement is heaven, and until we reach its shores, we must stay in the battle of changing the face of eternity. Older brother or sister, don't give up and don't give in! Be a Caleb, and ask for the hill country where the giants live. We may not be physically stronger than the young ones, but we are more experienced and "faith-toughened," and with God's help, more equipped to fight than ever before. Don't sell yourself (or him) short!

To Younger Disciplers

Second, a few thoughts for younger disciplers of older people: To begin with, *respect* them. To really do this, you must recognize the chasm between God's view of older people and society's view. In America, age is most often seen as a burdensome liability. However, God says,

> The glory of young men is their strength,
> gray hair the splendor of the old (Proverbs 20:29).

> Do not rebuke an older man harshly, but exhort him as if he were your father (1 Timothy 5:1).

> Young men, in the same way be submissive to those who are older (1 Peter 5:5).

As one who is older than the large majority of those in the Boston church, I encounter mostly respectful attitudes in disciples. But as would be expected, we come into the kingdom with attitudes affected (and infected) by the world, and some of us have not figured out God's heart on this one yet. Check your own heart out in this area. Do you really respect older disciples, or just act like you do? What's in the recesses of your heart? You are going to be one of us soon, and God's law of the harvest is that you will reap what you sow. Better to figure it out now rather than later.

Another thought for younger disciplers: *Trust* older disciples. Sometimes in our fear of being too sentimental or "soft" on them, we don't accept at face value what they tell us. We may be prone to think they are making excuses when they are actually sharing valid reasons for what they have done or cannot do. Suspicion is a harsh cloud under which to live. If you have difficulty accepting what another person says, be honest without being accusatory and ask for clarification. Say something along these lines: "I'm not sure I understand what you are saying or feeling, but I want to. Help me understand better." After you have seriously listened and tried to understand their perspective, then pray and do what you think best—or if unsure, get advice from another person. Just remember that love "always protects, always trusts, always hopes, always perseveres" (1 Corinthians 13:7).

Love also calls others to be their best for God. Don't be sentimental, and don't be overly fearful of being sentimental. Call it like you see it, but first understand age for what it is. Our bodies come from dust and will return to it, but our spirits come directly from God (Zechariah 12:1; Hebrews 12:9). They are essentially ageless, being capable of living eternally. Paul put it in perspective with this comment:

> Therefore we do not lose heart. Though outwardly we are wasting away, yet inwardly we are being renewed day by day (2 Corinthians 4:16).

Our bodies are wasting away (ouch!), but our spirits can stay young in Christ. It's a mind-set, and you need to help those older ones you disciple to keep thinking young.

Of all people, disciples should stay young longer. They have something to live for and something to die for. They are in a win/win situation: They can have their cake and eat it too. I remember George Gurganus belting out sermons well into his seventies, excited to be alive and excited to have a purpose in the kingdom. Let's not allow him to be a kingdom exception. Aging gracefully means that we are "full of grace." Paul was driven by grace to outwork all of his younger cohorts (1 Corinthians 15:10). Let's help older disciples to imitate his spirit!

Life-Situation Changes

Family Challenges

Through the years, many changes in our life situations will occur, especially regarding family. Singles will get married, and some marrieds will become single once again. Children will be born, and some couples will learn that having two children doubles the work load, while three *quadruples* it (or so I am told)! Nothing becomes simpler or easier, and often these changes usher in many new pressures and challenges far beyond anything anticipated. When life tumbles in on top of us, we must maintain our convictions as disciples, and get the discipling needed to not only survive, but thrive.

At each new stage of family change, the load will, at first, seem unbearable. In fact, when any part of life brings new levels of responsibilities, we will have to grow into the job.

When my friends are feeling overwhelmed by such challenges, I enjoy sharing a passage from Jeremiah with them. In it, the prophet was becoming burdened by a good case of the "whelms," and God had a rather surprising answer to his problem:

> "If you have raced with men on foot
>   and they have worn you out,
>   how can you compete with horses?
> If you stumble in safe country,
>   how will you manage in the thickets by the Jordan?"
>   (Jeremiah 12:5).

Wow! What a comforting thought! Was God simply taunting him? It may seem like that, but God is always solution oriented. He is forcing his prophet to face the sometimes harsh realities of life. Back when God called Jeremiah, he told him of the challenges he would be facing and promised to enable him to rise to the occasion. Read especially Jeremiah 1:17-19. God did not promise him a nice comfortable life free of challenges. He promised just the opposite.

The beginning place in dealing with the challenges is in deciding to grab life by the throat and refuse to let its problems win. Frankly, many of us have weak characters and are ill-equipped to handle the pressures life will certainly bring. But we are going to have to quit thinking like couch potatoes and toughen up! Life's problems may all be solved in the last fifteen minutes of a TV show, but we are not talking about life as we might wish it were; we are talking about reality. Countless generations of people have lived on this earth during times which were far more difficult than anything we might face. As disciples, we must be determined to become, with God's help, "a fortified city, an iron pillar and a bronze wall" (Jeremiah 1:18). Believe it or not, this determination is the beginning point in dealing with what feels like immense challenges brought on by family changes.

But now let's turn to the advice needed by disciplers who are trying to help others meet these challenges. When a person gets married, they have less time for other things, even good things. Paul said it quite plainly in 1 Corinthians 7:33-34. A newly married person cannot use this new responsibility as an excuse, but neither can a discipler have unrealistic expectations for them. When children come, more time must be given to the family, which, of necessity, leaves less time for former activities. The additions cannot interfere with our being disciples, but as disciples, our family responsibilities cannot be neglected. Neglecting family is simply not an option for a disciple. The tragedy of losing one's own children spiritually cannot be described in mere words. The word "balance" could be used to rationalize an uncommitted life-style, but it does convey a correct idea when trying to keep all of life's plates spinning at the same time.

Most problems in discipling those with increased responsibilities come when the discipler has less of these same responsibilities. If the family setting of the disciple and discipler are about the same, the discipler will understand the new responsibilities and will advise accordingly. However, if the discipler has less responsibilities in life than the one he disciples, misunderstandings are more likely to occur. In either case, talking openly about the demands on one's schedule will result in striking the right balance. The biggest need for the discipler is to develop the wisdom and discernment to accurately determine when a person is genuinely overwhelmed and when they just *feel* that way and need an attitude adjustment like God gave Jeremiah. A listening ear, an understanding heart, an honest tongue and a helping hand are the solution to discipling those facing such times. Life will not get easier; therefore, we must get stronger.

Occupational Challenges

Losing or finding a job introduces change and added pressures. The first carries the pressure of adapting to unemployment while trying to land a new job, and the other carries the pressure of learning a new job in the midst of a new environment with new associates. Who of us has never been "caught up" by career and finances? Who of us has never felt overwhelmed by the loss of a job or the challenge of walking into a new one? Maintaining our disciple's commitment in these situations requires much prayer and much help from those discipling us. If we don't stay strong, we may enter a spiritual "fog" and not emerge until months later, having incurred significant damage along the way.

For the most part, I think we disciple one another pretty well in these situations, because they are common to all of us, and we know the ropes reasonably well. However, if the discipler has a less demanding job than the one he disciples, he may not be as understanding as he needs to be. In such cases, the discipler should himself seek additional advice from strong disciples who have similar job challenges to the one being advised. Some careers are going to demand more time and energy commitments than others, but if we are going to reach people for Christ from all parts of society, we are going to have to be there to do it. However, some can handle the pressures of more demanding careers, while others cannot. All of us must keep evaluating our heart's involvement in our careers. Working to live is one thing, but living to work is yet another. Much talk, much prayer and much advice will ultimately provide the answers needed.

An important area which is often overlooked in discipling is how to advise disciples who are *underemployed*. We need to help people look farther down the path of their future than they may want to do. And we will need to adjust to their having less time available when they go back to school or get more training to put themselves on a real career track. If we are leading a ministry group, their reduced availability may leave some bases uncovered, but long-range planning is a must if we are going to disciple the "whole person." These situations are common and need attention, but the choices are often hard ones to make. Disciple, seek advice about this vital area of career future. Discipler, help your friend to live up to his potential in a career. He and the kingdom will be better off for it in the long term, in spite of some sacrifices in the short term.

Health Challenges

By now, many practical suggestions have been made for dealing with changes in life which definitely apply to health challenges as well. But in a young movement with a preponderance of younger disciples, we are mostly treading on new territory in this area, but "times they are a-changin'." Growing older is certainly related to facing health challenges, but there are some significant differences. Growing older is gradual, and reversals in health are often more sudden. Age can be seen by the gray hair and the wrinkles, but chronic health problems often cannot be seen on the surface. What should be our approach in facing serious changes in our own health, and what should be our approach to discipling those who are ill?

This question is a good one, for good health is not guaranteed forever, and unless we die suddenly, we are going to face serious and terminal illnesses. About a year ago, I attended our PC Ministry devotional. No, PC doesn't stand for either politically correct or personal computer: It stands for "Physically Challenged." The people in the group had a wide range of physical problems, from chronic fatigue syndrome, to permanent paralysis, to cancer. A number were in wheelchairs. I was introduced as a TAB, which, I was informed, meant "temporarily able-bodied." I laughed at the time, but I was sobered. How would I do in coping with MS or being a paraplegic or having terminal cancer? Most of us are going to find out at some point, aren't we? Probably all of us are going to disciple people with such challenges, if we are not already.

Earlier in the book I mentioned that I disciple Tom Jones, who has MS. This disease, like chronic fatigue and certain other illnesses, usually invades the body very gradually. It plays a mind game with you. Sufferers wonder, "Is it all in my head?" Worse, they wonder if *others* are wondering that. (And they find out that some are.) Self-doubts rise with the progression of the disease. In trying to assess the situation, they seek advice, and the advice received often varies from one person to another. "Take care of yourself and rest more," says one. "Push through and pay no attention to it," says another. These are tough times for disciple and discipler.

I remember going through times with Tom that left me in tears. My eyes are filling up right now thinking about it. He is as conscientious as any Christian I have ever known, and hard work is his middle name. In the early days after he was officially diagnosed, he needed encouragement just to rest longer without feeling guilty. He needed sensitive advice about making other necessary adjustments. It was not easy, and it still isn't, but God is blessing him and his family tremendously. He has taught me so much about life, and through his book *Mind Change*,[1] he has taught many to face serious challenges of all types with victorious faith.

Rather amazingly, I was interrupted in my first writing of this chapter by a phone call from Courtney and Arlene Russell. Courtney has endured some unusual health challenges for a decade and is suffering from lymphoma right now. His first bout with serious illness came ten years ago, when he was about thirty-five years old, in the form of an aneurysm in the brain. He came close to death, but thankfully survived. Since then, he has suffered from varied and strange diseases, and most recently from cancer. Through all of it, he has remained very spiritually active in people's lives and very faithful in the face of his various conditions. He nearly died again last summer, but the fifty of us praying in the hospital waiting room moved God to pull him through the ordeal. Now he is undergoing the most intense treatment I have ever heard about as the doctors are trying to clear his body, blood and bone marrow of this deadly disease.

As we talked tonight, I asked him to share with me (and you) his insights about the role discipling has played and is playing in his life. He said what he needed most were brothers with whom to share his heart and to pray. He went on to mention the importance of other people being willing to talk about his health condition and the possibility of his death without feeling weird. But he also said that even though his condition may be terminal, he and others still need to have faith that God can heal him. Surrender includes looking at the worst possible alternative and being willing to accept it if God wills, but then stating faithfully our preferences. This process of surrender, according to Courtney, is a daily affair.

He is one of those men who looks and acts well even when he is very seriously ill. He is not avoiding reality and putting up a strong front. He is just focused on trying to give to others no matter how he may be feeling. Of course, this is an admirable trait, but it means that we have to ask how he really feels and what he needs from us as we try to help bear his burdens.

Sometimes we think that bringing the subject up may cause the sick person to become emotionally down. Don't worry about that, because a person with cancer never gets it out of their mind anyway. They just need a friend who will share in their pain, their fear, their prayers, their faith, their family and whatever future God grants them. Courtney has had many brothers who have shared in his life, and in turn he has shared his life with them in a profound, faith-building way. Discipleship is no theory with people like Courntney and Tom. They would tell you that they would not want to live without being a disciple.

Conclusion

Make no mistake about it—changes can be challenging. As disciples, we must trust God, stay kingdom-focused, embrace the challenge of change and radiate a faithful spirit in all circumstances. As disciplers, we must learn to be as empathetic and sympathetic as possible in helping disciples face their challenges, without compromising Jesus' standard for discipleship in any way. As I think about both roles, it seems to me that spirituality is our greatest need the spirituality to stay focused and faithful no matter what comes down the highway of life. The spirituality to discern the whole life picture of those we are trying to help and to love them enough to pay whatever price is necessary in order to serve them. May God help us to grow and to help others grow, and to grow some more. Then we can face the challenge of change squarely and remain victorious, even when the change involves leaving this life and entering eternity. "So we fix our eyes not on what is seen, but on what is unseen. For what is seen is temporary, but what is unseen is eternal" (2 Corinthians 4:18). Amen!

15

GROUP DISCIPLING

✠

After years of trying to make it on their own, many people in our society are once again realizing their need for groups. We have support groups for those who are trying to lose weight, overcome addictions, adjust to the deaths of family members, or deal with a number of other challenges. We have special-interest groups of all types, and those conversant with the Internet have opportunity to tie in to others all over the world with the same interests. Independence will last only so long. Eventually, human beings feel the need to be in groups. God made us to need each other.

It should come as no surprise that groups in the Bible receive special emphasis. Group discipling was common in the ministry of Jesus. Relating to one's discipler is one thing, but relating to one's peers is yet another. Discipleship groups reveal some things about character which may not be revealed any other way. Unrighteous competitiveness is most likely to be exposed in such settings, as Matthew 20:20-28 well demonstrates.

The group dynamic enables everyone to help and be helped in a powerful way. The "think tank" setting spawns ideas through synergistic creativity which will help everyone to be more effective as disciples. Also, Jesus was able to simply save time in his training of the apostles by giving his more general directions only once. He did use individual times for meeting more specific needs, such as the conversation in John 21 with Peter. Perhaps an equally important benefit of group discipling is the humility demanded by being a part of such groups. Any setting which encourages humility is bound to have great potential for bringing blessings into our lives, for God always rewards this quality bountifully.

Jesus and His Use of Groups

The Book of Mark contains some very helpful examples of group discipling times. As we go through them, you will notice that a number of different lessons were taught in these settings. In each account, we will try to determine the chief reason for Jesus' use of group discipling.

Asking: What Did You Learn?

After Jesus had taught the crowds in Mark 7:14-23 about what makes men "unclean," he answered questions from the disciples in a more private setting. I am sure they appreciated the privacy since Jesus prefaced his remarks with the question, "Are you so dull?" The point is that Jesus was showing them how to deal with the tough issues in a large crowd setting, and they had missed the biblical application intended. The apostles had failed, but at least they had failed together! Joys are increased by sharing them with others, and pains are decreased by sharing them with others.

Why do you think Jesus used the group setting here? The text itself indicates that he gave the apostles a more detailed explanation than he gave the crowd. This should come as no surprise, since our basic premise is that most of what he did, even with crowds, was to prepare the apostles for their future work in spreading the gospel. One of the most effective ways to train others is to do something in a real-life situation and then ask those who observed what they learned. The approach works great whether a sermon has been delivered to a large group or a counseling session has been conducted with one or two people. Ask questions that cause the trainees to think, such as: "What did you learn?" "Why did I do...?" "Would you have done anything differently?" "Why?" Their answers will set the stage for the whole group to learn from one another. Never miss an opportune moment to teach following an activity.

Surfacing Needs

In the classic passage containing Peter's good confession (Mark 8:27-33), Peter went from hero to goat in a matter of minutes! He at least had the presence of mind to take Jesus aside to rebuke him, but perhaps he should have taken him further away from the other apostles! The text informs us that "when Jesus turned and looked at his disciples, he rebuked Peter. 'Get behind me, Satan!' he said" (Mark 8:33). The following verse says that Jesus called the whole crowd to join the disciples as he continued teaching the point Peter had missed.

Perhaps the key lesson from this group-discipling setting is that input from a small group helps the leader determine what is needed in larger groups. This principle is one of the most helpful for leaders, especially since we do not have the perfect insight that Jesus had. A select group gives you a "feel" for the larger groups in two ways. One, they are a representative sampling of the larger group. What they need is probably quite similar to what the whole group needs. Two, being a part of the larger group makes their input about the needs of the group valuable. A wise leader uses both of these avenues to gain insight into the larger groups he is trying to influence.

Dealing with Failure

In Mark 9:14-32, Jesus was focused on the process of building faith. When Jesus came down from his mountaintop experience of being transfigured, he quickly entered the valley of reality. His disciples had tried to cast a demon out of a young boy and had failed. Evidently they were arguing with the teachers of the law in self-defense. The whole situation frustrated Jesus, as verse 19 indicates: "'O unbelieving generation,' Jesus replied, 'how long shall I stay with you? How long shall I put up with you?'" He then turned to the father of the child and found that his faith was also weak. After censuring him for weak faith, he healed the boy and then took the apostles indoors for further teaching about the situation at hand.

He had allowed them to experience failure because of a deficiency in faith and then to observe another person (the father) with the same kind of deficiency. Now that the experiment was complete in the laboratory of life, they were prepared to see the point. They had cast out demons before, and perhaps were overly confident this time. Or maybe the exact opposite was true. Since Peter, James and John had been on the mountain with Jesus and his OT friends, the others may have been low on confidence in the absence of these key leaders. In either event, they had failed and wanted to know why. Jesus told them that the hard cases required a large amount of faith, which was only available through prayer. (Some manuscripts add "and fasting.") After a failure, nothing deepens the lessons learned more than a group debriefing session. The rest of this text shows that he was preparing them to have enough faith to deal with his impending death. Smaller defeats are often the path of preparing for larger victories, which appears to be Jesus' goal in this small-group setting.

Finding the Target

Mark 9:33-37 provides us with our next example of group discipling. Humility is one of man's greatest needs, and the higher we ascend in leadership, the more of a temptation we might have to become prideful. The apostles were once again arguing about which of them was the greatest! Jesus taught that the measure of greatness was not to be *served by* many, but rather to *serve* many. He drove his point home by using a little child as an object lesson. Can you imagine how the apostles must have felt? One minute they were filled with delusions of grandeur, and the next minute they were looking at a scrawny, dirty little kid and being told that they weren't as great as he or she. The same lesson taught in the midst of a large crowd would have lost much of its sting. Jesus wanted them to feel the full force of seeing where their pride had led them. A small-group setting allows a rebuke to pierce the heart without devastating it, teaching lessons which will never be forgotten.

Mark next gives us the well-known account of James and John seeking the two chief seats of leadership in Jesus' kingdom (Mark 10:35-45). These sons of Zebedee wanted these positions badly enough to enlist the help of their mother. (Actually, she may have volunteered!) The other ten apostles found out about it and were "indignant." Were they concerned over their two brothers' struggle with the pride of position and looking for ways to help them? No, they were in a jealous panic, thinking that they had been beaten to the punch! Groups have a way of revealing hearts. We also may be critical of the request of these two brothers, but we must admire the atmosphere Jesus had created among them, for they were quite open about their ambitions.

Jesus uses the occasion to teach further lessons about humility and servant leadership. Group discipling allowed him to take full advantage of the immediate circumstances. Lessons delivered to a large crowd are by nature somewhat hit-or-miss, in that the most urgent needs of each person cannot be met perfectly. However, in a small group, the target is well in sight and can be hit with pinpoint accuracy.

Reinforcing a Point

Jesus knew that pride and materialism were two of the biggest challenges men face. In Mark 12:41-44, we see him sitting down near the temple to watch for the ideal example of a person who was totally nonmaterialistic. When the poor widow came along and made her amazing sacrifice, he then called the apostles over for a little group session to teach them about financial giving as God views it. They certainly needed the lesson, but they didn't grasp it immediately. As they were leaving the temple area, the apostles were wrestling with what Jesus had just said. They called his attention to the beautiful temple buildings, which only could have been built by the rich and not by the copper coins of widows. Jesus' next statement must have come as quite a shock. He informed them that those beautiful buildings were about to be destroyed. Thus, he reinforced a point about materialism he had made earlier: "What is highly valued among men is detestable in God's sight" (Luke 16:15). Living as apostles would demand a total renunciation of any attachment to material things, a lesson he taught in the most striking way possible.

Inspiration in Groups

Groups not only provide an opportunity for special input and training, but they have a way of inspiring us to go beyond anything we would do all alone. Synergism partly explains what happens, but not completely. One of the most inspirational passages in the Old Testament is 2 Samuel 23:8-23, describing the exploits of David's mighty men. Their heroic feats were the topic of discussion around campfires at night, and the mere mention of their names raised chill bumps on the skin of bright-eyed young-sters all over Israel. David had his group of thirty mighty men, a group of three from within them, and several others for a grand total of thirty-seven mighty men. Without question, their awe-some courage was fanned into greater flames by seeing the deeds of others in the group.

Josheb-Basshebeth, chief of the Three, killed 800 men in one encounter (verse 8). Obviously, he was focused on the "Oddsmaker" and not the odds! Similarly, Eleazar ended up all alone against the Philistines after the Israelites first taunted them and then fled upon their attack (verses 9-10). He "put up" after refusing to "shut up"! When the battle was over, his hand was frozen to the sword, and the enemy lay slain at his feet. Shammah had this same spirit, for when Israel's troops fled from the Philistines, he stood his ground and single-handedly struck the enemy down (verses 11-12). It would seem apparent that the courage of these men gained fuel from the feats of their brothers.

Next came the three who demonstrated loyalty to royalty! David had only to mention his longing for a drink of water from the well near the gate of Bethlehem, and three of his mighty men broke through enemy lines to get it (verses 13-17). David was filled with such appreciation and amazement that he poured it out as an offering to God, calling it the "blood" of his men. In verses 18-19, we read about Abishai, who raised his spear against 300 men and killed them. In fact, even though he was not a part of the Three, he became more famous than they were and ended up being their commander. He was undaunted by the fact that he was not originally a part of this very select group, for he be-lieved that only the aimless remain nameless.

My favorite mighty man is Benaiah (verses 20-23). He was famous for some unusual feats of valor. He killed two of Moab's best fighting men, and struck down a huge Egyptian armed with a spear while he was armed with only a club. He also went down into a pit on a snowy day and killed a lion. I've always imagined that the army was taking a "snow day" off from their battles and were playing games back in the tents. Benaiah was not to be sat-isfied without a battle raging, so he wandered off in the snow looking for a fight. Finding none of the enemy to engage, he came across a lion who had fallen into a pit and couldn't get enough traction in the snow to escape. Behaiah's eyes brightened up, and he slid down the snowy bank of the pit, ready for action. I can picture the faces of the men back in camp when he arrived dragging the lion, covered with blood, grinning from ear to ear. In dynamic groups God can raise up more warriors like this one, who replaced his "zestlessness" with restlessness and went looking for a battle!

Groups have a remarkable ability to inspire courage. I can remember the first time I stood up on a little box and took my turn at public preaching in a park in London. I remember the rather hostile crowd, but I especially remember the small band of brothers with whom I stood. Later I took groups of brothers out to do the same thing, and it bonded us in a very special way. It may not be the wisest nor most effective way in our sophisticated society to sow the seed, but it definitely provides those who are doing it with an adrenaline "rush" and a great lesson in boldness. The thought of doing that kind of public proclamation all alone would be foreboding, but doing it in a group is an adventure. After such occasions, we felt like we were *Davids* fighting *Goliaths* as soldiers of the Most High God!

And the "thrill of victory" can be experienced in activities which are not by design spiritual activities (though we must all remain spiritual while doing them!). Several years ago, my wife, Theresa, was leading a discipleship group of single women leaders. Once, about midnight, she took them to Bob and Pat Gempel's home. At the back of their property, a rope swing hung from a tall tree that could be used to transport its rider high over a swamp. It was definitely exhilarating in the daytime, but doing it for the first time in pitch dark was just plain *scary*. Years later, that group of women still talk about that night when they literally jumped off the bank and out of their comfort zones. The courage and camaraderie developed together paid dividends later in spiritual settings. God needs some mighty men and some mighty women today, and we need to pray for ways to take our discipleship groups into the realm of adventure in order to build courage, character and closeness. Groups have great potential for this sort of thing—don't waste it!

Wisdom in Groups

Wisdom rises to the surface better in groups than through any other means available. Jesus referred to this principle of group wisdom in Matthew 18:19-20:

> "Again, I tell you that if two of you on earth agree about anything you ask for, it will be done for you by my Father in heaven. For where two or three come together in my name, there am I with them."

This statement followed his directions for dealing with unrepentant sin by ultimately taking it before the church, if nothing else induced repentance. For much of my life I have heard the last sentence used to show that God is with a small church or group, even if only two or three come together. That is not the context. God is also with less than two or three, if I understand my Bible— he is even with *one!* The context is the wisdom of a group and how God provides his wisdom through it.

Coming to decisions by the use of group consensus is God's plan. The reading of Acts 6 (where the seven are chosen to oversee the process of providing for the widows) and Acts 15 (the Jerusalem Conference) demonstrate how the early church followed this plan. I trust the wisdom of spiritually minded individuals, and the more spiritually mature they are, the more I value their opinions. But I value a group's opinion more than that of any one person, no matter who he is. When I first came to Boston, I was privileged to be in leadership groups with Kip and Elena McKean, Al and Gloria Baird and Bob and Pat Gempel—ground-floor leaders in the early Boston church. I learned much about *spiritual* group dynamics.

In the early Boston group, I can recall Kip making statements like this one: "Well, here is my idea of what I think is best, but you may throw me and my idea out the window!" And with that introduction, he would lead a lively discussion. Like all great leaders, he surrounds himself with strong and outspoken people who are willing to "mix it up" in discussions. But they are *spiritually* strong and can be persuaded with godly reasoning. Time after time, I saw consensus reached as God was allowed to lead the group to his decisions. For someone coming out of my background, it was quite remarkable and certainly faith building.

Through the years since that time, I have learned to trust the wisdom reached in groups far more than the wisdom of individuals, including my own. When I have faced some of my most difficult personal decisions, I have asked for the wisdom of our top leadership group time and time again. At points, I would have to bring my emotionalism and sentimentality under submission, because the decisions involved me and my family and were highly important to us. But looking back on the last nine years, my faith in God to work through a spiritual group has been rewarded in an unbelievable way. Sure, religious groups led by arrogant and self-serving leaders who neither ground their message in Scripture nor welcome input from others who are committed to Scripture, have resulted in some terrible tragedies in our world. And there will surely be more of these. But we should still trust the way God works through groups of godly men and women who are humble personally and privately. Collective wisdom is available in any discipleship group, and more importantly, God is available to bless the sharing of group wisdom with his own wisdom. My prayer in such group settings is for God to help us follow his agenda and reach his conclusions. Experience has proved to me that he has faithfully and repeatedly answered that prayer.

Practical Suggestions

Recently, I have been giving thought to some ways that ministry leaders could use groups to better move the work of the church forward. Some groups are formal, in that they are organized for a certain purpose—like a house-church-sized ministry group. Surely we need to utilize the power in such groups. But others are informal, in that people who share things in common tend to feel a certain connection. For example, single moms typically will find other single moms and become friends, for they face similar challenges. Newer disciples are drawn to others like themselves, and disciples who have been in the kingdom a long time will feel a bond with other "veterans." Of all the informal groups in the church, and there are a number, I am perhaps most concerned about this veteran group. I am not alarmed, but I ensure that they continue to contribute their best to the kingdom and that they do not develop the maladies of "spiritual aging" mentioned in Revelation 2 and 3. I have heard too many comments about those with spiritual longevity who are not living up to their potential. But what can be done about it? Groups, like individuals, have distinct personalities. Therefore, groups respond best to the same approaches that work best with individuals in the group. Simple enough, right? What kind of leadership motivates a person who has been a disciple for a long time and has lost some of his idealism and excitement (and who may have become downright cynical)? They cannot successfully be treated as young Christians who really don't know much. Being highly directive without providing them with the opportunity for input is certain to come up short in gaining the needed cooperation and participation. Let me hasten to add that pure hearts will respond well to immature or insensitive leadership, but why make it difficult?

If older disciples (spiritually older, not necessarily chronologically older) don't feel "pulled in," they will feel unappreciated and disrespected. Maybe it shouldn't be that way, but we are human and we have the need to be shown respect and appreciation. The writers of the New Testament addressed these needs repeatedly. To be treated like a neophyte does not sit well with those of us who are older in the Lord. If you expect those who are older in Christ to respond well to your leadership, you had better figure out some ways to seek their input. Even if they are not living up to their potential, they still have insights which could really benefit your leadership. And if you are a younger leader who sees this approach as either giving in to those you view as bothersome, or trying merely to placate them, you are being prideful and insensitive (and a bit dumb). Periodically, pull together different types of groups, especially the informal types, and seek input. You will be seen as a great leader by them, and you will become that if you are not already. It works!

Growth in Groups

Earlier in the book, I mentioned several discipleship groups of which I was a part and the profound effect they had on me. Some of the most radical and rapid growth possible comes through these kinds of groups. Within a few weeks of moving to Boston, Kip McKean invited me to be in a leader's group with about a dozen other brothers. Many of them were soon to leave Boston to lead mission teams that planted churches in faraway places. It was a wonderful opportunity to develop spiritual bonds with men who were to become my heroes in the faith. Perhaps because Kip knew that many would be leaving the group soon, he made sure that no time was wasted. In one of those early group settings, we had what is often called a "good point/bad point" or "strong point/ weak point" session. Stated more accurately, it is a session in which we help each other to see ourselves more clearly in respect to how we are most like Jesus and most unlike him.

That particular night, we started rather late after other activities were finished for the evening and the children were all tucked into their beds. We took the time to address what we saw in each person. Some in the group knew each other quite well, and others were new acquaintances. Both viewpoints were extremely helpful. Those who knew us best had a very good grasp of many things about us, but had learned to overlook some things (which is not all bad). Those who knew us least were really valuable in helping us understand the first impressions we were making on others. When the group finally ended, it was almost daylight. We were scheduled to meet for a ministry staff meeting in just a few hours, which we did. You might have expected that the staff meeting was dull that day, since a number of us had had almost no sleep. Not so! Spiritual electricity was in the air. We had been lovingly challenged to be more like Jesus, and we were "fired-up" to do it! Those nights will never be forgotten, for their highly positive effects will remain with us for eternity.

A number of different formats for strength/weakness discipleship groups can be used. To preserve time, you can choose to have only one person share about one other person in the group. For example, you can go around the circle and have everyone share about the person to their left or to their right. Or, the leader of the group may choose to do the bulk of the sharing. For younger disciples, go heavier on the "good point" part; and an occasional session with only positives stressed is very encouraging and helpful. But if you have not been a part of such a group, you will be amazed at how much a spiritual critique will be appreciated even in younger groups. In the world, critiques are usually dreaded and dreadful, but in the kingdom, they make us feel really loved. To be sure, pain is involved when the weaknesses are pointed out, but like a trip to the dentist, it does quit hurting after a while, and we feel great about having healthy teeth—or souls! It is an amazing phenomenon.

I remember one night at a leadership retreat with Randy McKean's discipleship group. He had informed us previously that we were going to have the group and that on this night he was going to do most of the evaluating. I was not doing great spiritually at the time, and frankly, I was dreading the group. He either asked who wanted to be discipled first, or talked about deciding who would be first. I definitely was not raising my hand! He started with another brother, and as he lovingly helped him to see his strengths and weaknesses, my sinful resistance started melting away. I can still remember wishing that he had started with me, because I was seeing how much I needed it. After my turn came, I felt very repentant and very loved, and for the rest of the retreat, I felt absolutely awesome. As I write this, I know that we need more of these groups to call us higher for God and closer to one another.

A related use of a discipleship group is found in Matthew 18:15-18. This text tells us that if a brother sins against us and does not respond well to our attempts to resolve the differences, then we should bring back one or two others to help reconcile the problem. Before moving to Boston, I preached for a congregation in San Diego. Gregg Marutzky worked alongside me, leading the campus and singles primarily, while I led the married group. We had desired to work together for years, and finally had the opportunity to do it. God blessed us in many ways. I did most of the preaching, and he did most of the behind-the-scenes work, which was at least as influential as my more visible work. He had been trained in discipleship and discipling far more than I, and frankly, he ended up making me look good!

Although we were the best of friends, we, at times, had our struggles. Being a number of years older than Gregg, I represented the good, bad and ugly of being a father figure. We both came to Boston for more training, with him preceding me by about four months. After I came and experienced the growth produced by participating in a few of the discipleship groups, I talked to Gregg about having Kip (who was discipling me) and Tom (the brother discipling him) sit the two of us down and help us see ourselves more clearly. Although we were actually doing pretty well at the time, Gregg said, "Fine." It was an unforgettable experience. We both saw ourselves as never before, and gained an amazing amount of insight about the underlying issues which had caused the tensions between us. At the end of a long session, he and I were both shedding tears of repentance (James 4:7-10), and since we were all sitting on a carpeted basement floor, Gregg and I walked on our knees to each other, and hugged while we wept. The sins between us were resolved and dissolved, and the bond between us was made permanent and strong. I truly believe that we would die for each other.

The growth prompted in groups is not at all limited to personal spiritual growth. Groups bear fruit together. We help each other learn how to become "fishers of men." We help build relationships and study with the non-Christian friends of our brothers and sisters in the group. No fruit is as sweet as "group fruit." Jesus discussed the shared joys of group fruit in John 4:36-37 in these words:

> "Even now the reaper draws his wages, even now he harvests the crop for eternal life, so that the sower and the reaper may be glad together. Thus the saying 'One sows and another reaps' is true."

Paul further described the same principle in 1 Corinthians 3:6-7:

> I planted the seed, Apollos watered it, but God made it grow. So neither he who plants nor he who waters is anything, but only God, who makes things grow.

The night I wrote this chapter I talked on the phone to my wife's brother Curt, who is a part of a discipling church in Dallas. Last fall (1996), I strongly encouraged my first cousin and his wife (from the other side of the family) to visit Curt and Janet and investigate the church. They made the 200-mile trip and became very excited about seeing discipleship in action. They began studying the Bible with Curt, Janet and a number of others in their ministry group. At the end of December, they were baptized into Christ and have changed about as much as any two people I have ever seen. That night I called Curt just to thank them for the way they have loved, taught and discipled Bill and Donna. He humbly spent some minutes telling about others in the group who have been an integral part of the team effort. Without question, my cousins were fruit borne to God out of a group effort, and without other people like Mike, Chris, Steve and Diane it would not have happened! (And based on my long-distance phone bills, I would add the names of Gordon and Theresa to the list.)

Now that is what it is all about—family reproducing family, a harvest group bearing fruit and a team winning souls to Christ! Praise God! And thank God for the power of groups to change our lives from darkness to light (1 Peter 2:9), and then to keep them changing as we "are being transformed into his likeness with ever-increasing glory" (2 Corinthians 3:18).

16

FAMILY DISCIPLING

The physical family provides us with the model for discipling relationships: Consciously or unconsciously, discipling occurs between husband and wife, parents and children, older children and younger children, and extended family members and their closer relatives. The training given in the family is very broad, ranging from the basics of personal hygiene to the most important moral values of life. Obviously, since spirituality is the most valuable type of training from God's perspective, spiritual discipling in the family must by necessity become the highest priority. The book of Deuteronomy describes this spiritual discipling within the family in many passages, including the famous *Shema:*

> These commandments that I give you today are to be upon your hearts. Impress them on your children. Talk about them when you sit at home and when you walk along the road, when you lie down and when you get up (Deuteronomy 6:6-7).

Such passages make clear why we would say that spiritual discipling is a process of passing on divine principles within the framework of a natural, daily life-style.

In this chapter, we will divide family discipling into three categories: families discipling other families; husbands and wives discipling one another; and parents discipling children. If these principles are practiced faithfully, our families will be bright lights shining in a dark world of dysfunctional, self-destructive families. Ultimately, everyone must come to God because he wants to deal with his sin and respond to God's love. But many begin this divine pursuit through an initial attraction to the marriages and families of disciples. We have, or can have, what the world wants and needs. They may not sense their need for God, but they are highly aware of their need for happy marriages and families. Therefore, let's make sure that we are using everything God has made available to us through discipling relationships. We will be abundantly fulfilled, and we will be magnets which draw others to the kingdom of God.

Families Discipling Families

Families who have been in the Lord longer must pass on to newer families what they have learned about building strong family relationships. Nothing helps newly converted parents learn to disciple each other and their children more than seeing it modeled. Without being able to observe a godly marriage and a godly family at close range, worldly dynamics will continue out of pure ignorance, no matter what the intentions. For this reason, couples should disciple couples, and couples with children should disciple other couples with children of similar ages whenever possible. Once you have gone through the "loop" of any part of life, you are in a most helpful position to lead others through it. Marriage and family dynamics are some of the most important in life, and we need help handling these relationships effectively. If newer converts grow in these areas, they likely will remain faithful to God and be productive in his vineyard. If they are not growing in developing spiritual families, they will often become disillusioned and get into a downward spiritual spiral.

Couples who disciple other couples will most often relate as brother to brother and sister to sister, which is well and good. However, at regular intervals (based on the nature of the marriage) the discipling time should be a foursome. My general observation is that this does not happen often enough in discipling churches. Each of us has his own perspective about our life and our relationships, and without question, our perspective is biased. I may think that I am doing very well, but my wife may have a different perspective. I may think our marriage is hitting on all eight cylinders, and she may think we are running on two! Sometimes those of us who disciple and counsel marriages describe a dynamic that others think is merely a humorous anecdote, complete with a bit of exaggeration to make it funny. But I have had some version of it happen numerous times. It goes like this: You ask the husband how their marriage is doing, and he says, "Great—couldn't be better!" You turn to the wife and ask her the same question–and she bursts into tears. Men and women very often have quite different expectations and evaluations of their marriages.

If you do not have some discipling times with the two couples together, you will not get the most complete picture of each individual. Marriage definitely reveals our inmost character, and our mates see our best and our worst. Therefore, those who disciple us can learn most about us from our marriage dynamics. But without hearing the perspective of both husband and wife together, you will likely have a distorted view, since we are all unwittingly biased.

Several cautions are in order if we are to deal with the inherent bias of all humans. First, accept the fact that you are biased, however unintentional it may be. When your mate describes you or an incident totally differently than you would, don't take it personally and become defensive.

Second, as the discipler, do not come to any strong conclusions by listening to one partner in the marriage. Be assured that the tendency to form those conclusions is real. After all, the person sharing his side of marriage issues is your friend and is sincere in his rendition of things. Keep in mind that each of us is biased, and that biases in marriages are probably the strongest kind. We get "hooked" emotionally in ways here that we do not in other settings, and our perspective thus becomes distorted. I remember my first marriage counseling session as a young minister. The woman came to my office first and described her marriage problems to me. As I took notes, I found myself thinking that her husband was a real lout who needed a swift kick in the pants! The next day when I met with him, and he began describing his marriage, I thought to myself, "Some mistake has been made–he must be someone else's husband." Since I hadn't known them before, I honestly thought that I was dealing with two different marriages. I tried to inconspicuously see the names written on my notes to find out if it was the same marriage or not—and it *was*. Do not underestimate the biases in marriage that all of us have, and don't fail to periodically spend discipling times as couples, gaining the most insight possible into each person's heart and life.

Third, keep the second caution in mind when discipling a person whose mate is not a Christian. Some very serious mistakes are made in this arena which simply must be avoided. A typical case would involve a woman whose husband is not in the church. She describes her marriage situation to the sister who disciples her, and the sister accepts her side of the story as accurate, as do other women in her circle of relationships. When the person describes problems with her non-Christian husband, they think "Poor little disciple. She is married to a terrible husband, and she is to be pitied for being treated unfairly by him." You see, her story sounds quite believable because *she* believes it's all true. But she is biased, and perhaps *very* biased!

Some years back, I was told about a woman in a typical situation of this type who was having serious marriage problems. As a church leader, I was called in to help give her counsel. However, her husband had already called me, even though he was not a member of the church. As might be expected, the two sides of the story were very different. Most of the women counseling the Christian woman were highly sympathetic to her viewpoint. I asked to meet with both husband and wife, which I was able to do. Individually, I heard both sides of the story, and then put both partners together. Without going into detail, suffice it to say that the woman had as much fault in the marriage as the man, and in my judgment, even more. But she was viewed by the women in her life as "poor little mistreated disciple," and as a result, she was neither discipled correctly nor helped. Do not fall into that trap! Disciple the Christian partner in these cases to go the way of the cross described in 1 Peter 2:18-3:7, no matter how poorly their mates may be treating them. And whenever possible, try to get time with both partners in the marriage in some setting. You will learn a lot and will be enabled to help the Christian much more than if you hear only one side of the story. Of course, there are situations where a Christian spouse is, in fact, being mistreated by a non-Christian husband or wife. And it is not true that every story you hear will be badly distorted. However, you must be careful and wise in coming to a certain conclusion.

Another dynamic of families discipling families is when a more spiritually mature family has a newer family into their home for family devotional times. Many men are reluctant to initiate family devotionals because they do not know how to lead them. Being able to observe another father leading his family in a "devo" is an immense help to the less experienced father. Families need to disciple by demonstration, and the need is *urgent* when a family is led by a single mother. One-parent families need to be included in activities of all types with two-parent families, but especially important are the activities which are more spiritually focused. Single parents face some unique challenges which can seem overwhelming unless others pull them into their families on a regular basis. Since we are all a part of God's family, we need to live accordingly. My encouragement to single parents is to ask for help and invite yourself over if others are not initiating this with you. Your children have a great need here. If medical help were required, you wouldn't hesitate to ask for it. Don't be shy about asking for spiritual help either.

Couples discipling couples and families discipling families will make us all family in a wonderful way. It is God's plan. Let's use it to the full.

Husbands and Wives

Weekly discipleship times in our marriages are essential for growing, happy marital relationships. Daily prayers are likewise essential. In giving instructions to husbands and wives in 1 Peter 3:1-7, Peter ends with the statement, "so that nothing will hinder your prayers." Certainly we are to pray as individuals, whether married or single, but this passage is directed at married people. The implication is that couples will be praying together. From simply a practical viewpoint, nothing solidifies a marriage like regularly praying together. Couples who do not pray together do not stay together emotionally and spiritually the way God intends, period. No exceptions. Just make the decision to do it and then follow through with your decision.

Weekly discipling times are bright spots in the relationship. Spirituality is a cultivated quality which cannot be maintained without consistent attention. Spiritual marriages cannot remain spiritual without this cultivation, for the "weeds" spring up fast and grow rapidly! A part of the recipe for growing marriages is working together as a couple in discipling and counseling less mature couples. Another part is working together in evangelistic activities—sharing your faith, building relationships with non-Christians and then studying with them. But an absolutely essential ingredient in a growing marriage is the regular (which means *scheduled*) weekly discipling time of at least two hours. The following format was suggested by Wyndham Shaw in a lesson on marriage, and it provides an excellent sample of what this weekly time should include.

- Commendations and compliments: Share what you really have appreciated in each other—and make it a great time of encouragement!

- Areas of need and/or problems: Share things that have bothered you about your mate. However, mention only one or two things per session. We are talking about having a discipling time, not a gripe session! Be sure to listen carefully without becoming defensive. No one knows you as well as your life partner. Therefore, be excited to get their perspective and learn from them. Humility is required and humility will be rewarded (maybe in some very exciting ways!).

- Plan your calendar and schedule for the week (or next week, if your discipling time is near the weekend). Talk about areas of shared responsibility such as child care, use of the car and other areas needing coordination between the two of you.

- Talk about your feelings—your goals, desires, dreams, frustrations, fears and anything else that really brings out your heart and inner convictions. For those who find sharing at this level difficult (are you listening, men?), some specific exercises may help to strengthen your "feeling-expressing muscles." One such exercise is to talk back through your lives together a year at a time. Anything you remember from the early years of your life is most likely remembered because it was associated with an emotional experience, either positive or negative. Sharing these memories together will bond you and increase your understanding and appreciation of your partner. Another exercise is to share with each other something you have never shared before. The more difficult it may be to share it, the more it will help the sharer and the marriage bond. Bottom line, learn to share your hearts together. Real intimacy is much more a matter of heart to heart than body to body.

- Household management: Talk about needs around the house (the "Honey-do" list)!

- Children: Talk about how you each feel about how the children are doing. Make sure that you are unified about discipline and other parenting concerns. Your unity as a couple in this area is more important than almost anything else. Stay spiritually focused and stay unified in dealing with your children.

- Plan for family devotionals and discipleship times with each of the children during the week.

- Finances: Make sure that adequate communication on all financial issues takes place, and that each of you feels unified about the financial decisions that are reached.

- Close out with a great prayer together!

I realize that this is quite a list and that you will not be able to cover all these areas every time. But husbands, as leaders, you need to look this over periodically and check your experiences against it. If something has been left out consistently, make sure you focus on that item the next time.

One caution is in order at this juncture. Depending on your longevity in the kingdom and your spiritual maturity, discussing some of these topics may generate some heat. If you cannot agree on children or financial issues or anything else, get help from the couple discipling you. Discipleship times between husband and wife should be very positive experiences, but you may well need help in moving them onto a positive track. Learning to talk through the tougher issues is vital, even if tensions are produced at first. All marriages (and I do mean *all*) will need outside help in resolving differences at times. Do not be surprised when you reach an impasse, and don't be prideful about asking for help. It is all included in the price of the ticket to the wonderful adventure of marriage discipleship. Pay the price and enjoy the growth!

Parents and Children

Ideally, each parent should have a weekly discipling time with each child. Some parents who have a number of children alternate every other week with a certain child, which insures that each child still has a weekly discipling time with at least one parent. If you do have several children, consistently spending this scheduled appointment together will take time. However, the time spent will be as important as any you spend during your hectic week. I have never heard a parent of grown children complain that they spent too much time with them during the growing-up years. On the other hand, I have heard hundreds of parents regretfully exclaim that they should have spent more quality time with their kids, and I am personally in that category. We did not become a part of a discipling church until our kids were teens, but no excuses are good enough. I still knew to do much better than I did. Now we have strong spiritual relationships with Bryan and Renee, praise God, but I would give anything to have spent more time with them in their early years. Please, parents of younger children—make the time available and make it spiritual and special. You and your children will thank God that you did.

As much as nightly prayer times and weekly discipling times with the children are vital, let me add that spiritual relationships are a twenty-four-hours-a-day, seven-days-a-week affair. You cannot relegate spirituality to a schedule, as important as those scheduled times are. In the Deuteronomy 6 passage quoted earlier, parents were told to disciple their children in God's truths by this means: "Talk about them when you sit at home and when you walk along the road, when you lie down and when you get up" (Deuteronomy 6:7). "Sitting at home" would include meal times, which are wonderful opportunities to deepen the family relationships. "Table times" (or "table talks") done correctly will develop family memories of the finest sort. This setting is a natural one for sharing our hearts with one another. Other times would also be included in the sitting-at-home category. Conversation times will be far more valuable than watching television. Obviously, some of us are going to have to turn off our television sets in order to follow God's teaching here, aren't we? At the risk of being accused of overreacting, I will have to admit I love the bumper sticker which reads: "Kill your television!" Why not substitute family reading for time spent in front of the tube and build some special family memories?

"Walking along the road" in our culture can be equated with riding along in "planes, trains and automobiles" (to borrow a movie title). As we travel, talking about spiritual topics should be a natural part of our conversations. The reference to "lying down and getting up" can mean that "beddie-bye" time (or whatever it is called in your family) should be a time of both talking about God, often with Bible storybook in hand, and praying. When we arise in the mornings, time should be planned for further spiritual input into your children's hearts before they go to school. Some parents have a quiet time with the older children before they leave for school, which helps arm them spiritually for the battles they will face. Satan will be waiting for them when they walk out your front door each day. Make sure that they walk out hand in hand with God. Discipling your children is not simply a matter of a set time and place—it is to occur at all times and in all places when you are together with them.

Having said that, let me move on to the need for having that weekly set time and place. Your kids hear you talking about your dp times (discipling times with your discipleship partner). If you are doing what you should be doing in that realm, they will also pick up on the importance of these relationships and the time you devote to them. If the children sense any less emphasis on the times you have scheduled with them, they will develop a negative view of discipleship. However, if you value the discipleship times with your children, and show it by protecting your schedule with them as diligently as with others, then they will absolutely relish discipleship. What you do and what you value will be transferred to your children's value system. Such attitudes and values are "caught" as much as "taught." Hearts transfer, so let's make sure we have the right things in our hearts!

What do you do in a set discipling time with your children? It depends on their ages, their interests and their present needs. At the younger ages, a trip to McDonald's will be an exciting venue for the morning, complete with a few planned spiritual comments about whatever they may need. The little guys will not sit still for long discourses on any subject. Plan for some "hands on" activities to teach them what they need to learn. As the children get older, do some fun things together (fun to them, perhaps not as much to you!). During those times, have in mind the spiritual message you wish to share and then share it in the context of your activity or on the trip to or from the activity. Sometimes you will need to sit down and do nothing but talk, but in discipling times with individual younger children, this will not prove to be an exciting way to conduct spiritual business.

Children often talk more freely in a setting without constant eye contact. They are easily intimidated by adults, even parents (at times, especially parents). Providing for a more relaxed atmosphere will help avoid the awkwardness in discussing things that are more difficult to talk about. For this reason, talking while riding in a car or while taking a walk together will prompt some of your most in-depth conversations. Just make sure that discipling times are not "heavy" or boring. Relax, loosen up and be "cool" (but not too cool, especially if your kids are teens—they will not appreciate your trying to act like a teen).

In a discipling church, your teens will almost always have discipling relationships with other teens or with teen ministry leaders. Be sure you encourage these times and expect them to be great. In some situations where families are very strong and the relationships with parents very good, the teens and their parents may feel less need for the teens to be discipled outside the home. As good as things may be at home, there is still great value in these relationships in the teen ministry. Trust me here: Teen ministry leaders will often see things you as a parent are overlooking. Furthermore, even if your teen seems to be quite open with you, discussing some things, like sexual temptations, is much easier with peers or teen leaders. These discussions will help teach teens the importance of becoming their own spiritual persons, rather than simply relying on their parents' convictions.

In addition to scheduling weekly discipleship times with each child, we need to schedule a devotional time at least weekly. Having a "devo" as one part of a family night is probably the best plan, for it allows a longer time together to deepen family ties as you pray and play together. Make it special, and make it fun. By all means, seek discipling in this area as you look for the best ways to conduct family devos and other family events. The length of family devotionals, the type of lesson shared, the means of sharing it and the amount of singing are all variables which depend on the ages of the children. Just be sure to get input about how to lead them well. When the children are grown, they will look back on devos, table-talk times and family nights with fond memories. And keep in mind that building memories is a specific aim of parents as they train their children.

One of my favorite ways to build precious memories is to have sharing times at holidays, birthdays and other special days. Children need much training in the fine art of feeling and expressing appreciation. Ingratitude is often the first step away from God, as Romans 1:21 indicates, and it is one of the most disturbing characteristics of youth in our day. Therefore, we have a family custom of sharing what we appreciate about each other at holiday times, or about a person having a birthday, or about a couple observing an anniversary.

Two Christmas seasons ago, we had such a sharing session in our family that none of us will ever forget. My mother was with us, as were Bryan and Renee and their "steadies" (now mates). We went around the family circle with everyone sharing about one person at a time. The emotions of love and appreciation were running high that day, and we literally used up half of a large box of tissues wiping away our tears. I think we all were anticipating the changes upcoming in the children's marital status, and we all were rejoicing at the way God had worked out their relationships. Spending the necessary time and energy to plan for those memory building occasions will pay marvelous dividends. The children will be grown and gone much faster than you think. Make the time count by building family traditions that will tie the heart strings in a triangle to one another and to God. You will all enjoy a bit of heaven here on earth.

THE MAGIC INGREDIENT

Reflecting back through the years and circumstances of learning about discipling has filled my heart with deepened convictions and precious memories. My personal search for these truths has been neither simple nor easy, but its rewards have been indescribably wonderful. The "missing ingredient" from my life has given way to the "magic ingredient," but it took me a while to get there.

As a trained Pharisaic skeptic in a traditional church, I originally had some negative reactions when I first heard about a young man named Kip McKean moving to Boston with some rather lofty goals, including building a great church of disciples there. I thought to myself "not in that cold place filled with traditional, formalized religion." After he began accomplishing what I had believed impossible, I looked for another excuse for my continuing skepticism. I remember reading a congregational bulletin announcing their plans for future plantings of churches in many of the world's most influential cities. *What unmitigated gall,* I thought. Somehow seeing a determination to follow the NT pattern of starting churches in major cities and then multiplying both disciples and churches from there didn't arouse much in me except envy. Sad, wasn't it?

Next, I heard about a church planting going out to London, and I started feeling better! This discipling stuff would never work in a foreign land, even though they speak a *form* of English. Alas, I was proved wrong again. "Well," said I, "these young guys may have experienced some early success there in that English-speaking place, but it will never work in a *real* foreign place." Then came Paris and cities that spread from India to South Africa to Asia to South America. Less then two decades later, well over 200 churches of disciples are flourishing in more than a hundred nations, and a number of them are the largest church of any type in their cities or nations. Dozens have more than 1,000 in attendance on Sundays, and several have over 5,000.

Thankfully, I buried my pride and skepticism long ago, and by God's grace, my hearing about a group of multiplying disciples became sight—and I joined in! The years since have been at once challenging, enlightening, frightening, exhilarating and rewarding beyond belief. I have witnessed dynamic church growth but have also experienced great personal growth. I have found the hidden treasure and the pearl of great price. I have discovered a purpose that fills every waking moment with direction and fulfillment enough to last a lifetime. I no longer daydream about what might be or could have been, for I am living out my dreams on a daily basis. I pray to be doing exactly what I am doing now for the rest of my life.

If you have been disappointed in discipling relationships and do not, at this moment, feel as enthusiastic about them as I do, my appeal to you is to keep applying the principles you have read about in this book. Many marriages have suffered through years of unmet expectations and disappointments before "hitting stride" and becoming truly great. For whatever reason, sometimes relationships do not gel easily or quickly. *Don't give up!* Pray for God to renew your faith and to enable you to apply yourself to discipling like never before. Refuse to worry about what might have been. I have often wondered why I did not find the discipling movement long before I did, but I have ceased worrying about it. I am just determined to drink the cup of life God has poured for me and savor every last drop of it! Discipleship is the plan of God. Love it and love him, and never give up on either.

APPENDIX

WHY THE CONTROVERSY?

by Thomas A. Jones

Discipling relationships as described in this book are based carefully on biblical teachings, but no one should think for a minute that such relationships are not controversial. As soon as efforts were made in the latter part of the twentieth century to return to discipling relationships, alarms were sounded in traditional religious circles. One of the most terrifying words in modern man's vocabulary was used to describe those who were seriously and daily attempting to practice the Bible's message of one-another relationships. That word was "cultic."

"Cultism in the Church" read the headline of a prominent religious paper, with the article going on to describe how "dangerous" certain practices were that were connected to discipling relationships. The primary argument was that discipling relationships result in people controlling other people, and for selfish purposes. Coming as it did in the late '70s after the Jonestown mass suicide, that article had a chilling effect. Who would want to be associated with anything that might be cultic?

Those who had begun to seriously reevaluate what Scripture was calling for knew there would be costs to pay. They knew that Jesus himself had been the object of much suspicion and criticism. (And just think what kind of stories the media would be doing on Jesus if he took twelve men today and trained them as he did then!) They knew Jesus had said that all who followed him would likewise come under attack. No one likes to be accused of being in a cult. It is the ultimate "slam" in this generation; but nonetheless, many have decided to be committed to Jesus and to the true nature of biblical relationships regardless of what the reaction might be.

Make no mistake about it—there are dangerous groups that practice dangerous forms of "spirituality." Jonestown and the Branch Davidians of Waco quickly come to mind. As we prepare to take this book to press, the world's newspapers are describing the mass suicide of thirty-nine people in a posh mansion outside San Diego, California. Strange videotapes made by the group members before their deaths are being aired on television. In their view, they were shedding this outer skin we call a body and going on to a higher level of existence. Somehow they expected to be picked up by a space ship that was hiding behind the Hale-Bopp comet. Not surprisingly, television networks and local stations are interviewing experts on cults, and warnings are being issued against any extreme forms of religion or spirituality.

Sadly, those who seriously follow Jesus will always be associated with such phenomena. In part, this will happen because there will always be men who will take the message of Jesus, pervert and distort it, and use it unscrupulously for their own evil purposes. Most people will not take the time to study the Scriptures carefully to sort out the pretenders from the genuine article. But such association will also happen because there is a radicalness in Jesus' message that most people choose to avoid. Most people are not at all willing to become what Jesus called us to become. The easiest way to dismiss his real call to cross-bearing and unselfish living is to label genuine NT practice as cultic.

Comparing the Two

Given the serious problems found in some religious groups and given the amount of media attention devoted to these groups, it is not surprising that many of us would have some questions about discipling relationships. Hopefully, from the things Gordon has written you are able to see how thoroughly biblical such relationships are. Hopefully, you are able to see that this is not a system contrived by man, but a way of relating that springs from the word of God. However, it may be helpful to compare genuine discipling relationships to the practices of dangerous cults. The differences are remarkable.

Ultimate Devotion to a Human Leader

First of all, cults are characterized by ultimate devotion to a human leader. Jim Jones, David Koresh, the Reverend Moon and the man from San Diego who called himself "Do" are some of the best known examples, but there are many others. While in some of these cases the Bible is touted, the ultimate authority in such groups is the leader himself. The Bible is not the standard by which the leader and everyone else is measured. The Bible is a tool used by the leader when it is useful to him and his goals.

This is in stark contrast to churches practicing biblical discipling. Here the word of God is the absolute standard, and everyone is measured by it. Strong leaders are needed. God needs more "mighty men" like those Gordon has described who worked with King David. But no man is above the word of God. Wherever there are true biblical relationships, everyone, including those in top leadership positions, are held accountable by other disciples for living according to the Scriptures. Everyone, including top leaders, needs discipling and gets discipling. A leader who begins to exercise authority in an unbiblical way is called to repent, even by those he leads. Those who are not servant leaders (Matthew 20:25-28) will not stay in leadership.

Thought Control

Probably no phrase is more associated with cults than "mind control." Through the use of various techniques, leaders of cults are said to gain control over the minds of their followers. There is no doubt that, in many groups, leaders with strong and charismatic personalities have overpowered the thinking of their followers. There is no doubt that people have been subjected to a bombardment of ideas for which they had little defense. Certainly, in various groups food or sleep deprivation is used to weaken resistance and make followers more receptive to the message.

In the practice of biblical discipling there is nothing remotely like this. No true disciple wants to have any control over the person he is discipling. His desire is to encourage the person in his relationship with God, so God will have the ultimate control. Certainly, any efforts to weaken a person emotionally or physically are totally rejected. Being a disciple is all about making a clear minded and completely voluntary decision to follow Jesus Christ. No discipler committed to biblical principles will ever try to manipulate someone to obey any command. Biblical discipleship is either completely from the heart or it is not real at all.

In biblical discipling, there will be consistent encouragement for the people involved to be studying the Bible on their own and to be coming to their own convictions. Everyone is reminded often that the Bible is the standard and that everyone should regularly study the Bible to see that the things they are being taught are true (Acts 17:10-11). People are specifically taught, as Gordon Ferguson has taught in this book, that no one should ever do anything they are told to do if (1) it violates the word of God, or (2) it violates one's conscience that is being trained by the word of God. This is a message you will not hear from the dangerous cults of our day and age.

Inward Focused

Because the mentality in cults is not biblical, it is self-serving and inward-focused. Cults are not known for their service and their sacrifice for the needs of others. They are known for isolating themselves from society. They develop a bunker mentality. They become far more concerned about their own "salvation" than the welfare and salvation of others. This has been seen in the extreme in a number of cults where the whole thing ends with mass suicide.

Where true biblical discipling is being practiced, friends are yoking themselves together to encourage one another to be like Jesus. Being like Jesus means dying to selfish goals and being outward focused. It means being concerned about the spiritual and physical needs of people around you. Discipleship partners following a biblical model will be encouraging each other to meet the needs of the poor and the needy, and also the needs of those who are spiritually separated from God. Instead of isolating themselves from society, disciples will be encouraging each other to go deeper and deeper into the situations of those around them to offer love and support. Where there is biblical discipling there will, of course, never ever be a call for people to take their own lives. Nothing could be more in opposition to biblical principles.

On the contrary, disciples will be called to give to others all they have to give for as long as they have something to give and to trust God to bring them home when he desires.

——◆——

We should not think that we will ever be able to present the case for biblical discipleship in such a way that the world in general will appreciate it.

No one lived what we are trying to live more than Jesus. He did it perfectly. What was the result? He was regarded as a dangerous man, as a demon, as an insurrectionist. Those who followed him were called madmen, atheists and cannibals.

Like the misjudged early Christians, we should make our best effort to explain ourselves and to show the correctness of our standard, but there will always be many (even a majority) who will doubt our motives or distort our teaching. The true practice of discipleship is dangerous—dangerous to traditional religion that wants God on human terms. Traditional religion took the greatest offense at Jesus. He was Public Enemy Number One. We can expect something like that reaction until he comes back. Our task is to return good for evil and love for hate. Jesus calls us to pray for those who oppose and persecute us and to keep giving unselfishly—physically and spiritually—to a world that desperately needs help.

The relationships described in this book will never be popular with the majority, but they will help all who accept them to love the world even as God so loved it when he gave his only Son (John 3:16).

NOTES

Chapter 1

1. Robert E. Coleman, *The Master Plan of Evangelism* (Old Tappan, New Jersey: Fleming H. Revell Company, 1963).
2. Gary Collins develops these levels of relationships in more detail in *How To Be a People Helper* (Santa Ana: Vision House, 1976).

Chapter 4

1. Roy H. Lanier, Sr. *The Timeless Trinity* (Denver, Colorado: Roy H. Lanier, Sr. Publisher, 1974), 46.
2. For further study on the nature of the church see the excellent discussions in *Glory in the Church* (Woburn, Mass.: Discipleship Publications International, 1996).

Chapter 5

1. For a more detailed treatment of this passage, see my book, *Victory of Surrender* (Woburn, Mass.: Discipleship Publications International, 1995), 75-85.

Chapter 6

1. Thomas and Sheila Jones, *Jesus with the People* (Woburn, Mass.: Discipleship Publications International, 1996).
2. Regarding priorities, see my comments about evaluating, regulating, and amputating in my book, *The Victory of Surrender* (Woburn, Mass.: Discipleship Publications International, 1995), 83.

Chapter 7

1. For additional information on this topic, see: Marty Wooten, *Power in Weakness* (Woburn, Mass.: Discipleship Publications International, 1996).
2. See: G. Steve Kinnard, *The Call of the Wise* (Woburn, Mass.: Discipleship Publications, International, 1997).
3. I think you would find my booklet and tape set, *Justified* (Woburn, Mass.: Discipleship Publications International, 1994) very helpful along these lines.

Chapter 9

1. Some years ago I heard my friend Joe Woods draw a helpful distinction between the weak and the uncommitted. Some of Joe's thoughts on this can be found along with other useful material in *The Disciple's Handbook* (Woburn, Mass.: Discipleship Publications International, 1997), 130.

Chapter 11

1. Mike Leatherwood, Brenda Leatherwood, Declan Joyce and Joanne Randall, *Some Sat in Darkness* (Woburn, Mass.: Discipleship Publications International, 1997).

Chapter 14

1. Thomas A. Jones, *Mind Change: The Overcomer's Handbook* (Woburn, Mass.: Discipleship Publications International, 1995).

INDEX

New from DPI

THE
DISCIPLE'S HANDBOOK

Valuable tools all in one handy spiral-bound volume

Includes:

PART 1 - STUDIES

First Principles
Additional Studies for Making Disciples
Deep Convictions - thirteen weeks of quiet times
Doctrinal positions of various groups and denominations

PART 2 - RESOURCES

The Medical Account of the Crucifixion
Church History in Miniature
Listing of International Churches of Christ
Frequently Asked Questions about the ICC (from the WWW)
Other helpful lists and resources

PART 3 - IDEAS

Helps for discipleship partners
Ideas for singles' households
Thoughts to begin the day
Great ideas for children and families
Fifty songs for family devotionals
Other helpful suggestions for a variety of needs

PART 4 - PLANNING AND EVALUATION

Fourteen worksheets on a variety of topics, including:
- Your ten deepest convictions
- Your personal mission statement
- Fifty things you want to do before you die

PRACTICAL EXPOSITION SERIES

Life to the Full
A study of the writings of James, Peter, John and
Jude
by Douglas Jacoby

Mine Eyes Have Seen the Glory
The Victory of the Lamb in the Book of Revelation
by Gordon Ferguson

Power in Weakness
Second Corinthians and the Ministry of Paul
by Marty Wooten

The God Who Dared
Genesis: From Creation to Babel
by Douglas Jacoby

The Call of the Wise
Introduction and Topical Index to Proverbs
by Steve Kinnard

The Victory of Surrender
An in-depth study of a powerful biblical concept
by Gordon Ferguson

True and Reasonable
Evidences for God in a skeptical world
by Douglas Jacoby

Raising Awesome Kids in Troubled Times
by Sam and Geri Laing

Friends and Lovers
by Sam and Geri Laing

Friends and Lovers Study Guide
by Mitch and Jan Mitchell

Take Hold of Life! A Devotional Book for Teens

Mind Change: The Overcomer's Handbook
by Thomas A. Jones

ESPECIALLY FOR WOMEN

She Shall Be Called Woman
Volume I: Old Testament Women
Volume II: New Testament Women
edited by Sheila Jones and Linda Brumley

The Fine Art of Hospitality
edited by Sheila Jones
The Fine Art of Hospitality Handbook
edited by Sheila Jones and Betty Dyson
(two-volume set)

Our Beginning: Genesis Through the Eyes of a Woman
by Kay Summers McKean

For information about ordering these
and many other resources from DPI, call
1-888-DPI-BOOK
or from outside the U.S.
617-938-7396.

World Wide Web
http://www.dpibooks.com